Distributed Object Architectures with CORBA

Managing Object Technology Series
Barry McGibbon, Series Editor
SIGS Publications, Inc.
New York, New York

Additional Volumes in Preparation

Distributed Object Architectures with CORBA

Henry Balen
with Mark Elenko, Jan Jones, and Gordon Palumbo

PUBLISHED BY THE PRESS SYNDICATE OF THE UNIVERSITY OF CAMBRIDGE
The Pitt Building, Trumpington Street, Cambridge, United Kingdom

CAMBRIDGE UNIVERSITY PRESS
The Edinburgh Building, Cambridge CB2 2RU, UK   www.cup.cam.ac.uk
40 West 20th Street, New York, NY 10011-4211, USA   www.cup.org
10 Stamford Road, Oakleigh, Melbourne 3166, Australia
Ruiz de Alarcón 13, 28014 Madrid, Spain

Published in association with SIGS Books

First published in 2000

Design and composition by Andrea Cammarata
Cover design by Tom Jezek

Printed in the United States of America

A catalog record for this book is available from the British Library.

Library of Congress Cataloging-in-Publication Data is on record with the publisher.

ISBN 0 521 65418 1 paperback

To Renée

Biographies

Henry Balen:

Henry has been designing and implementing object-oriented systems since the mid-1980s, when the technology was still in its infancy. His work emphasizes parallel and distributed processing. Since moving to the USA, Henry is involved with distributed object projects for the financial community at the epicenter of capitalism, Wall Street. Henry has been a frequent speaker on the subject of CORBA and distributed systems at various conferences. Henry co-founded Xenotrope in 1997. In his spare time he sleeps.

Mark Elenko:

Mark has concentrated on Java-based design and development since 1995, working on all types of systems. He has a B.A. from Columbia University, an M.S. from New York University, and an apartment full of modular origami. Mark is professionally fond of objects but tries to avoid them socially.

Jan Jones:

Jan has designed and developed applications since 1993, including client-server application, trading system development specializing in math intensive algorithms and user interfaces, and web-based distributed systems using Java and CORBA. She has a B.S. in Electrical Engineering from the Georgia Institute of Technology. When not working at Xenotrope she can be found performing with Fuscia Dance.

Gordon Palumbo:

Gordon has been entrenched in the CORBA front lines since 1995, and has designed and implemented CORBA– and Java–based systems for major financial institutions. While not working with computers, he can be found practicing his other avocation, juggling.

Contents

Foreword

When we started the Object Management Group a decade ago, we could only hope that writers of the caliber of Henry Balen would take up the cause. I can remember those early days where we spent most of our time trying to explain to anyone that would listen why object technology was important. In the last ten years it has become an ever increasingly complex world, one where homogeneity of platforms is almost unheard of, and where legacy applications continue to be an integral part of the mix. It has become apparent that the old does not always make room for the new when it comes to enterprise applications. It has also become apparent that understanding the architectural issues involved in designing and structuring systems based on distributed objects is one of the major keys for successful deployment. The industry consolidation behind such standards as Common Object Request Broker Architecture (CORBA), the Unified Modeling Language (UML), and the Meta Object Facility (MOF) have immensely helped to make analysis and design easier. Moreover, there are better tools out in the market than ever before, but we have yet to automate architecture—which provides good job security for those who understand the issues!

Henry Balen's efforts in this book should provide a jump-start to those who are planning on building distributed systems using object technology. The importance of architecture cannot be overemphasized. Many projects have not achieved the desired results or in some cases even failed because of the lack of time or lack of skills spent up front on the analysis and design of the system architecture.

Achieving the stated project requirements, achieving the targeted return on investment, and making the time to market window are the key measures of an application's successful deployment. Good analysis and design work done up front has emerged as an important ingredient for helping to achieve these goals. This book provides a very useful guide with valuable insights, from lessons learned, which will hopefully save the reader both time and money, and increase the probability of designing and implementing enterprise-wide distributed systems using object technology.

William Hoffman
President and COO
Object Management Group

Acknowledgments

No book is written in a vacuum, nor is it a complete work. This book could have easily been trapped in a continuous cycle of revision to reach "publishing nirvana." During the long process of writing I have received support, without which this book would not exist, from colleagues and loved ones. I would like to thank my spouse, Renée, for her patience and confidence during the long days. I would also like to thank Marvin Wolfthal for his time reviewing each chapter and subsequent valuable advice. I also thank my colleagues at Xenotrope for their support, and help with the production of the book. Finally, I would like to thank Lothloríen and the editorial team at Cambridge University Press.

Chapter 1

Introduction

Over the past few years, I have been giving presentations on distributed systems and CORBA. My focus has been on the design and architecture of such systems. In each presentation I refined my ideas and thoughts. It seemed the next logical step to produce a book on the same subject. If the audiences I have seen are indicative, there is a definite need to share information on the construction of distributed systems. Our field improves with the flow of information: the ability to learn and build upon each other's experience. This book is a contribution from my coauthors and me to the codification of the principles of distributed object architecture.

Software architecture, by its nature, is rather ephemeral and not easy to write about. There are various *ad hoc* approaches to architecture, and it has only been in recent years that we have seen increase in work to codify architectural principles. Part of this codification is the adoption of design patterns from the work done in real-world architecture by Christopher Alexander. There is a growing literature on design patterns, and the use of patterns goes some way to helping with the construction of complex distributed systems. We will now take a quick look at what architecture means for the world of software and lay the groundwork for the rest of the book.

What Architecture Is

If you were to look up the definition of *architecture* in a standard dictionary, you would find that architecture is the "art and science of designing and constructing buildings." You could say likewise that software architecture is the art and science of designing and constructing programs; however, the design and construction of programs is not a mature science. The construction of software systems lies somewhere between a craft and an engineering discipline!

Architecture also refers to the style of a building; when you refer to Gothic architecture, a certain style and method of construction is evoked. Likewise, with software architecture, we use the term to refer to the structure of the system and the style used in its construction. The terms "component based architecture," "object-oriented architecture," "pipeline architecture," and so on, refer to ideas and ways of constructing systems that have evolved during the short history of software engineering.

The tools for software construction are relatively accessible. Just as practically anyone can construct a chair, anyone can write simple programs. However, the design and construction of complex programs can be more akin to the design and construction of a cathedral. Unfortunately, it is not difficult to find software systems constructed with shaky foundations. The choices we make when specifying our architecture and its principles will determine the foundation of our eventual system.

Software architecture, unlike its real-world analogue, resides in a fluid world of bits and bytes. It is a world not seen by the majority of computer users; you can not walk down the virtual street and admire the Corinthian columns or the flying buttresses. However, just as in its real-world counterpart, principles of good software architecture have developed. Some of the principles of software architecture have become philosophical beliefs, many of which are ingrained within the gestalt of the developer community.

Why Architecture Is Important

We live in a time of constant and rapid change. With the rising popularity of the Internet and electronic commerce, we are seeing higher expectations for systems created in short time frames. The number of users of a Web-based application increases rapidly, and can be difficult (if not impossible) to determine at the outset. These systems have to adapt, be flexible, and take into account constant change and new demands.

With all this in mind, it is even more important that we develop systems with good architectural principles. If we do not, then the cost will be high. We will need to redesign, rewrite, and reinvent, all of which introduces risk to the business. Our goal is to create a system that can be extended so as to expand and encompass change.

In addition to the above concerns, systems are also getting larger. It is no longer possible for one person to understand every component of a system. It is necessary to adopt guiding principles that are shared among the development team. The architect (or architects) of the system can determine the principles that will be used, but they also need to convey their ideas to the developers.

A good architecture should facilitate the construction of your system. The quality of your architecture can be determined by its support for abstraction, extensibility, scaleability, interoperability, and components.

The architecture should support the types of abstraction necessary to model your business. It is not good if your model contains business objects that represent financial instruments and your architecture only deals with socket-based communications. On the other hand, you do not want your architecture to be overly complex; if it is too complex, your development team will not adopt it. Another aspect of good architecture is its simplicity—that is, its ease of understanding.

Your architecture should support interoperability. Most modern environments contain a mixture of machines. Your architecture must consider this. Adopting open industry standards within your architecture helps in this process.

Good architectures allow you to extend your system. It should facilitate the addition of new components, and the use of existing components for new applications. A good architecture will also allow your system to scale—that is, to take into account increasing number of users by possibly replicating services.

Architecture is an important aspect of your system because it enables you to provide a framework for construction, embody principles in your system that developers can follow, and support future enhancements. As much of the literature will point out, we are in the early stages of turning computing from a craft into a science. Currently, books like this one help convey the folklore and codify architectural principles.

Distributed Architectures

The importance of good architecture is greater when constructing a distributed system. With more disparate components interacting, the complexity of the final system increases. A good architecture should help you manage that complexity. Also, that elusive goal of the object-oriented world, reuse, is realized within distributed architectures. Each of our distributed services may be used by client applications in ways that were unforeseen by the original implementers.

Figure 1-1 illustrates the evolution of software systems from the monolithic to multi-tiered and distributed components. The construction of each of these systems would not have been possible without support from the underlying technologies, and as the level of abstraction embodied within those technologies increased so did the sophistication of the systems produced. You should note each enabling technology's implementation usually builds upon functionality provided at the lower level of abstraction.

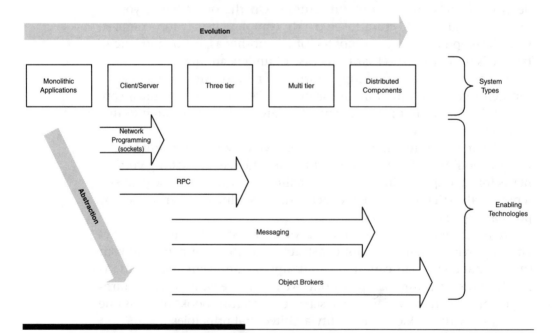

Figure 1-1. *Evolution of distributed systems*

A distributed architecture is not complete without a set of services. These services support the functionality necessary for the success of a large system. Services that are core to the success of a distributed system cover the functionality of directory, persistence, security and transactions. Directory service allows you to locate remote objects. Persistence provides you with the mechanisms to store an object for long periods. Some form of security is necessary in any network, and transaction support allows you to ensure the integrity of information. You can usually purchase these services, or tools that help with your own implementations.

Distributed objects facilitate the construction of multi-tiered architectures. The object-oriented concepts of encapsulation and polymorphism translate well to the world of network-based components. When we look at each distributed object, we see that it provides a public interface to the network. The actual implementation hides behind this interface, and there is no way that a user of the object can see the implementation. With this in mind, it should be relatively straightforward to switch the implementation of the object without affecting the users.

The OMG and CORBA

The Common Object Request Broker Architecture (CORBA) is an open standard that provides infrastructure to support the construction of distributed systems. CORBA is independent of computer languages and operating systems, and is the best solution available if you want to build a heterogeneous system of distributed objects.

In the late eighties, many people and organizations were developing infrastructures to support distributed objects. Then in 1989 the Object Management Group (OMG) was founded. The OMG is a standards body with a mandate to define a standard for systems composed of distributed objects. It is probably one of the largest standards bodies, with over 800 member companies. Its vision of interoperating distributed objects was achieved with the advent of CORBA 2 in 1996. Since then the OMG has expanded its effort and come up with standards that extend the base features of an ORB.

The 800 or so members of the OMG vary from vendors (such as IONA, Inprise, BEA and so on) to users (such as Boeing, Motorola, Cisco and so on). The OMG provides a forum in which the users of the technology interact with the vendors. This melting pot of the computer world is responsible for a vision of a world of distributed objects based on open standards. While the membership of the OMG contains organizations with many viewpoints, it would be fair to say that the vast majority agrees upon the need of open standards.

Many groups are working in parallel within the OMG to define standard interfaces to objects supporting vertical markets (or Domains) and to define and adopt specifications for analysis and design. There is now a Domain Technical Committee within the OMG with subgroups in Healthcare, Telecommunications, Finance, Electronic Commerce, Life Science, Transportation, Manufacturing, and Business Objects. The Analysis and Design Task Force within the OMG was responsible for adopting the Unified Modeling Language (UML) as part of the OMG specification.

All of this leads to a grand vision of a single architecture that permeates the software engineering process from design through implementation and deployment. Central to this vision is the Object Management Architecture (OMA). The OMA is illustrated in Figure 1-2. At its core is the Object Request Broker (ORB). The core ORB provides the basis for location and

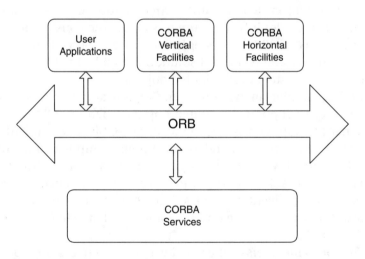

Figure 1-2. *The Object Management Architecture*

communication between distributed objects, it supports the definition of object interfaces and brokers requests for remote method invocations.

The CORBA Services define basic services that most distributed object systems need; these include naming, security, transactions, persistence, and others. The CORBA facilities build upon the ORB core and the CORBA Services; in fact, if you look at the OMG call for proposals (CFP) you will find that responses to requests for new facilities should state how they fit into, and build upon, the OMA. There are two types of facilities: horizontal and vertical. Horizontal facilities are not domain-specific; the Meta-Object Facility is one such example. Vertical facilities are domain-specific, such as Currency and Party Management in the Finance domain.

CORBA is probably one of the most important technologies of recent years. It has helped us realize complex distributed systems. As the standard evolves, we will see more facilities that support higher levels of abstraction. It will become an enabling technology for the enterprise.

Purpose and Scope

Development of multi-tiered systems using technologies such as CORBA and Java has increased. Unfortunately, the software community currently suffers from a shortfall of people with the skills necessary to build flexible, distributed, object-based systems. In addition, the demand to produce such systems within many industries is increasing, especially with increased interest in providing systems that work on the Web. In conjunction, there has been an attitude of "learn the technology and the system will follow." Because of organizational issues and unrealistic expectations, however, programmers spend little time on the overall design of a distributed architecture. This has led many people to produce inflexible systems that do not perform well when systems need to expand.

Distributed systems are more complex than monolithic programs. There are more interacting parts that rely on a physical network for communications. There is greater potential for parallelism. There are synchronization and integrity problems unique to the nature of distributed systems. These systems are also less tractable and harder to debug.

This book is about the architectural issues involved in the design and structure of distributed systems based on distributed objects. Principles of building a distributed object system are similar, regardless of whether you use CORBA or some other technology (such as RMI or DCOM). You will still need to tackle the issues of interface design, transactions, persistence, life cycle, and so forth. I picked CORBA since it is an open standard with plenty of implementations, with both commercial implementations and public domain versions available on the Internet.

The goal of this book is to help you learn different aspects of distributed architectures. Architecture encompasses the organization and composition of a system, assignment of functionality, development and use of frameworks, selection of design, and decisions for deployment. The composition of your system is determined by your interface design; we shall take a closer look at aspects of interface design and how it affects your distributed architecture. All of these will be explored in the context of building a distributed object system.

In this book, we are going to explore distributed object architectures, both as a type of architecture for a software system and the principles for the design and construction of such systems.

Intended Audience

I wanted to produce a book for a wide audience, but not be another introduction to CORBA or object-oriented techniques. There are plenty of other texts that will provide you with more detailed information about CORBA (see the references for some). My aim is to take an architectural viewpoint to the construction of distributed systems without being yet another patterns book. The book is also meant to be practical. The information contained within is based on the experience of building such systems.

If you intend to learn about or develop a system of distributed objects, or are developing such a system, this book is for you. Whether you are a manager, system architect, application designer, or programmer, you will find information of use in this book.

Organization of Contents

This book has been organized to take you through a description of distributed objects and help you understand the design issues, then look at the various aspects of a distributed object system. Nowadays, no book is complete without some mention of the Internet; we look at how CORBA relates to the Internet, especially some of the new standards that are emerging and will influence future CORBA-based systems. We finish off by taking a look at what is involved when you wish to deploy a system using CORBA.

Here are brief summaries of the rest of the chapters in the book. Most chapters are fairly self-contained, so if you prefer to go through the book in a semi-random manner, you can use this as your guide.

Chapter 2: Distributed Objects

Distributed objects provide good support for the construction of multi-tiered systems. Here we look at what a distributed object is. Then we see how CORBA supports the construction of distributed object systems, and where CORBA can do with some enhancement. We finish the chapter by looking at how existing systems can be integrated using object wrappers, in particular existing systems are classified into three types: database, library, and application. Each of these present their own challenges for integration.

Chapter 3: Partitioning, Interfaces, and Granularity

The key to building a successful distributed system is in the design of your interfaces. These are the aspects of your distributed objects that are seen by all users. The decisions you make when designing your interfaces have a direct impact on the flexibility and performance of your final system. We shall see why it is not sufficient to take an object model and just distribute it on the network.

Chapter 4: Meta-Information

Meta-information holds the key to the production of flexible systems. We take a look at meta-information within CORBA and how you can use it.

Chapter 5: Life Cycle and Persistence

Objects in your system have a life cycle. They are created, moved, and destroyed. Sometimes the life of an object exceeds that of the process in which it is created; in this case the object must reside in a persistent store.

Chapter 6: Transactions

Transactions provide us with the mechanism to maintain the integrity of information within our system. Transaction monitors work in conjunction with our databases to do just this. The CORBA standard has integrated the functionality of transaction monitors within its Object Transaction Service. We take a look at what transaction processing means for distributed objects.

Chapter 7: Security

Any computer system that is part of a network can be vulnerable to misuse and attack. Security services are needed to help minimize the possibility of misuse. In addition, systems that perform electronic commerce require security features that guarantee privacy and non-repudiation. The CORBA security service provides a lot of the necessary functionality in a relatively nonintrusive manner.

Chapter 8: CORBA and the Internet

With the importance of the Internet, we would be remiss not to look at how CORBA and the Internet work together. We look at how CORBA fits in with the Internet, and in particular, we look at architectures to extend a CORBA-based system across the Internet. We will also take a brief look at new standards such as XML and see how this is complementary to CORBA.

Chapter 9: Architecture Considerations for Deployment

Once you have developed your system, you will need to deploy it. How do you monitor what is going on? How do you handle failure and load balancing? Here we will investigate some of the mechanisms that you can use to help with the deployment of the final system.

Appendix: COM/CORBA Integration

It is the goal of the OMG for CORBA to be inclusive; this means that it should work with other technologies. The OMG has defined mechanisms for integration with Microsoft's COM. For completeness, we look at the OMG specification. When you decide to obtain a product to help in this area, you will know what is involved.

References

Alexander, Christopher et al. *A Pattern Language: Towns, Buildings, Construction.* Oxford University Press: New York, 1997.

IEEE Software, *Special Issue Architecture* 12, no. 6 (November 1995).

IEEE Software, *Special Issue Object Methods, Patterns, and Architectures* 14, no. 1 (January/February 1997).

Mowbary, T and R. Malveau. *CORBA Design Patterns.* New York: John Wiley & Sons, 1997.

Orfali, R., D. Harkey, and J. Edwards. *The Distributed Objects Survival Guide.* New York: John Wiley & Sons, 1996.

Shaw, M and D. Garlan. *Software Architecture.* Prentice Hall, 1996.

For further information on the Web:

http://www.omg.org—here you can find the CORBA specification and the current work of the OMG.

Chapter 2

Distributed Objects

Why would you want to implement a system using distributed objects? Maybe you have written a client/server system using other technologies (such as TCP based sockets, RPC or DCE). You may wonder what the motivation is to move to "distributed objects"? To answer that question, we will first review the benefits of object-oriented technology; then we will see how these benefits are utilized when object-oriented technology is taken to the network.

Object-oriented concepts, tools, and techniques have been with us for the best part of three decades. During that time the technologies based on object-oriented principles have matured: languages, development environments, case tools, and databases. Applications have become more distributed in nature. Development tools have matured to support the construction of distributed systems.

Quick Review of Object-Oriented Concepts

This book doesn't aim to teach you object-oriented concepts. In this section we will merely review some of the salient aspects. For further information, I recommend that you read one of the many books on object-oriented design such as "Object-Oriented Software Engineering" by

Jacobson et al. (See References at the end of this chapter.)

Over time, systems have increased in complexity. Software construction had to match that complexity. The object-oriented paradigm enables us to manage the complexity of modern systems. Complexity is handled through classes, inheritance, polymorphism, and objects.

Objects, classes, and inheritance

Every day we classify objects as a mechanism to help us make sense of the world. When I ask you if you have trees in your garden, you understand what I mean by the term *tree*. *Tree* is a classification that we use to represent objects such as the oak tree that is in Renée's garden. (Renée's garden is an instance of *garden*, but we will get to that later.) This helps us communicate and share our model of a complex world. I do not have to iterate through all the types of trees to ask you that simple question. In object-oriented terms, tree is a *class*. Oak and maple trees are both a specialization of the class tree and are themselves classes.

An object is an instance of a class. Objects are concrete realizations of the type defined by the class. The oak in Renée's garden is an *object* (an instance of the class *oak*).

In an object-oriented model, we represent the specialization of oak and maple from tree by using an inheritance relationship. Figure 2-1 illustrates the inheritance relationship of oak and maple to tree. You should note that inheritance should be considered a relationship we refer to as "kind of."

An oak is *a kind of* tree.

A maple is *a kind of* tree.

Some programming languages enable you to develop classes that can inherit from more than one parent. This is called *multiple inheritance*. Over the past few years, debate about the usefulness of multiple inheritance (or lack thereof) has taken on the intensity of religious warfare. My advice is that you remember that inheritance models "a kind of" relationship. Ask yourself if the child class is "a kind of" the parent class. If it does not seem to be a match, then you may want to model the relationship by use of composition rather than inheritance. We would indicate whether a tree is deciduous by use of an attribute of the class *tree*.

All instances of a class display similar behavior, properties, and meth-

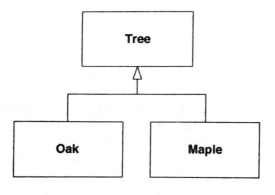

Figure 2-1. *Sample inheritance relationship*

ods. The specification of a class exposes only its interface to public view; its underlying implementation is hidden, or "private." The interface defines the methods (a method is the object-oriented term for a function) that are used when we interact with an instance of the class. The private implementation contains the code that is executed whenever one of the public methods is invoked. Other entities within the system interact with the object through the interface defined by the class. Only the person who provides the code for the implementation is concerned with how the internals of the object work; the user is only concerned with the interface.

When we define a class, we provide a public interface (set of methods) and an implementation. When we use inheritance, the child class (*maple*) inherits the methods and implementation from its parent. So when we want to model the difference between deciduous and coniferous trees, should we use an inheritance relationship or should this be an attribute of the class *tree*? The answer to this will probably best be determined by the model that you develop as your solution.

You should note that CORBA does not support implementation inheritance. Though you can define an inheritance hierarchy in IDL, this is interface inheritance. The method definitions are inherited—not the implementation!

Encapsulation

The principle of encapsulation is not new to object-oriented programming; structured programming made use of encapsulation. Encapsulation refers to hiding the implementation of an object (or component) behind a well-defined interface.

Switching to another analogy, most people today know how to drive a car. They expect that the clutch, accelerator1 and brake pedals are located in the same relative positions. It is not necessary to know how to build a car in order to use it. This separation of interface (the driving) from implementation (the construction) in object-oriented parlance is *encapsulation*. Encapsulation enables us to understand an object from its interface; we do not need to look at the internals.

Polymorphism

We may wish to model part of a transportation system with different modes of transport. We have a general *Vehicle* class from which we inherit *Boat*, *Car* and *Plane*. Figure 2-2 illustrates this inheritance from *Vehicle*. *Vehicle* defines the method *drive*; thus, it is possible to drive a vehicle by invoking this method. Each of the subclasses also define this method, they each provide an alternate implementation. What happens when you drive a boat is different from what happens when you drive a car. Instances of *boat* and *car* understand what you mean when you say *drive*. This is *polymorphism*.

To support this type of software construction we need concepts that support our methodology as well as our implementation language and tools. Although we can write an object-oriented system in a non–object-oriented language, the impedance mismatch between design and implementation will present a severe problem (and may indeed define a circle in Dante's Inferno).

Patterns and components

Now that the construction of systems using object-oriented techniques has matured, techniques are emerging to build upon the object-oriented foundation. A recent technique is the use of Patterns. There are patterns

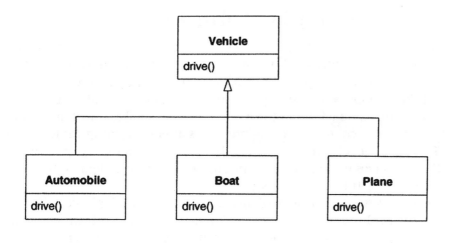

Figure 2-2. *Types of Vehicle*

of design and patterns of analysis. Developers noticed that they were using recurring solutions when building software systems. They therefore borrowed an idea from the field of architecture: that there are patterns reused in the design of buildings. The aim of the pattern movement is to document a recurring solution; we then have a knowledge repository that can be referenced and used in future designs (and analysis) that may be applicable. The seminal book for patterns is by the "gang of four" (Gamma et al 1994). Patterns for design and analysis provide a supplementary mechanism for conveying information about the system.

Recently we also have witnessed the emergence of component models. These build upon the object-oriented paradigm to provide as a mechanism of construction standard objects that can be "plugged" together to provide a working system. A component model defines a set of methods that a component should support; these enable components to interact with each other in a standard manner.

Object Based Distribution

No computer is an island, for we have become a networked world. Whether it is an Internet, Intranet, or Extranet, we are constructing networks of machines to share and exchange information and resources. As with other applications systems, distributed systems are also becoming more complex. In addition, the modern business makes use of many different types of computers and applications; there is a strong desire for all of these systems to work together. Therefore, it makes sense to leverage the advantages that accompany the object-oriented paradigm to the production of distributed systems.

Getting systems to work together is only one reason for building a distributed application. You may want to distribute the work among a set of processing resources: some of the computers may be better suited to manipulation of large amounts of data, whereas others are better at fast graphical display. You may want to share information across a corporate network (or the Internet): the company's sales force may be in different locations but need to see the same information. You may want to reduce the cost of software distribution in your organization by providing thin clients, while the business logic resides on remote services. The term *thin client* became more promient soon after the introduction of Java; a thin client is one with minimal code, usually just a user interface and all the business logic resides at a server. Thin clients can be easily distributed on a as demand basis and thus reduce the cost of maintaining large numbers of machines running the same application.

A distributed object is an object that can reside anywhere on the network. The client does not know the implementation language (C++, Smalltalk, or Java) that we used, nor does it need to know. We communicate with the distributed object by using a proxy; this proxy enables us to view the distributed object as if it were local to the client application. It is not necessary for the user of the proxy to know the location of the corresponding distributed object. The infrastructure provides an object bus, a transport that supports requests from the client to the distributed object. The infrastructure to support distributed objects brokers the communication from the client to the distributed object.

We are seeing architectures for distributed systems being composed of many tiers. The client/sever architecture of the '80s is a two-tier archi-

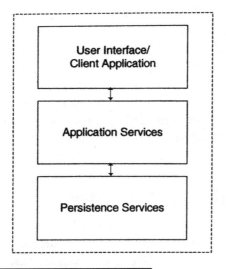

Figure 2-3. *Components of a three-tier architecture*

tecture, the first tier containing the client application and the second tier the database service. Now we are seeing architectures that utilize three or more tiers. Figure 2-3 illustrates a typical three-tier architecture. We separate the user interface from the application logic and the data persistence services. The Persistence services provide the means to make an object persistent, to save its state. We implement the persistence by using an object database, or providing a layer than can translate from your object model to other storage (like a relational database).

Distributed objects provide natural support for implementing three-tier and multi-tier architectures. By decoupling these layers, we provide a system that facilitates the reuse of the distributed objects implemented in the application and database layers. This allows us to view the distributed objects provided by the application services as network-aware components, which we can reuse in a variety of clients.

The infrastructure needed to construct such a system of distributed objects is a piece of middleware software called an Object Request Broker (ORB).

We can build a basic distributed object system on top of the functionality provided by the basic ORB. If we support large applications, we will need other services: a directory service to find objects on the network, a security service that manages access and encryption, support for distributed transactions, and notification of significant events. Further discussion of the services to support the production of a distributed object architecture will be covered in later chapters of this book.

Distributed objects bring to the network the benefits that we first realized from using object-oriented techniques. When we distribute an object, we make its interface (methods) available to clients via an object bus. Middleware tools such as an ORB provide us with this ability.

What CORBA Provides

The Object Management Group (OMG) has defined an open standard for ORBs: the Common Object Request Broker (CORBA) standard. CORBA has gone through a series of revisions since it was first introduced. The version currently in use is CORBA 3. We shall soon see ORB implementations incorporating the new features.

Describing what CORBA provides as a specification, and what is available to purchase from your local vendor, is a moving target—a target that moves slowly, however. The standards process that the OMG goes through is constant, with meetings every couple of months throughout the year. Several books will give you an in-depth description of CORBA. I am going to provide a brief description of the highlights that you should be aware of before you continue with the rest of this book.

CORBA provides us an open standard for the production of distributed object systems. This insures interoperability across programming languages, machines, and products. We can all see the benefits of standards in our life: electrical sockets and plugs, music CD formats, road signs, and railroad tracks. Without these standards, we would run into problems while attending to our everyday business. In a similar manner, the use of standards in the production of distributed object systems help us.

With CORBA, we have a mechanism where objects can communicate with each other regardless of where they are located. Objects may be located within the same program, within different programs on the same machine, or on separate machines. Also, since CORBA provides mappings from OMG Interface Definition Language (IDL) to all major programming languages, we can choose to implement our objects in the language and on the hardware of our choice. You can now find products such as IONA's Orbix for MVS that enable you to implement CORBA objects on the mainframe!

CORBA provides us with a standard model for distributing objects across our network. CORBA also defines a rich set of services that facilitate the construction of distributed object systems. The ORB is the plumbing that enables the operation of distributed object architectures. Like all plumbing, the ORB should be transparent to the application. To realize this it is necessary for there to exist services that use the plumbing and facilitate the construction of distributed architectures.

OMG IDL

CORBA requires that we define our objects using Interface Definition Language (IDL). Recall that we want to provide a system of distributed objects in which the infrastructure is independent of the programming language, operating system, and other implementation-specific details. CORBA specifies how IDL is "mapped" to a variety of widely-used programming languages. Every CORBA implementation supplies a code-generation utility for some subset of the supported languages. Thus, we may think of IDL as a kind of "universal" high-level language for specifying the interfaces to networked services. When we use IDL, we provide a "contract" between the distributed object and its users. We are obligating the distributed object to conform to the interface that we have defined. The client can see what methods are supported by the distributed object and knows what information it needs to send to that object when it wishes to invoke one of the methods.

As a quick comparison, Microsoft's DCOM also provides an IDL (Microsoft IDL). However, you do not have to use MIDL, since the tools provided by Microsoft will generate IDL for you. Java Remote Method Invocation (RMI) does not use an IDL. RMI is a distributed object system for Java servers and clients; since there is one homogeneous programming language, there is no need to abstract the interfaces from the implementation language.

IDL is a declarative language; you explicitly declare your interfaces and types. You may wonder, "Why should I learn another language?" Take heart; IDL is very similar to other programming languages and its constructs are easy to understand (especially for those of you already familiar with C++ and Java). Listing 2-1 provides an example of some IDL code.

Listing 2-1: Example IDL code

```
struct SearchCritera {
    string documentType;
    string criteria;
};

interface DocumentLocator {
    exception NotFound {
      string reason;
    };

    string FindDocument(in SearchCriteria criteria)
        raises(NotFound);
};
```

Once you have written your interfaces in IDL, you will use an IDL compiler supplied by your ORB vendor. The IDL compiler will generate code in your target programming language; the produced code handles the details of how the client and server communicate across the network and consists of a client "proxy" and a server "skeleton." Your client uses the proxy to interact with the remote object in a transparent manner. You will implement the distributed object by providing an implementation for the skeleton.

CORBA Interoperability

CORBA Interoperability specifies how different implementations of the standard communicate with one another, thus guaranteeing vendor-independence in the area of networking. The General Inter-ORB Protocol (GIOP) defines a protocol for all messages sent across the network. Like IDL, GIOP is a high-level abstraction. Specific implementations are built on different network transport protocols. The Inter-ORB Interoperability Protocol (IIOP) is an implementation of GIOP using the ubiquitous TCP/IP. ORB implementations wishing to comply with the Interoperability portion of the CORBA standard must support IIOP.

The ORB vendor may implement other protocols. These are called Environment-Specific Inter-ORB Protocols (ESIOP) and allow the ORB to bridge different networking protocols. One such ESIOP is based on DCE (Distributed Computing Environment Common Inter-ORB Protocol).

In the IIOP protocol, information about the network location of an object is contained in an Interoperable Object Reference (IOR). You usually obtain an object reference from a directory service. The ORB takes care of resolving the object reference to the actual distributed object; your program will not normally be concerned with the details. CORBA also enables the programmer to convert an IOR to and from a text string representation. We can store and communicate this string to other processes using a variety of methods.

Object adapters

For the ORB to manage remote objects in a manner transparent to the client, an object adapter is required. Object adapters are responsible for creating and activating a distributed object, and for invoking its operations or methods. Figure 2-4 illustrates the components of an ORB that are involved when a client invokes a method, of a remote object.

There can be many different types of object adapters. CORBA 2 defines a basic object adapter (BOA) that ORBs provide to fulfill this functionality. Though the specification defines the behavior of the object adapter, it does not specify a portable application programming interface (API). With CORBA 3, we will see the introduction of the Portable Object Adapter (POA). The POA provides a standard interface to object adapters that is vendor-neutral.

Services

As of this writing the CORBA standard defines fifteen services, all of which are meant to help with the construction of a distributed object system. You will be hard pressed to find all services implemented by any one vendor, although a core set of services are available for most commercial ORBs. These are:

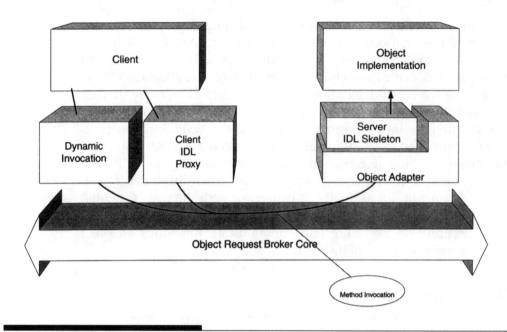

Figure 2-4. *Remote method invocation*

- **Name Service**—The name service provides a directory mechanism. We use this service to store references to remote objects in
  a directory structure so that a client can find them by name.
  There is no assurance, however, that the object you are trying to
  access is active.

- **Event Service**—The event service defines a mechanism for suppli-
  ers to broadcast information to a set of consumers by the use of
  event channels. The event service allows you to use push or pull
  protocols (or even a combination). You can even set up channels of
  filtered information. The CORBA standard, however, does not guarantee any quality of service; this is provided by the implementers
  of the event service (this is a way that distinguishes vendors).

- **Transaction Service**—The Object Transaction Service (OTS) provides a way to manage distributed transactions. This is similar
  to—or the same as, depending on the vendor—a mechanism used

by transaction monitor products such as Tuxedo from BEA, or Encina from Transarc. The OTS provides us the means to ensure transactional integrity for the persistent information within the system. It also manages the database resources used by the system, allowing the system to perform database commits or rollbacks depending on the success or failure of the transaction.

- **Security Service**—The security service provides a mechanism to implement all aspects of security, from user validation and authentication, to access control, encryption, and non-repudiation.

- **Trader Service**—The trader service provides a "yellow pages" for the system. Like the name service, it is a means by which we can locate an object. However, instead of using a name, we search for an object by criteria. Each service registered with the trader has associated attributes that characterize the service.

We will be revisiting some of these services in more detail as we proceed with the discussion of distributed architectures in this book.

What CORBA Does Not Provide

The last section gave us with a quick review of what CORBA provides. Here we will cover some of the services and facilities that vanilla CORBA does not yet provide that would help when producing a production system. Implementations of the next revision of the OMG standard, CORBA 3, will soon emerge; these will provide us with improvements (such as an Interoperable Naming Service, Objects by Value, Messaging, and so on) that address some of the issues mentioned.

Despite the missing features, we can still produce a viable architecture using CORBA for our infrastructure. We can compensate in the design and implementation of our system, by either adjusting our architecture or providing homegrown versions of the missing features.

Semantics

We use IDL to define the interface of our distributed objects, but IDL does not capture the behavioral semantics of those services. We know what methods an object provides, its arguments, what it returns, and what exceptions it can handle. We do not know what preconditions may exist before we use any particular method supplied by the object, nor what postconditions may exist. We do not know the precise relationships between the distributed objects or what relationship (if any) exists between different methods in the interface. Currently CORBA does not provide a mechanism to capture this information.

UML

The Unified Modeling Language (UML) is the leading modeling language for object-oriented analysis and design (OOAD). UML was primarily the work of Grady Booch, Ivar Jacobson, and James Rumbaugh (the "three amigos" of Rational Software Corporation) who brought together elements of their Booch, OOSE, and OMT methods. The UML standardization effort was taken up by the OMG, which approved UML as a standard in 1997. The OMG has continued to maintain and revise the standard and has used it as the basis for other work.

UML is used as a graphical notation; it is not itself a methodology for OOAD. Although Rational Software promulgates the Unified Process, UML is basically process-independent. That said, UML provides the language for the software blueprints that are the working elements of any OOAD method. UML can describe how a system is to be used, how its classes are related and packaged, how it runs, and how it is physically deployed. UML serves as a means of communication in OO development—among people working on a system, and between people and CASE tools.

Figure 2-5 is a sample UML use case diagram of some interactions between a user and a document system. The user can find or format

documents, both cases involve authenticating the user. Finding a document is a generalization of finding by keyword or id. Changing the view type of a document is an extension of the ability to format a document. This diagram captures some of the functional requirements of the system, and can be used to derive design elements and test cases.

UML includes several types of diagrams:

- *Use case diagrams* capture interactions between actors and the system.
- *Class diagrams* show classes and interfaces and their relationships.
- *Object diagrams* illustrate object instances and their relationships.
- *Sequence diagrams* show the sequence of messages between objects.
- *Collaboration diagrams* elucidate the structural relationships between interacting objects.
- *Statechart diagrams* are state machine diagrams for classes, use cases, and systems.
- *Activity diagrams* are activity flowcharts.
- *Component diagrams* show components and their relationships.
- *Deployment diagrams* show relationships between hardware and software elements.

A solution is to implement a repository of metadata information that describes a system. Rather than implement a repository, we may achieve the same goal by providing an IDL interface to a repository supplied with a CASE tool. The use and access to metadata by the application at runtime enables us to produce dynamic systems. These systems can discover and use new distributed objects as they are introduced with minimal or no code change.

The OMG's meta-object facility (MOF) will provide us this functionality. The MOF provides an interface to a repository in which we can store the object model for the system being implemented. In the future we should be able to produce dynamic systems that can utilize the metadata within the MOF. For example, we can produce applications that will query the MOF to discover the capabilities of a distributed object.

The metadata stored within the MOF can be expressed using the Unified Modeling Language (UML). UML is a standard adopted by the OMG; it provides a modeling language for the analysis and design of an object-oriented system. UML is becoming the standard language used to express object models regardless of methodology.

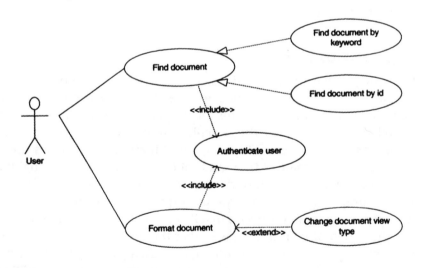

Figure 2-5. *Sample UML use case diagram*

Interoperable naming service

You have provided a distributed object and you want others to use it, so you advertise its object reference using the naming service. This service allows us to name an object and associate its object reference with that name. Now a colleague from another department wishes to make use of your object. The problem is that the other department is using an ORB supplied by another vendor.

Simple, you say: CORBA defines interoperability—we do not have to do any work. In practice, you discover that there is a bootstrap problem. How does your colleague's application get that initial object reference to your object? The IOR for your object needs to be made available to the application.

You can use a variety of mechanisms to publish the initial object reference. One could be that you both make use of the same name service. Whatever mechanism you end up using, even if it involves passing around string representations of the object reference, you will have a small amount of initialization and configuration to handle.

The mechanism of object activation, as performed by the object adapter, is not standardized. When the ORB infrastructure receives an object reference it needs to resolve, it will make use of an object adapter to perform activation.

Interface versioning

Okay, now you have your interface defined and you have provided an implementation. Now the business requires some enhancements to the system: what do you do? Does this mean that you need to change your IDL? What happens to all those deployed clients? Is updating client installations a costly exercise? For large multinational companies this is the case; also, the update of thousands of clients distributed throughout the world can take several months. So how can CORBA help you? The plain and simple answer to this question is that it does not help!

The more complicated answer is that if you spent enough time and energy on the design of your interfaces so that the system is extensible, then you will have less of a problem. However, even then you may need to introduce change. CORBA does not provide a mechanism to support multiple versions of an interface; this was dropped from the OMG specification a couple of years ago. The official OMG approach is to use inheritance.

Providing a mechanism to version interfaces is complicated. However, some object-oriented databases have managed a similar process with the ability to version schema. The lack of a version control mechanism for interfaces increases the complexity of the development process.

Objects by value

With IDL, we define the interfaces of our distributed objects; however, we can only define simple types and structures as arguments to the methods of a distributed object. It is currently not possible to pass a CORBA object from one process to another (we can only pass object references).

Our main problem of passing objects from one process to another is how to pass the implementation of an object across different programming languages. Java RMI solved this problem by just supporting the one programming language.

A solution is for the implementation to be available to all processes— maybe in a shared (or dynamic) library. Then we just need to transfer the state of the object.

The object-by-value specification that the OMG recently adopted provides a mechanism to pass objects. Unfortunately, though, it does not provide a mechanism for the migration of a distributed object. It would be nice to be able to transfer a distributed object from one process to another in a way that is transparent to the client. This would facilitate management tasks: for instance, when we need to take a production computer system down without interrupting service.

Messaging

Messaging-oriented middleware (MOM) products are a class of product that facilitates asynchronous communication. MOMs provide control over the quality of service, guaranteed message delivery, and mechanisms for load balancing and specifying priority of messages.

Currently the CORBA Event service provides some of the abilities of MOM products. You can even find some implementations of the Event service that sit on top of other MOM products. However, current ORB implementations do not provide us with the full capabilities of a MOM product.

With CORBA 3, we will see all the capabilities provided by MOM products as part of an ORB. This will provide us with a standard interface for true asynchronous communication with distributed objects. Clients do not need to block when invoking a method on a distributed object. We can deliver messages with certainty even after the client is no longer active. Your client can receive messages when reestablishing a connection to the network after disconnection. Messages can be given a priority and servers can process those messages according to a predetermined scheme.

System management

The area that is seriously lacking with ORBs is the management of a production system. At present, the OMG has not specified any mechanisms to manage a system of distributed objects. Solutions for system management are invariably homegrown. Some of these we will discuss later in the book.

ORBs need to obtain the functionality provided by transaction processing monitors: load balancing (distributing server loads across multiple systems while appearing as a single system to the client) and fault tolerance (when a server fails, transparently routing messages to a new server). We are seeing ORBs with these features emerge in the market with the introduction of ORBs by TP monitor vendors such as BEA.

We also need services that enable us to monitor the distributed objects in our system, manage those processes (shutdown and object migration), and interact with network management tools.

Service-Oriented Architecture

Because we define distributed objects by their interface (IDL), each distributed object can be considered to provide a service. As we saw, the OMA defines four categories of services, starting with the base CORBA services (such as naming, security, and so on) and then the horizontal and vertical facilities. Additionally, we have those services defined by the application you develop. By defining the distributed objects you produce as services, you will produce a set of reusable components.

You will see as you work through this book that it's a good idea to design a distributed object system as a set of cooperating services. This does not mean that we are going back to a remote procedure call–like model: remote processes providing services with a flat interface of functions. We still provide a distributed object model. We should be cognizant, however, of the limitations as well as the capabilities of the technologies that we use, including the network and the ORB infrastructure.

We will see in the next chapter that the granularity of our IDL interfaces will also affect the performance of the system that we are implementing: the more fine-grained the distributed interface, the more network overhead. Now, some would argue that as networks improve and that fiber optics become more prevalent, this will no longer be an issue. In my opinion, this is a problem similar in nature to memory-hungry applications; just because memory is cheap, that does not mean large applications are justifiable. To satisfy the needs and expectations of the users of the system, you need to be aware of the limitations of your technology.

Integration Strategies with Existing Systems

Most of the time we do not develop a new system in a vacuum. There exists some code or system that our business uses and wants to integrate with the new application. We want to retain our investment in the development and production of the existing system while moving into the New World of distributed objects. Quite often, the literature refers to these pre-existing systems as "legacy." *Legacy* always brings to mind COBOL code written decades ago, but today the legacy system could have been developed last year. Therefore, I prefer to use the term *existing system*.

We can separate the types of existing systems into three categories: database, library and application. In all of these categories, the system usually has embedded business logic. It is the business logic that we wish to keep and make available to the new application, while allowing the old application to continue working. In all categories of existing systems, we need to have or obtain an understanding of the business problem that we want to model.

Integration occurs by providing a façade, otherwise known as an object wrapper. Figure 2-6 shows a schematic of an object wrapper. The wrapper itself will be a distributed object defined using IDL. The implementation of the wrapper manages the interaction with the existing system. There is no "correct" way to produce such a wrapper, although you should be

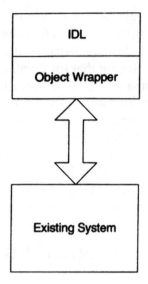

Figure 2-6. *Object Wrapper*

aware of some concerns and techniques. I will try to give you a flavor of these so that you will be better armed when you are in the position of integrating an existing system with your distributed architecture.

Beware of creating an interface that just maps to the functions of the existing system. While this may seem like the easy course in the short term, you will produce an inflexible system. It is worth the extra effort to produce a façade (set of object wrappers) that provides the model that you want to expose to other parts of the system and hides the old implementation. A layer of abstraction should encapsulate the existing system, one that provides a more intuitive object model.

There are three steps to the production of object wrappers.

- Analyze the business problem. Just as you would begin any project analyzing the problem, you should understand the business problem thoroughly. You will then have a domain model.

- Specify the interfaces. You will first produce a design model from which you will extract the distributed objects. These distributed objects model the problem domain used by the client applications. By specifying these objects in OMG IDL, you will have a model of your existing application with which other parts of your distributed system can interact.

- Provide an implementation. This is a deceptively easy task. Depending on the complexity of the interface to the existing code base, this task may be quite complex.

The cost of interfacing directly with the existing system may be too much. A solution may be to provide an implementation with an indirect interface; for example, your distributed object may work on data files produced as output from the existing system.

Integration strategy for a database

As relational databases became popular we saw the introduction of such features as triggers and stored procedures. These enabled the programmer to ensure the integrity of the data within the database by embedding business logic into the actual operation of the database. This increased the complexity of applications. Applications, which access the database, do not necessarily have a uniform business model.

You may want just to provide an object model on top of the data model through which the application performs all access. In this case, it will be necessary to implement a layer that maps the data model into the object model. As mentioned above, this database interface would form part of the data services layer of a three-tier architecture.

I have found an implementation of the OMG query service to be a simple, yet useful way to wrap a relational database. The query service can also be used to wrap other data sources. While this does not provide an object model, it facilitates access to the database via a standard CORBA-based interface. The query service provides all the functionality of the relational model (see the OMG specification for more details). You can then provide the new business logic in the application layer of the architecture.

Other tools on the market enable you to map from a relational model to an object model. One such tool is the eponymously named Persistence. Some of these tools will also generate OMG IDL, though you should be aware of the issues related to interface granularity when dealing with machine-generated code (these will be discussed in the next chapter).

Regardless of the method you chose to map from the relational (or network) model to an object model, you should still design the public IDL interfaces to reflect the business logic used by applications.

Integration strategy for a library

Typically, a library (if object-oriented) will already present a set of classes that are used together to solve specific business problems. You will need to look at how the classes are used and gain an understanding of the dependencies. There will be a straightforward manner to map from the functionality provided by the existing library to that provided by your IDL.

For a non–object-oriented library, you can still perform the same process. However, it will be necessary to be aware of the strong dependencies or coupling that may occur among the functions.

It is also important to know whether the library with which you are integrating is thread-safe. Your distributed objects will probably exist in a multi-threaded server to increase the performance of your distributed application. If the library is not thread-safe, then you will need to ensure the integrity of the system by providing locks. If this becomes a problem with performance, then you may wish to replicate instances of servers.

Integration strategy for an application

Integration with an existing application is probably one of the hardest tasks to achieve. Success will depend on not just how well you understand the business domain, but also how well the application is structured.

Depending on how the existing application is structured, it may have various mechanisms you can use to communicate with it:

- Use an application programming interface (API).

- The application understands some form of network messages. It may be the server part of a "traditional" client/server system.

- The application is a batch program with file-based communication.

The existing application may consist of a monolithic piece of spaghetti code. If this is the case, then your task may be next to impossible, unless there is some way to interact with the application without touching the application's internals. If the code for the user interface is tightly coupled with the business logic, however, then you have your work cut out for you.

If you need to extract the business logic from the application code, you will need to refactor the code (refactoring is a means to change the internal structure of the program through a series of small steps). Refactor to create a consistent interface that will support the desired business model.

I have seen some clients present applications that have been developed and deployed using systems such as Paradox or PowerBuilder. Their jump to distributed object architecture is driven by the desire to leverage their business by using some of the "cool" technologies that they have heard about (such as Java and CORBA). Sometimes, after looking at their system we see that the business logic is so dispersed within the application that it would be simpler to rewrite the system. The justification for integration may be insufficient to match the cost of integrating the existing system.

It should now be apparent that, when implementing a distributed application, you should spend enough time and energy on your IDL interfaces. These are the public faces of your distributed objects, with which all the other parts of your system will interact. As far as the clients are concerned, the implementation behind those interfaces can be anything as long as they behave as advertised.

Summary

In this chapter we reviewed object-oriented concepts and looked at distributed objects, in particular the OMG's CORBA standard. We discussed how CORBA-based products help with the construction of a distributed object based system. In addition, we looked at some of the features CORBA provides to help construct such systems, and we discussed what will be forthcoming in the OMG's "CORBA store."

Most of you have existing systems that provide functionality that will be incorporated into your new "state-of-the-art" system. We discussed the integration of existing systems. The different types of existing systems were classified into database, library, and application. We then looked at each of these and discussed how integration may (or may not) be realized.

References

Fowler, Martin. Analysis Patterns: Reusable Object Models. Reading, Massachusetts: Addison-Wesley, 1997.

Gamma, E., R. Helm, R. Johnson, and J Vlissides. *Design Patterns*. Reading, Massachusetts: Addison-Wesley, 1994.

Jacobsen, I., M. Christenson, P. Jonsson, and G, Overgaard. *Object-Oriented Software Engineering*. Reading, Massachusetts: Addison-Wesley, 1992.

Orfali, R., D. Harkey, and J. Edwards. *The Distributed Objects Survival Guide*. New York: John Wiley & Sons, 1996.

Meyer, Bertrand. *Object-Oriented Software Construction*. 2nd Edition, Hemel Hempstead, UK: Prentice Hall, 1997.

For further information on the Web: http://www.omg.org—here you can find the CORBA specification and the current work of the OMG.

Notes

1. In America, the accelerator is the gas pedal. This shows that the use of terminology in your object model is important. Use terms and words that are common parlance for the domain that you are modeling.

Chapter 3

Partitioning, Interfaces, and Granularity

Building a system based of distributed objects is not the same as constructing a single object-oriented program. We need to take into account the effects of the network, the fact that we can have tasks interacting while running in parallel, and the possibility of partial failure. Implementing mechanisms to handle failure and coordination of concurrent processes (which will be covered later in the book) may be extremely important; however, the choices we make when designing distributed objects profoundly impacts the performance and flexibility of the system.

It's not enough to take an object model and just distribute arbitrarily, placing objects throughout the network without further consideration. Once we have decided on how to distribute the functionality of the system, we need to spend time and energy defining the interfaces to the distributed objects. Additionally, new users to distributed objects and CORBA commonly encounter problems in identifying the best level of granularity for their distributed objects. Incorrect identification can make the resultant system performance far from satisfactory. Finding alternatives may be too late when you no longer have the time or resources for improvements.

When you initially design your system's distributed objects, you will be concerned with each object's interface, the object model's granularity, and how the complete system is partitioned. The granularity of the object model refers to the scale of abstraction and tasks embodied by the objects and their associated methods. Partitioning refers to where you are going to locate your objects; that is, in which server processes and where on your network. All the decisions you make for these aspects of your distributed object system have effects that you should understand.

In this chapter we will be looking at the issues involved in developing a distributed object model and the production of a corresponding set of interfaces. First, we will have a quick look at where this process fits into the project life cycle. Then we will look at interface design, granularity and partitioning. Finally, we will examine how this applies to an example of a document publishing system.

The Project Life Cycle

Object-oriented software development takes places in phases. The various stages in a project life cycle are analysis, design, development, implementation, testing and deployment. However, we do not go through each of these stages in a straight line. Within each phase, we look forward and we reflect back, tweaking the models that have been developed to incorporate current discoveries and make refinements.

The models developed at each phase of the project represent an abstraction of a real-world problem. This abstraction provides us with a vocabulary, in object-oriented terms, of the system we are developing and help with the production of code. Different methodologies have used various names to describe the various models. This book doesn't aim to provide a methodology, but rather to help you with the production of a distributed system. Typically, the output of the analysis and design stages of the project life cycle is the conceptual model of the system. We then translate this to an implementation model, which is in effect the code we are writing.

The conceptual model provides a description of the system. It also includes static models (such as class and object models), dynamic models (such as sequence and state diagrams), usage models (such as use cases), and architectural models (system composition). Plenty of work has been done over the past couple of decades on how to produce all these models. The design and construction of object-oriented systems, within a single address space, is well understood (for further reference see the books by Booch and Jacobson).

Let's assume for this project that we've decided that our system will be distributed. This may have been a requirement inherent to our problem, or we may have determined as part of our analysis that we needed a distributed system. Once we've made this decision, we need to design the distributed object model and make choices as to the interfaces of its objects.

Production of distributed object systems is relatively new, and introduces new factors into the design process. This requires us to build an additional model: a distributed object model. There are three aspects that we should be aware of when producing such a model:

1. System partitioning.

2. Interface design.

3. Granularity of the distributed object model.

Each of these has an effect on the other. Figure 3-1 illustrates the interdependence of these three aspects of interface design. It is difficult to deal with issues of partitioning, interface design, and granularity in isolation. A well-designed system will balance the forces from each of these areas, providing interfaces at a suitable level of abstraction and granularity.

Partitioning

In the course of designing a distributed system, we create a lot of objects. How do we distribute the things in our object model? We could take our objects and just haphazardly scatter them across the network; however, we would end up with an inefficient system, because we would have introduced an unnecessarily high level of interaction among the objects across the network.

One of our goals when we "partition" our system is to create an architecture that will support evolution. New requirements can be incorporated when they are discovered. The system should also be flexible enough to support the reuse of components so as to provide new functionality. Why reinvent components later on when you can design a system now to maximize the reuse of its parts?

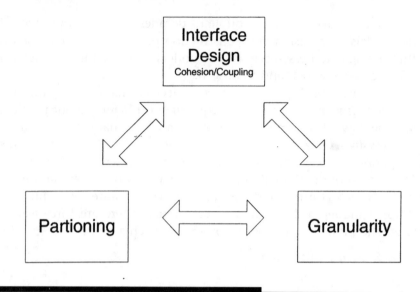

Figure 3-1. *Forces in distributed object model design*

The distributed system we are building will probably be decomposed into a set of subsystems. Each subsystem is composed of a set of distributed objects that support the functionality of that subsystem. Partitioning consists of the choices we make in dividing functionality into subsystems, and the subsequent placement of distributed objects. We may also choose to locate some of the objects in these subsystems on the same machine, and even within the same process, depending on deployment and performance issues. We can use a guiding set of principles to help us arrange the distributed objects into the various subsystems.

By design, the subsystem should be cohesive; that is, the distributed objects within the subsystem should support the object-oriented concept represented by the subsystem. For example, a distributed object that represents a printer should be just a printer; it should not control a microwave.

Each subsystem should be coherent; that is, we design classes to make them represent a well-defined abstraction. They should support a well-defined concept, or set of concepts, derived from our business model. For example, a subsystem that provides functionality for a print facility should contain only distributed objects that support that functionality (like a printer and print scheduler).

It is useful to consider each subsystem as providing a service. We would produce subsystems for data access services, print facilities, account management and so on. Taking this approach, our distributed system uses an architecture based on a set of cooperating services.

This partitioning also affects the interface choices for distributed objects that compose the subsystem. We should examine the flow of control among the subsystems so that no one subsystem becomes a bottleneck. We can look at our use cases and determine how each of the subsystems may be used in the application. From these, we derive scenarios making use of the various subsystems we have identified. We will then have an initial idea of how each of the parts of our system interact, and we can adjust our decisions regarding partitioning if it looks unbalanced.

In addition, we can refine our decisions regarding partitioning based on the examination of a sequence diagram. Sequence diagrams (such as that in Figure 3-8 later) capture the interaction among the objects within your model, and are a good indicator of the amount of communication necessary to perform the tasks required by the system. If a lot of communication is necessary to perform a task then we should examine the objects that are used for that task. These objects are good candidates to be located within the same sub-system.

We have now defined partitions of subsystems containing distributed objects. For each distributed object to be accessible by users of the subsystem, we need to define an interface for it using IDL. This set of interfaces then becomes the public face of the subsystem, and the functionality defined by them is supported by the implementation within the subsystem.

Interfaces

You will recall from Chapter 2 that an interface is a collection of methods and attributes. Interfaces are the expression of our distributed object model and the public face of our subsystems. Our subsystems can contain many distributed objects, so they can support multiple interfaces. The structure of our interfaces will affect the performance and reusability of components of the system.

In the process of developing the distributed object model, we identify the various subsystems, which may be located in disparate parts of the network. Each of these subsystems will support one or more distributed objects. Each of these distributed objects will provide a public interface that we express in IDL.

Interfaces may represent both entity objects and process objects. An entity object represents a thing, such as a document. A process object provides an abstraction of a process; for example, a process object may be a document locator.

We have to deal with many issues when we design an interface:

- The interface should be cohesive; it must support a single concept.

- We should minimize the coupling—a measure of the dependency between different parts of the system—between the implementation of the interface and the clients.

- We must define exceptions—standard methods of handling error conditions.

- We must decide what use to make of polymorphism—the reuse of common definitions of interfaces to serve different objects.

Cohesion

The concept of cohesion as applied to software construction was formulated, concurrent with the work on structured programming, in the late 1970s. At that time cohesion was defined as a measure of the logical relationships and connectivity between different parts of a software module. When we bring this concept to the object-oriented world, cohesion is defined as the measure of the logical relationship between the methods within a class and the measure of logical relationships within a subsystem. We refer to the cohesion of a class (or object) and the cohesion of subsystems. For a distributed object model we refer to the cohesion of interfaces and subsystems. A cohesive software module helps support maintainability of the system by expressing the parts of a system as easily understood units.

During the initial work on cohesion, different types were identified (Yourdon and Constantine 1979, and Myers 1978). To help with this discussion, here is a quick overview of some of the types of cohesion as applied to an object model, in order of desirability:

Coincidental cohesion—A class and its elements do not represent a coherent abstraction. For example, a class that is defined as a set of unrelated methods is coincidental.

Logical cohesion—Actions performed by a method vary according to a switch passed as a parameter.

Temporal cohesion—Methods are grouped together to be executed at a certain time. For example, methods to perform initialization tasks are only connected occasionally.

Procedural cohesion—A class is defined specifically for one application. A method of such a class is a sequence of functions executed when a condition is met.

Sequential cohesion—The input of one method depends on the results of a previous method.

Functional cohesion—All elements of a class work together, supporting the class's well-defined abstraction.

When we produce a cohesive distributed object model, we find that each of the interfaces represent essential concepts. Each object is easier to understand; the overall system is more maintainable; and the components that comprise the system are easier to reuse. All of this contributes to reducing the overall cost of the system.

The following guidelines will help us produce a distributed object model consisting of functionally cohesive interfaces:

- Each interface should embody an essential concept (abstraction) and all the elements of an interface should be strongly related to that abstraction. This implies that an interface should correspond to either a real world or logical entity.

- Each of the methods should perform a single coherent function or task. That is, if a method adds two numbers then it also should not set the timer on your microwave.

- Each of the subsystems of our distributed architecture should themselves be cohesive. For a subsystem to be cohesive then all the interfaces that comprise that sub-system should also be cohesive and support the object-oriented concept represented by that subsystem. For example, we may provide an interface for a document locator so that a client can find documents on an ad-hoc basis for later perusal. The document locator interface should provide us with the necessary functionality to locate the document, but it should not provide us with the functionality to examine a document's content (an interface to the document would do that). Additionally, how the locator retrieves the document is of no concern to the user of the locator.

Coupling

Whereas cohesion is a measure of the connectivity between related elements within a software module, coupling is a measure of the strength of dependency between different software modules. The stronger the coupling, then the stronger the interdependence of the different parts of the system. And this is bad. Some level of coupling is unavoidable, but we want to minimize it as much as possible.

Many levels of coupling can occur when you design an interface. When we are dealing with an object model we are concerned with coupling that exists between the different classes of the model and the coupling between the items within a class. Likewise for a distributed object model we are concerned with the coupling between distributed objects and coupling between the components of a distributed objects interface. Strongly coupled distributed objects will affect the flexibility of our system. The stronger the coupling the more brittle (inflexible) the system will be. As we will see later, the granularity of our object model also has an impact on coupling.

In *Object-Oriented Design Heuristics*, Arthur Reil details the various types of coupling that can occur:

> **Nil coupling**—there is no dependency between the two classes.
>
> **Export coupling**—one class is dependent only on the public interface of another.

Overt coupling—a class is dependent on the implementation details of another class, with permission.

Covert coupling—a class is dependent on the implementation details of another class, but no permission was given.

While we want to reduce the amount of coupling between components of a system, it is not possible to construct a system with nil coupling. That is, as soon as two or more components need to interact there will be some degree of coupling. Objects will always be related in some matter. Also, for the same reason, we do have export coupling because the different parts of our system interact by making use of the semantics defined by the distributed objects interfaces. However, the strength of that coupling will be determined by the choices we make when designing our interfaces.

It is the other types of coupling that cause us the most problems. Overt and covert coupling introduce dependencies that subvert our desire to produce a loosely coupled system. Since IDL only expresses the public interface of a distributed object and the internals are not exposed we avoid covert coupling. Additionally if the interfaces of a sub-system are at the same level of abstraction then we avoid overt coupling. If we provide interfaces within a sub-system at lower levels of abstraction then we expose unnecessary details of the internals of the sub-system. Then we have a form of overt coupling.

A distributed system can also contain an **implicit coupling**, based on shared knowledge between the components of the system. This occurs when the distributed object and its clients depend on mutual knowledge that is not captured in the semantics of the interface. In other words, the interface may not explicitly define the form of information passed between the user of the interface and the implementation; however, the form of that information is captured within the implementation of both client and server. This causes both the client and server to be coupled by relying on implicit knowledge as to the form of information.

It is possible to design a system that provides what at first looks like weak coupling, while actually providing strong implicit coupling. I have seen this done in a system as a means to solve the problems of interface versioning and management. Here one simple interface is provided for all distributed objects. Listing 3-1 shows a portion of the IDL for this type of coupling.

Listing 3-1: *IDL with strong implicit coupling*

```
interface Object {
  any doit(in long version, in string method, in string
    arguments);
};
```

The *doit* method of the object contains the information as to what method to call and a set of arguments. This creates two problems. First, this defeats the reason for using IDL, because we are no longer using IDL to specify the interface to our distributed objects. Second, this imposes a strong implicit coupling: both the client and the implementation of the object need to know the correct formats and allowed types. Instead of the interface of a distributed object being defined in the IDL, the interfaces are embedded in the actual implementation. Knowledge of the interface for any distributed object is now implicit, since it includes our decisions for the protocol used to represent the method and its arguments. This knowledge is shared among the components of the system and is not made explicit, so we have created a system that defeats the purpose of IDL, for which we still have the same design issues (cohesion, coupling and granularity), but in which the description of each interface is embedded within code.

Exceptions

An exception enables you to define a uniform mechanism to report error conditions for each method within your IDL. Exceptions can happen whenever a remote method is executed. This helps the user of a distributed object determine the source of failure; also, the caller of a method, which throws an exception, is forced to handle that exception.

You should make use of exceptions in your IDL, as this will help with the process of trace and debugging. When you define your own types of exceptions that are more meaningful to the application, then not only do you gain knowledge as to what went wrong, but you can also provide code to handle the error condition in a graceful manner.

Some programming languages provide constructs to handle exceptions, in which case CORBA exceptions map to the mechanism provided by the programming language you are using. If the language does not have an exception mechanism, then an alternate mechanism is provided. This allows you to check the state of any possible exception as defined by the CORBA mapping.

Polymorphism

Polymorphism refers to the ability to have many forms. In the object-oriented world, this refers to the ability of an object to be many different objects. For example, in our object-oriented programming language, our code may refer to an object that represents a scanner; we can then use this code to handle different types of scanner.

It is interesting to note that the class and type of an object are intertwined in many object-oriented languages. The class contains both the interface definition and the implementation. However, IDL only allows us to specify interfaces and says nothing about implementation. We can view these interfaces as specifying a type. We can utilize the feature that the interface is separate from the implementation. We can provide many different implementations of the same interface. Moreover, our clients can treat each of these implementations in a polymorphic manner.

An example would be an interface to a search engine. We could provide various implementations, one for a relational database, another for an object database. Since each of these implementations provides the same interface, our client can utilize both with no code change.

CORBA includes two mechanisms to provide polymorphism. You may have more than one implementation for a specific interface; both implementations can be treated in the same way. Also, an object reference to a specific interface may refer to an implementation of that interface, or an implementation of a derived interface.

Granularity

Granularity refers to the fineness, or coarseness, of your object model. Fine-grained models are composed of many small objects, each cooperating to provide an implementation that solves your business problem. On the other hand, coarse-grained models provide large controller-like objects that represent large concepts.

When designing your interfaces, it is important to be aware of the granularity of the distributed object model. The fact that the objects reside in different locations does add another dimension to the decision-making process. Fine-grained distributed object models have a negative impact on performance due to a high level of interaction. This increased amount of detail knowledge causes an increase in coupling.

If we take the naïve approach of distributing the full domain object model, we will produce a very fine-grained system. Conversely, if we provide a single interface to each remote process, we will end up with a course-grained system. There is a cost associated with both approaches. A fine-grained system will affect performance: more interactions between objects are required to perform a single task. A course-grained system will introduce problems with cohesion, usually because you are embodying more than one concept from the domain model within a single interface. This reduces flexibility, as the interface becomes more restrictive in the ways it can be used.

Granularity and coupling

I mentioned above that a fine-grained distributed object model increases the amount of coupling among the distributed components. The amount of knowledge required by the client of a set of distributed objects is simply greater. Another way to look at it is that a fine-grained model provides an insufficiently high level of abstraction.

A low level of abstraction can create a stronger amount of coupling among the different parts of the system. The user of the interfaces comes to rely on the application-specific knowledge embodied within the interfaces. We will have produced a distributed system that solves only one problem, and one in which the distributed objects are not reusable. In addition, this will affect the extensibility (the ability to add new functionality) and flexibility (ability to reuse parts of the system in previously unforeseen ways) of the system. You may hear such a system referred to as a "stove pipe," an allusion to a system that has a very narrow focus and a vertical problem.

The code illustrated in Listing 3-2 provides a simple example of a fine-grained model. Here the IDL represents the document as a collection of chapters, each chapter as a collection of paragraphs, and so on. Not only does this affect the performance (as we discuss later), it also provides us with an inflexible system. For example, what if we want to have sections in our document?

Listing 3-2: Example of low abstraction

```
exception NotFound {};
exception CannotInsert{};

typedef sequence<string> Sentence;

interface Paragraph {
    readonly attribute long nbrSentences;

    void addSentence(in long posn, in Sentence sentence)
                        raises(CannotInsert);
    Sentence readSentence(in long posn) raises(NotFound);
};

interface Chapter {
    readonly attribute long nbrParagraphs;

    void addParagraph(in long posn, in Paragraph paragraph)
                        raises(CannotInsert);
    Paragraph getParagraph(in long posn) raises(NotFound);
};

interface Document {
    readonly attribute long nbrChapters;

    void addChapter(in long posn, in Chapter chapter)
                        raises(CannotInsert);
    Chapter getChapter(in long posn) raises(NotFound);
};
```

One cautionary note: we can easily produce "stove pipe" systems when we use development tools that generate IDL. Currently these tools aren't sophisticated enough. They perform a simplistic mapping from an object model (usually a model of the domain) straight to IDL. This does not take into account constraints like the effect of communications over the network. To avoid the "stove pipe" problem, the user must add the sophistication by handcrafting the IDL.

The details conveyed by the interface directly affect the coupling. For example, if an interface to a remote printer has in it methods that directly relate to the capabilities of a specific model of printer, then the client is closely coupled to that specific type of printer. It is not a simple task to replace the printer in this system with a different one, and new printers would require new interfaces. However, if the printer interface provides us with a model of a generic printer, then we can easily provide different a printer implementation and the client is not coupled to any specific implementation.

Granularity and performance

Computers may be fast and communication overhead between two objects on the same system may be infinitesimal; however, when you multiply objects by the thousands, distribute them over a network, and constrict the bandwidth, the cost adds up. It takes a significant amount of time for communication to happen on our network, whether it is fiber optic or modem. On top of this there is the overhead imposed on communications from the ORB infrastructure. The ORB has to transform the request into a standard communications protocol (IIOP) and then translate the request for the destination platform. All of these factors contribute to network latency.

Moreover, every method invocation has a cost. If this cost exceeds the cost to execute the remote method, then we have a problem. This is further compounded by any task that requires numerous remote method invocations. The responsiveness of the system will be adversely affected.

What are our options? Of course, we could get a faster network. However, for most people this is not feasible, nor does it make business sense. The answer is to design our interfaces so that the cost of communications does not overwhelm the cost of execution. Granularity affects the communications performance of the system, especially the granularity of the methods within an interface. We do not want to make the distributed objects too fine-grained because of the resulting increase in network communication. We could coarsen the system, but if it is too coarse then our desire to produce a cohesive system is negated. This is a difficult problem to solve. You will find that the craft of good interface design will improve with experience. Being aware of the issues will help.

Example: Document Retrieval

To illustrate the issues raised in the previous sections, we will now look at a document retrieval system. First we look at the object model for the system, and then at the ways the system can be partitioned; then we derive an initial interface definition. After a short critique of the first set of IDL, we will refine our choices and develop a new set of interfaces to provide a system that is more flexible and maintainable, while retaining the cohesiveness of the object model. We will return to, and expand on, this example later within the book as we discuss other issues such as persistence and transactions.

Currently we are just concerned with the requirement for a user to find a document using an *ad hoc* query and peruse its contents. It would be useful later if we can add other sources of documents, and the ability to transform the content of a document into many formats. We will also take this into account as we progress through the example and produce IDL that captures these requirements.

An example of the effect of granularity is where we have an interface to a remote document in which every word is a separate distributed object. Any meaningful task would require a huge amount of network traffic. There would be a high cost of network communication to perform simple string manipulation, which normally takes a very short time to execute in local address space. A solution would be to locate each of the objects that compose the document within the same address space, not expose them as individual distributed objects, and provide an interface at a higher level of abstraction (Document).

Object model

Figure 3-2 is a diagram of the high-level classes within our system. These include a document locator, document store, and the documents themselves. Here is a brief description of the components.

Document—provides a representation of a document within memory. A document consists of document elements.

Document Store—provides persistent storage for documents. For example, this could be an object database. The store needs to provide the ability to find a document using an ad-hoc query. Once found the document is translated from the stored form into the form required by our object model.

Document Locator—takes a query and coordinates with the document store to find the requisite document.

Formatter—enables us to transform a document into a format suitable for the browser. It will be clearer as we proceed through this example where this class fits in, and we will alter what depends on it accordingly.

Display/Browser—this is a client side program that allows a user to interact with the system.

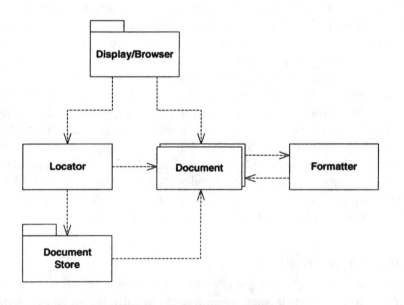

Figure 3-2. *Static class diagram for a document location system*

We can refine our object model further to provide more detail. Each of the above components will also contain and collaborate with other objects. However, for the purposes of our discussion it is currently sufficient for us to work with the above set of components.

Figure 3-3 illustrates part of a class hierarchy that can be use to model instances of documents. This is based on a composite pattern: documents are composed of document elements, and a document is itself a document element. This enables us to create quite a complex document by building a tree-like structure with instances of these classes. Figure 3-4 provides an example of such a structure.

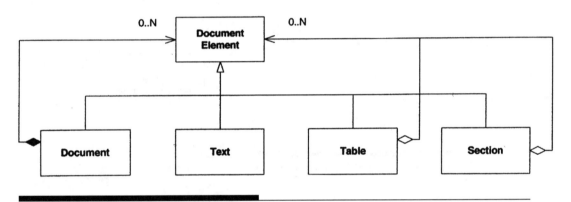

Figure 3-3. *Partial class diagram for document*

It should be noted that this is a relatively simple object model, but it is sufficient for the purposes of this example. As we proceed we will see that we can provide a rich set of functionality.

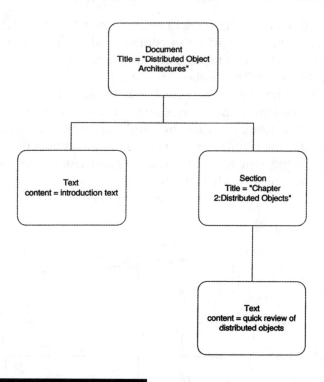

Figure 3-4. *Partial document instance*

Partitioning

Before we can design the interfaces to the remote objects, we need to decide how we are going to partition the system. Figures 3-5 to 3-7 illustrate the various partitioning schemes that we are now going to discuss.

> **Scheme 1**—Here we have one monolithic server. We can implement the various components of the server (document, locator, store etc.) as a standard object-oriented application. Only the user interface has been separated. Our server will be multithreaded to help it handle many simultaneous requests for document retrieval.

> **Scheme 2**—This is similar to the first scheme; however, we have separated the persistent store into a separate sub-system, thus providing a three-tier architecture. This enables us to define a standard

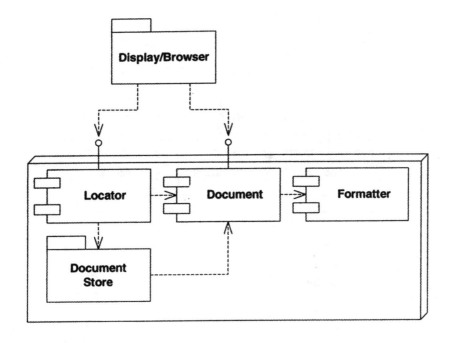

Figure 3-5. *Partition Scheme 1*

interface to the persistent store and to choose alternate stores if we like. For example, the locator could talk to more than one store to find a document; given that all the stores implement the same interface, the locator will be able to communicate to all of them. We also could replicate locators if one locator wasn't enough to handle the volume of requests.

Scheme 3—Here we have separated the formatter into its own subsystem. This allows us to define different types of formatter, to produce different output without having to touch the subsystem containing the locator and document.

Our choice of partitioning scheme will depend on our future vision for the system. We will proceed using the third partitioning scheme, as it offers us the most flexibility: it holds the promise that we can plug in new implementations of each of the components with minimal impact.

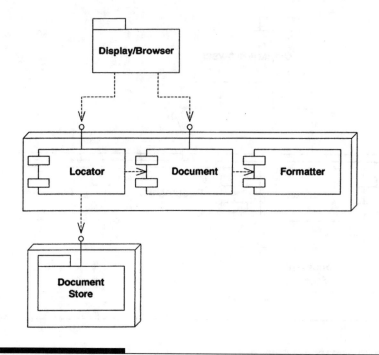

Figure 3-6. *Partition Scheme 2*

Initial Interface Definition

We will now develop interfaces to our distributed objects. Listing 3-3 shows interfaces for the locator and document model within a document management module.

The locator enables us to find a document given a query. Once a document has been found, we obtain an object reference to the remote document. If the locator does not find a document, then an appropriate exception is thrown; we need to handle this case within our client program.

Listing 3-3: Initial IDL for the document model

```
module DocumentManagement {
    exception NotFound {};
```

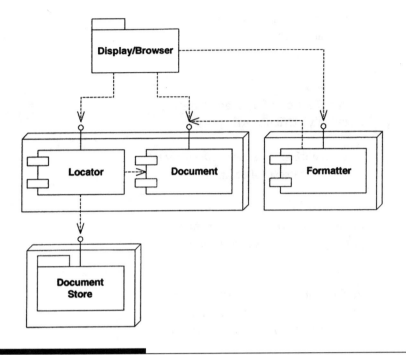

Figure 3-7. *Partition Scheme 3*

```
interface Document;

interface Locator {
    Document find(in string query) raises(NotFound);
};

exception NoContent {};
exception NoDocument {};

interface DocumentElement {
    readonly attribute string type;
};

typedef sequence<DocumentElement> DocumentElements;
```

```
interface Document : DocumentElement {
    DocumentElements getSubDocuments()
            raises(NoDocument);
};

interface Section : DocumentElement {
    readonly attribute string title;

    DocumentElements getSubDocuments()
            raises(NoDocument);
};

interface Text : DocumentElement {
    string getText() raises(NoContent);
};

interface Table : DocumentElement {
    readonly attribute long rowSize;
    readonly attribute long columnSize;

    DocumentElement getCell(in long row, in long column)
            raises(NoDocument);
};
};
```

Once we have a handle to the document, we can start to examine its content. You can tell the type of document element, and hence the content, by looking at the *type* attribute. We could provide a very fine-grained interface to the document model by defining methods that allow us to access the contents of a document character by character, though this would incur a lot of network traffic.

If we decide to add more document elements to our object model, we will need to extend the above IDL. It will then be necessary to regenerate code from the IDL and adjust the logic in our client program appropriately. The client program is coupled to the server by the amount of detail in the object model expressed by our IDL.

We should also be aware of some performance issues. Figure 3-8 shows a part of a sequence diagram to examine the content of a document. In the process of extracting the content of a document, there are many method invocations. Inevitably, this will increase with the size and complexity of the document. It would be fair to expect an increase in the cost of communications to correspond with an increase in the size of a document (because of the amount of information transferred); however, we also impose a cost on the perusal of a document's content, because the mechanism to navigate and extract information from a document is done as a combination of small steps.

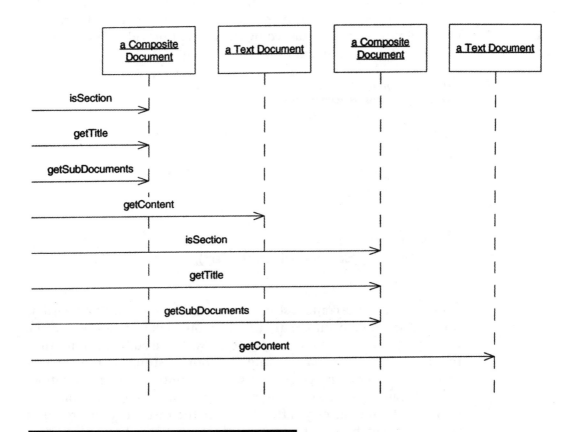

Figure 3-8. *Sequence diagram for content extraction*

Refinements

We will now refine the IDL to produce an interface that will facilitate flexibility and grow with our needs. We also want to reduce the cost of extracting the content of a document.

In the previous IDL, if we needed to add a new document element type (such as an image), then we would inherit the new document interface from the document element. Not only do we need to update the server to support the images; we also need to manage the IDL. This complicates the support necessary for the implementation and users of the interface.

If we view all document elements as content providers then we can factor out content provision as an interface. Listing 3-4 illustrates the IDL for a content provider interface. Note that we use an IDL structure to contain the content returned by the content provider. This structure can support many different formats of content.

Listing 3-4: IDL for the content provider

```
exception NoContent{};

struct Content {
    string format;
    any data;
};

interface ContentProvider {
    Content getContent() raises(NoContent);
};
```

In the listing, the content structure makes use of the CORBA type *any*. An *any* can contain information built upon CORBA types; *any* is the CORBA equivalent of a C++ *void* pointer, with the addition of runtime type information. You may ask why the "format" string has been included within the structure given that we have runtime type information. This is because the type of the information returned might be constant; however, the format may differ. Consider the case where we return a string representation of the content: the format may be some markup language or it could be PostScript.

The content structure does introduce some implicit coupling, because both the implementation and the user of the interface need to agree as to the form of the content. However, the structure contains some self-description that can be used by the user to decide what to do. In my opinion, the resultant flexibility outweighs the implicit coupling; and the semantics of the interface are not hidden. This is the type of decision that you will find yourself making when designing your interfaces.

Now we will return to the interface for documents. We can provide a generic interface for a document, one that captures the functionality we need for all types of documents and document elements. Listing 3-5 shows such a generic document interface. You will notice that there is no longer a document hierarchy defined in IDL; our clients only need to understand the one interface for all documents. To support different types of documents, then, we just provide different implementations.

Listing 3-5: Revised IDL for the document interface

```
interface Document;

typedef string SectionName;
typedef sequence<SectionName> SectionNames;

typedef sequence<Document> Documents;

interface Document : ContentProvider {
    attribute boolean isSection;
    Documents getSubDocuments() raises(NoDocument);

    SectionNames getSectionNames() raises(NoDocument);
    Document getSection(in string name) raises(NoDocument);
};
```

Our document interface provides the ability to navigate a document hierarchy, get the content of a document, extract sections of documents by name, and determine what sections a document may contain. Once we have determined what part of the document to get, we can then obtain the corresponding content.

Now I will extend our system by introducing a new component, the formatter. You use a formatter to transform the content of a document into another form. For example, we may wish to implement a PostScript formatter that will take a document and output PostScript. Alternately, we may have a formatter that produces the document in a form suitable for display, such as HTML.

It would also be nice to be able to make the functionality of a formatter available to future applications. The formatter then becomes a good candidate to become a distributed object. Listing 3-6 illustrates IDL for such a formatter. In it, you can see that the formatter just needs to understand content providers. We can plug any content provider together with the formatter of our choice.

Listing 3-6: IDL for the formatter

```
exception FormatError {
    string reason;
};

interface Formatter {
    Content format(in ContentProvider provider)
        raises(FormatError, NoContent);
};
```

We can provide implementations for different formatters, all of which conform to the defined interface. For example, we may have a formatter that can transform a document to HTML for online viewing, or we may have one that produces PDF. Maybe we will provide both! Our options are open. By defining the interface in IDL, we can plug new formatters into our architecture in a seamless manner. We can use other kinds of service, such as a name service, to help us find the instance of the formatter that we want to use.

We can implement a version of the locator, still conforming to our IDL, that utilizes other locators. Each of the other locators could either provide a degree of parallelism for finding the document within the same store, or they could search many different stores for the requested document. This is a federation of locators, each independent but working in parallel to perform the task.

To achieve this we do not need to change our client, nor do we need to alter our interfaces. We just provide a new implementation of the document locator that uses and coordinates the search process with other locators. Figure 3-9 illustrates such a system.

We can also do the same for the formatter, if a formatter does not understand part of a document then it in turn can utilize another formatter that does. Again we can utilize parallelism by farming different sections out to many formatters.

We have just gone through the development and evolution of interfaces defined in IDL to provide a mechanism to locate and publish documents. We have seen how our choices affect the flexibility of the final system. Now we have a version of IDL for document location and formatting that provides loose coupling and flexibility and supports future scalability. This provides a solid foundation for the future of our system.

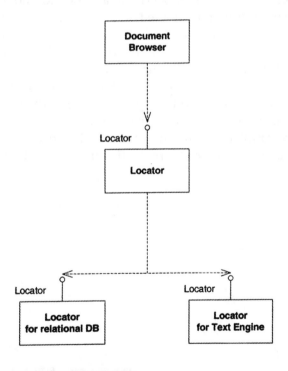

Figure 3-9. *Federated document locators*

Summary

We have discussed how to partition a distributed system, the design of the interfaces for the distributed objects and the effects of granularity. We also have seen how these are inter-related. Moreover, we have had to be aware of the computational versus the communication cost of any task to be performed. Inefficiencies will compound.

Designing a system of distributed objects and their interfaces is a heuristic process, though after reading this chapter you should now have an idea of some of the guiding principles. There is no one best solution; this will be determined by the requirements that have been set for your system. However, it is a common desire to produce a distributed system that is maintainable and flexible.

We have learned that a good object model is not necessarily a good distributed object model. Not all models that are good for monolithic applications translate well to a distributed system. We need to identify those objects that will have interfaces made public over the network. The level of granularity chosen for the distributed object model will have a direct effect on the flexibility and performance of the final system.

Be careful when you create your IDL. Fine-grained distributed object models have a direct impact on the performance of the system. Coarse-grained models produce interfaces that are less cohesive, and therefore lose flexibility. Think of the future when you design your IDL. Your system will probably need to grow and be flexible in ways that are difficult to predict.

References

Booch, Grady. *Object-Oriented Analysis and Design with Applications.* Redwood City, California: Benjamin/Cummings, 1994.

Jacobsen, I., M. Christenson, P. Jonsson, and G, Overgaard. *Object-Oriented Software Engineering.* Reading, Massachusetts: Addison-Wesley, 1992.

Myers, G.J. *Composite/Structured Design.* Van Nostrand Reinhold, New York, 1978.

Riel, Arthur J. *Object-Oriented Design Heuristics.* Reading, Massachusetts: Addison Wesley, 1996.

Yourdon, E., and Constantine, L.L. *Structure Design: Fundamentals of a Discipline of Computer Program and System Design.* Prentice Hall, Englewood Cliffs, New Jersey, 1979.

Chapter 4

Meta-Information

Meta-information is information about information. Now you have the definition, what does this actually imply for computational systems? There are occasions where you naturally make use of meta-information: the schema of your database, directory services, information about a system's configuration, and so forth. Meta-information in each of these cases allows us to increase the flexibility of the system. For example, if the schema for a database is embedded within your application, then you have negated any possible reuse of the information in the database. Separating the schema from the application allows other applications to make use of the same information.

The more flexible our systems are, the greater the chance of survival they have in the ever-changing environment of the modern computing system. To be flexible, you need to support dynamic discovery and incorporate new services when they become available. The key to providing flexible systems lies in the amount of self-description within the system. Some programming languages support such self-description (a good example is reflection in Java). There is also support for dynamic discovery of objects and meta-information within CORBA. In this chapter we will explore why meta-information provides such flexibility and how existing facilities can provide meta-information.

A lot of work done has been done in the past couple of decades on reflection in object-oriented systems. Reflection is the ability of a system of objects to reason about itself. This requires the use of a semantically rich meta-model—a description of the system—that can be queried programmatically. The ability of systems to be self-describing brings in the possibility of adding dynamic and flexible capabilities.

Most component models require a mechanism for reflection, because if you add a new component to the system, the current system needs a way to discover the capabilities of the new component. As systems increase in sophistication, we will see more use of meta-information at the programming level. Also, if the model of the system is stored within a repository, maybe using design tools, this helps with the documentation of the system, allowing other programmers/designers to gain access to the same information and hence produce other components that are consistent with the model.

The downside to building a system using meta-information is the increase in complexity. The more generic a piece of code is, and the more reliance on runtime information, then the greater the chance of unexpected error situations. As with all architectural and design issues, you need to weigh the expected benefits with the costs. With this in mind, let's take a quick look at meta-information in CORBA.

Examples of Using Meta-Information

Before we proceed, we'll look at a couple of examples that illustrate the use of meta-information. The first example is a document repository: meta-information is used to describe the documents held in store and how they may be interpreted. In the second example, we will see that the forthcoming CORBA component specification makes use of meta-information to describe components for deployment.

Document repository

In this example, we have a repository for many different types of documents. The system needs to be flexible and provide support for new document formats when they are released. Users can browse the documents in the repository, check them out for editing, add new documents, and perform criteria based searches for documents.

Alongside the documents in the repository, we keep meta-information about each of the documents. Some of this information pertains to types of documents. Each document type supported by the repository has an associated description; this description may contain information as to the format of instances of that document type. Each document instance has associated information containing details about the author, some key words for classification, the date of publication, the document status, its expiration date, and so forth. This system is illustrated in Figure 4-1.

For other components of the system to understand the information within a document, they must able to interpret the meta-information. Since the meta-information about document types contains information about the

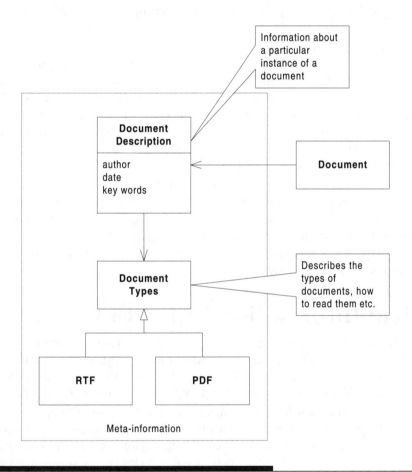

Figure 4-1. *Meta-information in a document repository*

document's format, it is possible to extend the system to understand new types of documents. When you want to add a new document type to the system, you add a description of the document type to the system's meta-information. Other system components can utilize this information to determine how to look at the contents of the new document type.

Package descriptions

Another example of the use of meta-information is the "Package Descriptor" that forms part of the CORBA component submission. This is an extension of the vocabulary described in the W3C note on Open Software Description (OSD).

A package consists of one or more implementations of a component and an associated description. The description contains a "Software Package Description" and a "Component Description." These descriptions cover the implementation of the component, the deployment environments supported, the components characteristics, and so on. You would then use a deployment tool that takes the component package and deploys the individual components. The deployment tool would use information within the description to determine where to install the components contained within the package. This mechanism provides a standard for the distribution and installation of components. As it is still a work in progress at the OMG I suggest that you visit their Website to review the current state of the Component Specification. This system is illustrated in Figure 4-2.

Meta-Information in CORBA

The CORBA standard defines various sources of meta-information as part of the core architecture and as additional facilities. The Interface Repository comes standard with an ORB; using this, you can obtain meta-information about the CORBA objects on your network. Recent additions to the CORBA specification include the Meta-Object Facility, which helps you to capture richer meta-information about your system of objects. You can publish and locate CORBA objects using the Naming Service or look up the CORBA "yellow pages," the Trader Service, to find an object that meets your criteria.

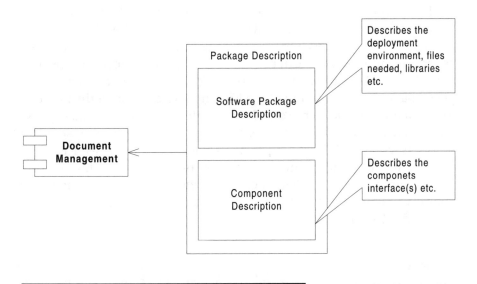

Figure 4-2. *Package descriptor for a CORBA component*

All these services and facilities give you the tools to construct a flexible architecture. The choice of which of these you use, and how you use them, depends on your requirements, the need for flexibility, and potential complexity of the system. We will take a quick look at each of the mechanisms for meta-information in CORBA and see where they may be useful.

Naming Service

For one object to talk to another, you need to know the target object's address, just as if you were to send a letter you need the address of the intended recipient. In CORBA, the address of an object is its object reference, of which there is a version that works across ORBs, the IOR. However, IORs can be quite difficult to remember. Most CORBA products have propriety mechanisms that enable you to "bind" a proxy to a remote object. This usually involves specifying the remote machine and the interface name of the object, and works in conjunction with an object activation daemon.

The Naming Service provides a mechanism for the publication and dissemination of object references. Rather than reinvent the wheel, or more appropriately a directory service, the CORBA Naming Service specifies a generic IDL interface that can be used to wrap standard mechanisms such as LDAP, DCE Directory, NIS, and so on. Your ORB vendor probably supplies a basic implementation of the Naming Service, though the interface to the Naming Service is reasonably straightforward and it would not take long to create your own implementation by wrapping another standard service (such as LDAP) with the OMG IDL for the Naming Service.

You can view the Naming Service as providing meta-information about your distributed system; it gives you the ability to name and locate your distributed objects. Also, you can structure the name space to suit the needs of your business.

Review

Anyone using computers over the past few decades will be familiar with the concept of a directory (or folder) structure for the computer file system. This structure allows you to organize and retrieve information in the form of files. The CORBA Naming Service can provide a similar structure for the name space and provides a way to map from a name to an object reference; however, you should note that the name space is more like a directed graph than a tree.

The Naming Service contains a database of mappings between names and object references. Using the OMG terminology, this mapping is called a binding. The service provides you with the functionality to find a name, create new bindings, delete bindings, and so on.

Listing 4-1 illustrates the essential interfaces for the Naming Service. As you can see, each name in the name space consists of a sequence of name components (represented by the IDL structure *NameComponent*) and each name component can have an associated user-defined type. By structuring names in this manner, the Naming Service does not impose any "standard" separators upon the user (like slash, /, for the UNIX file system and backslash ,\, for DOS). Name components are said to be equivalent if the name and ID of one component is the same as the name and ID of the other.

The key to navigation through the name space is to use naming contexts. Each node of the name space consists of a context; each context can contain name bindings. These bindings can be to other contexts or object references. Naming contexts are similar to directories (or folders) in a file system.

The top of the name space is the "root"; you can obtain the root naming context as an initial reference and navigate from there. All names you resolve are relative to the naming context that you use.

Using the *list* method, you can iterate through all the names at the next level down from the current context and dynamically discover what is bound to them. Additionally, the naming context interface also enables you to create new contexts, bind names to objects and contexts, remove bindings and so on.

Listing 4-1: *Essential interfaces for the Naming Service*

```
module CosNameing {

typedef string Istring;

struct NameComponent {
Istring id;
Istring kind;
};

typdef sequence<NameComponent> Name;

interface NamingContext {
    Object resolve(in Name n)
        raises (NotFound, CannotProceed, InvalidName);
    void bind(in Name n, in Object o)
        raises (NotFound, CannotProceed, InvalidName,
            AlreadyBound);
    void rebind(in Name n, in Object o)
        raises (NotFound, CannotProceed, InvalidName);
    void bind_context(in Name n, in Naming Context nc)
        raises (NotFound, CannotProceed, InvalidName,
            AlreadyBound);
```

```
        void rebind_context(in Name n, in Naming Context nc)
            raises (NotFound, CannotProceed, InvalidName);

        void unbind(in Name n)
            raises (NotFound, CannotProceed, InvalidName);

        NamingContext new_context();
        NamingContext bind_new_context(in Name n)
            raises (NotFound, CannotProceed, InvalidName,
                AlreadyBound);

        void destroy() raises (NotEmpty);

        void list(in unsigned long how_many,
                out BindingList bl,
                out BindingIterator bi);
    };

    enum BindingType {nobject, ncontext};

    struct Binding {
        Name binding_name;
        BindingType binding_type;
    };

    typedef sequence<Binding> BindingList;

    interface BindingIterator {
        boolean next_one(out Binding b);
        boolean next_n(in unsigned long how_many,
                    out BindingList bl);
        void destroy();
    };
    };
```

You can also have federated Naming Services—that is, instances of a Naming Service running on different machines. Each Naming Service can refer to the other, and the navigation from one to another is transparent to the user. The way to achieve this is to bind a context from one name service into another. Figure 4-3 illustrates a federated name space. Each name service may be running in a different geographical location.

Simple example

We shall now look at an example using the Naming Service for a set of Formatter objects. Figure 4-4 illustrates how we will structure the name space. We have a location in the name space where we can find references to formatters. We further structure the name space to indicate the type of the formatter.

Initialization

Before you can do anything with the Naming Service, you need to obtain a reference to the root naming context. This enables you to navigate the name space. Listing 4-2 shows code for obtaining a root naming context. The *resolve_initial_references* method is used to obtain an

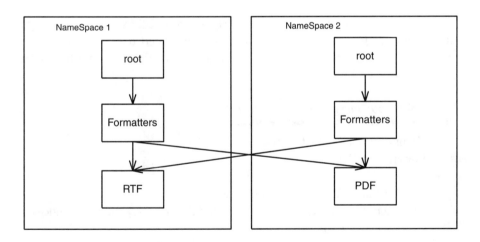

Figure 4-3. *Federated CORBA name space*

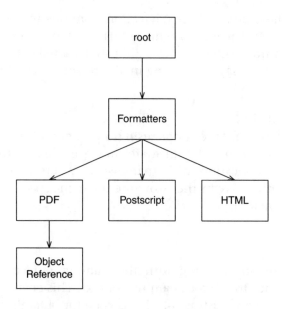

Figure 4-4. *Multiple Formatters for different document types*

object reference to the root context of the current ORB's Naming Service. Since the method returns a generic object, we need to narrow it to the type that we are interested in. (If the narrow operation is invalid. then an exception will be thrown.)

Listing 4-2: *Obtaining a root naming context*

```
NamingContextRef rootContext;
ObjectRef initRef;

try { // Find initial naming context.
   org.omg.CORBA.Object initNCRef = ORB.init().resolve_initial_references
   ("NameService");

   rootContext = NamingContextHelper.narrow(initNCRef);
}
```

Publishing

The code in Listing 4-3 shows how an object reference is inserted into the name space. In the example we are binding relative to the root context, though you should be aware that the *NameComponent* is relative to whichever context we use. For example, if we created a context at the point Formatters in the name space, then the *NameComponent* would only contain one element ("PDF"). You should be aware that the context for "Formatters" should already exist in the name space.

Listing 4-3: *Inserting an object reference into the name space*

```
// allocate a sequence for the name
NameComponent[] name = new NameComponent[2];
name[0] = new NameComponent("Formatters",
                "Formatters");
name[1] = new NameComponent( "PDF",
                "Formatter");


try {
// pdfFormatter is an instance of Formatter
    rootContext.bind(name, pdfFormatter);
}
```

Resolving

The code in Listing 4-4 shows how a client would extract a reference to the PDF formatter from the name space. Again, since the name space contains a generic object, you need to narrow the selection to the type of object you expect to get (and again, an appropriate exception will be thrown if there is an error).

Listing 4-4: *Extracting a reference to the PDF formatter*

```
NameComponent[] name = new NameComponent[2];
name[0] = new NameComponent("Formatters",
                "Formatters");
name[1] = new NameComponent( "PDF",
```

```
              "Formatter");

    org.omg.CORBA.Object objRef=null;
    Formatter pdfFormatter = null;

    try {
      objRef = rootContext.resolve(name);
      pdfFormatter = Formatter.narrow(objRef );
    }
```

As you can see, it can get quite clumsy creating *NameComponents* and populating them. Especially when you have a deep name space. As an alternate, you could establish a naming context closer to the point in the name space in which you are interested.

If you devise a standard separator for names (such as the forward slash), then you may want to wrap the functionality of the Naming Service to provide lookup and publish functions that take names that are more intuitive.

Implementation Repository

It is the responsibility of the ORB to ensure that an implementation of a distributed object is active when it receives a request for that object. To do this, the ORB also needs to keep track of which object implementations are available, and whether they are incarnated or etherialized. (*Incarnate* and *etherialize* are part of the new CORBA terminology, respectively referring to the activation and deactivation of an object by an object adapter. See the next chapter on life cycle for more details.)

The ORB keeps an implementation repository to assist with its housekeeping. The information in the implementation repository would consist of the name of an executable, how to start the executable, what interfaces it supports, and so on. When a request comes to the ORB for an instance of the Document Locator, it can then look at the implementation repository and run the executable containing the Document Locator if it is not already running.

As you have probably figured out, this information can be very operating system-specific. CORBA implementations can exist on a variety of machines, from the mainframe to embedded devices. The needs of the implementation repository will vary from OS to OS and from machine to device. As such, different ORB vendors may implement the Implementation Repository in different ways. Considering this, the CORBA specification does not standardize the implementation of the Implementation Repository. Also, since Implementation Repositories are vendor-specific, how you get information into the repository is not standard. Some vendors provide you with a set of administration tools that allow you to manipulate the contents of the Implementation Repository.

Distributed objects may be transient or persistent. Transient objects are those that are created at run time and do not outlive their creating process. Persistent objects are those that can outlive their creating process. Your client may have an IOR to a persistent object, and then, when the client binds to this object, it is the responsibility of the ORB to work in conjunction with the Object Adapter to incarnate the object. This indirect binding allows for greater flexibility at the expense of a small performance overhead.

You may also have more than one implementation of a given server. Each implementation may be located on different machines. This information can be incorporated within the Implementation Repository and used by the ORB for load balancing. The Implementation Repository itself may also be distributed and replicated among a set of machines, allowing for redundancy in case an Implementation Repository is unavailable. In this case, the IOR of an object will contain the addresses of the various Implementation Repositories.

Interface Repository

In the previous chapter, we discussed the design of the interfaces for your distributed objects using IDL. We can view IDL as both a contract and as meta-information. IDL is a description of the interfaces to your distributed objects. Remember that our distributed objects are only accessible through their interfaces, so if you have a description of the interface, you have a description of the distributed object from the user's point of view. Once you insert IDL into an Interface Repository, you can obtain this information at run time. The Interface Repository was the first CORBA mechanism to provide run-time meta-object information.

The downside, as I mentioned before, is that IDL does not capture the semantics or nature of dependencies between your distributed objects. You can not know the pre- and postconditions for each method of an object just from its IDL. Although all is not lost, for some applications you can still go far with just the information in the Interface Repository. If you need access to a richer meta-model, you may want to consider using the more recent Meta-Object Facility.

How you insert your IDL into the Interface Repository is vendor-specific. Sometimes you will find that the ORB vendor supports options to their IDL compiler that insert the interface into the Interface Repository. Other vendors may provide you with a set of tools that allow you to manipulate the repository. You will need to refer to the documentation for your ORB for details; however, the programmatic interface to the Interface Repository is standard, and, as with everything CORBA-related, defined in IDL.

A quick overview

The contents of the Interface Repository are instances of CORBA objects. There is a close mapping from the IDL types to the CORBA objects defined within the Interface Repository. Figure 4-5 shows the main types in the Interface Repository and illustrates their containment relationships.

You can navigate the Interface Repository and interrogate each of the instances to get a description of the object that it represents. For example, an *InterfaceDef* will contain objects that define its operations (*OperationDef*), attributes (*AttributeDef*), and so on.

You can modify the contents of the Interface Repository through its CORBA objects. Using this mechanism, it would be possible to write a tool to help with the administration of the Interface Repository (if your ORB vendor does not supply one).

Five abstract interfaces define the operations and attributes necessary to create a representation within the Repository. These are *IRObject*, *Contained*, *IDLType*, *Container*, and *TypeDef*. Figure 4-6 shows part of the inheritance hierarchy for the interfaces in the Interface Repository. You can navigate the bulk of the Interface Repository through the *Contained* and *Container* interfaces.

To help make this concrete, let's look at the IDL defined in the previous chapter for *Content* and *ContentProvider*.

```
exception NoContent{};
exception NoDocument{};

struct Content {
    string format;
    any data;
};

interface ContentProvider {
    Content getContent() raises(NoContent);
};
```

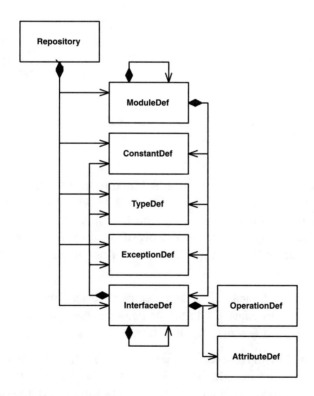

Figure 4-5. *Interface Repository types*

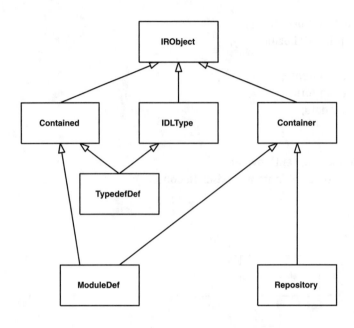

Figure 4-6. *Partial inheritance hierarchy for the Interface Repository*

Figure 4-7 illustrates part of the instance representing this IDL in the Interface Repository. As you can see, both the *Content* and *ContentProvider* are contained within the *Repository* and the operation *getContent* is contained within the *ContentProvider*. Now, if we were to extract the definition of *ContentProvider* from the Interface Repository, our code would look like the following.

```
Contained contained = ifr.lookup( "ContentProvider" );
InterfaceDef interface = InterfaceDefHelper.narrow( contained );
FullDescription description = interface.describe_interface();
```

Other mechanisms to extract information from the Interface Repository consist of iterating through all the elements of the Repository from the top node, or, if you have an object reference, obtaining the name of the interface from the object.

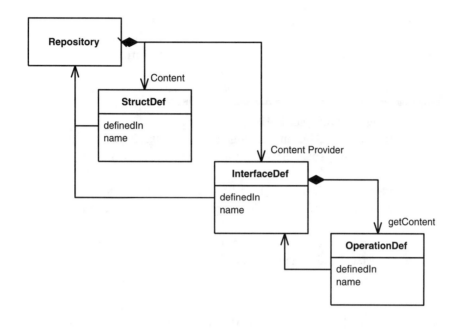

Figure 4-7. *Content and ContentProvider representation*

A simple example

To use the Interface Repository you first need to get a handle to it. As far as your client application is concerned, the interface repository is just another server. You can obtain an object reference to the Interface Repository through the method *resolve_initial_references*. After this you can treat it just like any other object reference.

If you have a reference to a remote object, you can then use this to obtain the name of the interface that the remote object implements. Once you have the name of the interface, you can then to extract further information about the object from the Interface Repository. Then, with this information you can construct a request using the Dynamic Interface Invocation mechanism (more on this later) to invoke one of the methods of the remote object.

Listing 4-5 illustrates the code to extract the full description of an interface from the repository. First we get a handle to the repository, then we lookup the interface we are interested in by name. Once the interface is found, we then extract the full description.

Listing 4-5: Extracting a full description of an interface

```
org.omg.CORBA.Object initRef =
    ORB.init().resolve_initial_references("InterfaceRepository");
Repository ifr_repository = RepositoryHelper.narrow( initRef );

Contained contained = ifr_repository.lookup( interfaceName );
InterfaceDef interfaceDef = InterfaceDefHelper.narrow( contained );

FullInterfaceDescription fullDescription =
    interfaceDef.describe_interface();
```

Dynamic Interface Invocation

In most cases, when you implement a client application that communicates with CORBA objects, you create client proxies for the remote objects by compiling the IDL definitions of the CORBA objects. These client proxies take care of the details of translating your request to a remote method invocation. The type and nature of the remote objects are known at the time of implementation. CORBA also provides a more dynamic mechanism wherein you do not necessarily know the interface to the remote object you are using until run time.

Dynamic Interface Invocation (DII) provides you the tools to create and invoke requests at runtime. You may have several reasons to take this approach. You may be implementing a system with rapid changes and additions to the servers, where the clients are more "intelligent" and discover interfaces at runtime. In addition, DII could be used as part of a gateway between two different protocols (more on this later). You should note that the server does not know whether the client is using DII or generated proxies from IDL, nor does it need to know. Let's now take a look at what is involved with using DII.

Steps to use DII

To use DII, you need to obtain a description of the interface to the remote object upon which you are going to invoke methods. You may see many simple examples where the information is embedded in the sample program. However, to be practical you will need to obtain the information from a source of meta-information, such as the Interface Repository. If you do use the Interface Repository, you will need to register the interfaces of the distributed objects and make the repository visible to the client application.

You would take the following steps when performing a DII operation and using the features of the Interface Repository:

1. Obtain the name of the interface.

2. Get the definition of the method you wish to invoke.

3. Create a request.

4. Invoke the request.

5. Extract the results.

We will now take a look at what is involved in the various steps.

Step 1: Obtain the name of the interface

Every CORBA object provides functionality to support reflective information when used in conjunction with the Interface Repository. You can obtain the name of the interface associated with the remote object and use this to extract further details from the Interface Repository. This is achieved by invoking the _get_interface_ method.

```
InterfaceDef interfaceDef = ((org.omg.CORBA.Object)obj)._get_interface();
```

Step 2: Get the definition of the method you wish to invoke

To make a useful dynamic program, you need to obtain a description of the method you wish to invoke. You must then use this description to create the necessary arguments for the request. You can either implement your own mechanism to get the method description, use a MOF, or use the Interface Repository. In this example, we make use of the Interface Repository.

```
Contained[] opSeq = interfaceDef.lookup_name(
    "getSection",
    1, // just the current object
    DefinitionKind.dk_Operation, //
    false // exclude inherited
);


// test to see that the opSeq contains the operator for
// the getSection method
if ( opSeq[0].name() == "getSection" ) {
    // then extract the definition of the method
    OperationDef opRef = OperationDefHelper.narrow( opSeq[0] );
}
// otherwise we have a problem
```

As an alternative, you could use the *describe_interface* method to get a full description of the interface. In the above example, we know what method we are looking for. However, if we were writing an interactive application, we could use the full description of the interface to construct a menu for the user to select the method (and enter values for the arguments).

Step 3: Create the request

You can employ two possible mechanisms to construct your request. You can either create your request object fully populated (using the *_create_request* method) or create an empty request object that you then populate. Both of these methods are defined as belonging to the CORBA Object, and so have definitions in all the language mappings. The following are the Java definitions of the *_create_request* and *_request* methods:

```
// Both these methods are defined on the class Object, they allow
// the programmer to create an instance of the Request object
public org.omg.CORBA.Request _create_request(
    org.omg.CORBA.Context ctx,
    String operation,
```

```
       org.omg.CORBA.NVList arg_list,
       org.omg.CORBA.NamedValue result
);

    public org.omg.CORBA.Request _request(String operation)
```

We will now look at both approaches, and apply them to invoke the *getSection* method of the *Document* interface introduced in Chapter 3. The first method, *_create_request*, takes as parameters a context object, name value list of arguments, and an object to hold the result.

```
String operation = "getSection"; // name could be obtained by other means

NVList argList = _CORBA.Orbix.create_operation_list( opRef );
NamedValue arg = argList.item(0);
if ( arg.name() == "name" )
    arg.value().insert_string("Chapter 4");
// note – we could also check the type

Context ctx = ORB.init().get_default_context();

org.omg.CORBA.Any return_val=_CORBA.Orbix.create_any();
return_val.type( opRef.result() );

org.omg.CORBA.NamedValue result =
    _CORBA.Orbix.create_named_value(null,
                        return_val,
                        org.omg.CORBA.ARG_OUT.value);

// Create the actual request
org.omg.CORBA.Request request =
    obj._create_request( ctx, operation, arg_list, result );
```

In the code we needed to instantiate objects to represent the context, arguments, and contain the result before we can create the request. As you can see, the code is clumsier that just invoking a method through a generated proxy.

We can simplify some of this by using a more compact form as follows:

```
org.omg.CORBA.Request request = obj._request("getSection");
request.add_named_in_arg("name").insert("Chapter 4");
request.set_return_type(
        orb.get_primitive_tc(org.omg.CORBA.TCKind.tk_string )
    );
```

Step 4: Invoke the request

Perhaps the simplest part of the whole operation is invoking the request. This is done by calling the invoke method on the request object.

```
request.invoke();
```

Step 5: Extract the results

Once you have invoked the remote method, you will want to extract the results. You will need to test the request object to see if either the ORB infrastructure or the remote object raised any exceptions.

```
if( request.env().exception() != null ) {
    // process the exception
} else {
    // process the result
    // request.return_value();
}
```

Deferred synchronous method invocation

CORBA does not have a mechanism to make asynchronous method invocations, though some of the services, such as notification and event services, do provide you with a mechanism to send information in an asynchronous manner. You should note that the oneway IDL mechanism is not actually asynchronous, and its implementation is vendor-specific. When you use DII, you can make deferred synchronous method invocations; here, you send the request to the remote object and test for return results as a separate step.

```
request.send_deffered();
```

You can then get the response using the *get_response* method (which blocks) or you can poll for the response using the *poll_response* method. Once you have received the response, you can process the results as in step 5 above.

DII summary

DII enables you to write dynamic clients. Examples of cases where you may want to make use of this mechanism include:

* Writing a generic test harness

* Writing part of a gateway between different protocols

* Providing a scripting tool, where dynamic discovery of interfaces may be necessary

The disadvantage of using DII is that to be truly dynamic, you need to use the Interface Repository and interpret the meta-information. This causes method invocation to be considerably slower (because of the extra network traffic) than using a statically generated interface. A possible optimization would be to transfer the meta-information for the target object at the time that the client binds to the target. This may be done using an interceptor mechanism (for a description of Interceptors see the discussion in Chapter 6), where the information is captured using a homegrown mechanism. This would optimize the reception of meta-information, though it would not be a standard procedure.

Dynamic Skeleton Interface

While the DII mechanism enables you to write dynamic clients, what about dynamic servers? CORBA provides us the Dynamic Skeleton Interface (DSI). This enables us to write generic servers that can respond to method invocations without including code generated from the IDL. You can use DSI to implement a generic server that can respond to a variety of requests.

To implement a dynamic server—that is, one that uses the DSI—you need to write an invoke method. When a request comes in, the *invoke* method is called. The method will then look at the request and the name of the operation, and invoke the corresponding method in the actual implementation.

Your *invoke* method needs to decode the arguments that have been passed in as parameters. This is like the inverse of the DII mechanism. Instead of dynamically creating a request, you are pulling apart the individual contents of a request to determine subsequent actions and associated parameters. The code in Listing 4-6 illustrates the skeleton for a generic gateway using DSI.

Listing 4.6: *Generic gateway skeleton using DSI*

```
class MyServer extends org.omg.CORBA.DynamicImplementation {

    // process incoming requests
    public void invoke(org.omg.CORBA.ServerRequest _request)
    {
        // extract the name of the operation
        String _opName = _request.op_name() ;
        // extract the name of the interface ...
        org.omg.CORBA.Object target = _request.target() ; // return the tar-
get object ...
        target._get_interface(); // get the interface for IFR processing

        // we now know the interface and operation ...
        // we can use the IFR to extract the contents of the
        // request and build a suitable server-side invocation...

        // in Java we may use a class loader to load a
        // suitable server-side implementation...
    };

}
```

Since the interface details are not compiled into the server-side code, you can start to provide more flexibility in your server. If we use Java for the implementation, we can make use of a class loader to bring into memory the actual implementation of the server-side object. Then, combining Java reflection with the reflective capabilities of the Interface Repository, we can map between the incoming request and the method invocation on the Java implementation.

You will find that most if the time you will not make use of DSI. This mechanism is useful for those of you that need to write a bridge between different protocols and CORBA or a gateway.

Meta-Object Facility

The Meta-Object Facility (MOF) is a recent addition to the expanding set of services provided by the CORBA specification. The MOF provides a richer meta-model than the Interface Repository: the Interface Repository only described CORBA types, not relationships. The MOF provides the necessary functionality to describe relationships.

The goal of the MOF is to provide an integration of CORBA applications with development environments. It was envisioned that a development environment would consist of a modeling tool and associated repository. By making the information in the repository available to applications at run-time, we can provide self-describing CORBA frameworks and components.

You can expect a MOF implementation to supply you a server, repository, and associated tools. You must be able to populate and manage the repository. The MOF contains a simple meta-metamodel that can be used to define meta-models, though for practical purposes you will find that MOF implementations come with a meta-model that supports the core UML. While the MOF does not have all the modeling constructs (if it did, the standard would probably still be in committee) it is far richer than the Interface Repository.

One of the goals of the MOF is to fill the holes left by the Interface Repository. The Interface Repository only understands the CORBA interface type system and does not represent relationships between the distributed objects. The MOF provides a "complete" solution for representation of meta-information within a CORBA environment. The MOF was also designed to be useful to those of you that do not wish to use CORBA.

Here are some highlights of the goals that the designers of the MOF had in mind:

* Share semantically rich meta-data.

* Support self-discovery, reflection.

* Allow the integration of tools with a CORBA environment (such as a CASE tool).

* Support for the forthcoming CORBA components standard.

* Integrate with the Business Object Facility (BOF)[1].

The MOF can also be used outside of CORBA! The meta-models that the MOF supports can encompass a wide variety of object-oriented systems. This means that the information captured within the MOF's repository does not need to be limited to a CORBA system. Consequently, we are seeing the development of tools that utilize the MOF for the development of other object-oriented systems (such as those based on Java beans).

Probably the most promise for the MOF lies in its use to support component-based infrastructures. Components that are expressed in terms of the MOF will provide reflective capabilities and can be understood by the rest of the system.

Another use for the MOF is in an Enterprise Application Integration (EAI) tool set. The goal of EAI is to integrate application across your enterprise; if you model existing applications and insert the model into a MOF, you can then incorporate those applications as components into the rest of your infrastructure.

There is a standard mapping from the contents of the MOF to IDL. This means that if you generate your business model using a standard CASE tool and insert it into a MOF-compliant repository, you can generate the IDL for your distributed objects. I would raise a caveat here in that you should be aware of the issues regarding interface design raised in Chapter 3.

In addition to the MOF, the OMG has passed a standard that allows the interchange of meta-information between repositories. The XML Metadata Interchange (XMI) provides a vendor- and system-independent mechanism to represent meta-information from a MOF repository. XMI is an instance of an XML grammar (see Chapter 8 for a brief description of XML), and as such is easily parsed by both applications and humans.

Trader

The Trader Service does what its name implies: it allows you to find other objects on the network that match a set of criteria. Unlike the Naming Service, wherein you publish objects by name, with the Trader you can associate an object with a set of properties. For example, you may advertise a Formatter object by its capabilities (PDF, RTF and so on) and an indication as to how busy the Formatter service is at the time of the request. Rather than locating an object based on its name (Naming Service) you can locate an object based on its capabilities. Given this functionality, some people have likened the Trader Service to a "yellow pages" for distributed objects. We'll take a brief look at the Trader Service.

A Trader works by taking an *exporter* and matching it with the requirements of an *importer*. Exporters are objects that advertise their services with the Trader. Importers are clients that use the trader to find objects that match their requirements.

To advertise (or export) the capabilities of an object, you must give the following information to the trader: the object reference, the service type name, and a list of properties. The object reference is the standard CORBA object reference. The service type name is the name you use to advertise the service and is held within a type repository. The properties are a list of name-value pairs that describe the capabilities of the object; you can indicate which properties are mandatory or optional, and properties can also be computed dynamically.

An importer will make a request for a service, such as the Formatter, to a Trader using a the "trader constraint language." The constraint language is a simple language consisting of Boolean expressions specifying constraints on the possible properties. You would use the Lookup interface to issue a query. Here you specify the type of service you are interested in as well as the constraints (you can also indicate what information to return, the order of the offers and so on). It is possible to obtain more than one offer as a result of a query; each offer represents an object that meets your criteria. You may also receive offers from objects that are derived from the type you were originally looking for.

You can easily see that Traders can be an important component to large distributed systems that require dynamic discovery. Since the properties of an exporter can be dynamic, you can base your search on the state of the object you want to use. For example, you may be looking for a Formatter that can produce PDF and is currently formatting less than ten other pieces of content.

Traders can also be federated. This allows us to link the offers from different traders (possibly in different parts of the organization) together to provide a larger pool of potential offers. Traders can provide the core mechanism for the dynamic use of distributed objects.

Summary

Meta-information is used in various guises in the modern software system. By realizing and making explicit the use of such information, we can improve the flexibility of our system and help ensure a long and useful life. To help learn about meta-information, we looked at examples that illustrate its use. Then we looked at meta-information with CORBA.

The usefulness of meta-information within your system is not limited to CORBA or distributed objects. However, CORBA does provide support for meta-information at various levels, from the implementation and interface repositories, through the naming service, to the MOF. With the introduction of the MOF, we are seeing a standard mechanism to share models from repositories. This provides an open software framework to support software construction from analysis and design through to implementation. I hope this chapter has inspired some ideas for making use of such information within your future (or current) systems.

References

Crawley, S. et al. *Meta-meta is better-better!* Presented at DAIS, Germany 1997.

Object Management Group. *CORBA Specification.* Available at http://www.omg.org

Component Specification, vol. 1, http://www.omg.org/cgi-bin/doc?orbos/ 99-07-01

Component Specification, vol. 2, http://www.omg.org/cgi-bin/doc?orbos/ 99-07-02

Component Specification, vol. 3, http://www.omg.org/cgi-bin/doc?orbos/ 99-07-03

van Hoff, Arthur, Hadi Partovi, and Tom Thai. "The Open Software Description Format (OSD)" http://www13.w3.org/TR/NOTE-OSD.html, August 11,1997

Notes

1. The BOF has metamorphosed into the BOI

Chapter 5

Life Cycle And Persistence

A key part of object-oriented software development is mapping design model entities to implementation model classes. Although we are used to thinking of object instances as the primary players in a runtime system, it is in fact the conceptual entities that they embody, not the instances themselves, that are truly important. Objects come and go, but what they represent lives on in the "minds" of clients. For example, a client invocation may require activating a service and instantiating a new object; or a single entity might be represented by objects in multiple processes in a system with load balancing; or a business entity can exist in a persistent data store and then be incarnated as objects in multiple services. Thus, what appears to be a single perpetual entity to clients may not currently exist as a physical runtime object, or may exist as multiple objects.

This difference between conceptual entities and the objects that serve as their vessels lies at the heart of the areas of life cycle and persistence. Questions raised by the entity/object duality that must be applied to every entity include:

- How is the entity identified so that objects know what they are implementing?

- What process or processes should the implementation objects live in?

97

- Does the entity exist only when an implementation object is created?

- Where and how is an entity's state stored if it exists beyond the implementation object?

- Can an implementation move?

Life cycle and persistence are architecturally core topics in their own right and will serve as the base for load balancing and failure recovery. Life cycle largely addresses what it means to implement an entity that may exist beyond the scope of a single process. Persistence is chiefly concerned with what it means for an entity to exist when its implementation does not. The two topics are complementary and closely entwined. We will cover life cycle first, during which we will assume the ability to persist an object's state.

Life Cycle

Objects in the world have temporal boundaries; they come into being and they meet their ends. In between they perform actions, get shuffled around, change state, form and break relationships, and so on. The life and times of an object exhibit a panoply of different aspects. Applying this to our software object models, several aspects can be modeled in a generic and useful way. Services can be created to observe and manipulate aspects such as the object's relationships to other objects (Relationship Service), its modes of behavior (state models), its internal makeup (persistence), how other objects view it (Property Service) and more. The notion of life cycle refers to the changes in an object's context within the system.

When developers refer to the life cycle of an entity, it is usually in one of two contexts: intraprocess or interprocess. Intraprocess life cycle describes how an implementation is disconnected from and tied to the system entity it is implementing. When talking about intraprocess life cycle, we talk about the instantiation of an object, how it might persist data, exposing it as a remote object, and in general, managing real resources.

Interprocess life cycle is what we consider distributed object life cycle. We do not so much consider the implementation object as manipulate which part of the system is allowed to manage the implementation of the system entity. Depending on how "part of the system" is defined, this could mean which process has the right to instantiate an implementation, or which department has this employee on its payroll.

Life cycle support implementations

Even if there is no support to remote the manipulation of object life cycle, some intraprocess life cycle support must be in place in order to simply create objects. Most basic support for intraprocess object life cycle in the ORB core lies within the object adapter. This will be evident in the initial discussion below, which will explore managing the relationship between the system entity and the runtime instance life cycle at the intraprocess level.

Life cycle transitions

Every entity has four main transition events in its life cycle: creation, activation, deactivation, and destruction. These define the changes in accessibility of the object in a system (Figure 5-1).

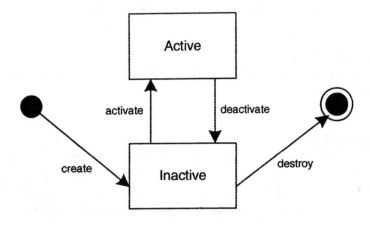

Figure 5-1: *Life cycle transitions*

Creation is when the entity first comes into being in the system; for example, the first time the object is entered into the database. Some objects, like services, are never explicitly created; they exist from the moment of deployment. In such a case creation is when the object is entered into the directory service.

Activation defines when the runtime instance is connected to the system entity. It represents the point at which the object is truly available to accept invocations.

Deactivation is when the object returns to a dormant state. Normally the runtime instance is freed and the entity reverts to a limbo state of existence, possibly back to the data store.

Destruction involves removing the entity altogether, such as deleting the row in the database, or removing an object from the namespace.

The runtime instance of an object goes through its own life cycle during activation and deactivation. The instance needs to be instantiated, have the entity information loaded from the data store, and have the object reference exported so it can be referenced remotely. From the system view this is all part of activation and the reverse process is all part of deactivation. Vendors will provide, to varying degrees, support for these aspects of activation. The persistence section will cover details of mapping the instance to the entity in the data store.

Activation/deactivation

We will now take a closer look at the mechanism of object activation and deactivation within the ORB.

Activating objects

When a client makes a request using an object reference, the ORB finds the correct process and passes the invocation to the object adapter in that process. The object adapter in turn needs to find the correct implementation object internally and pass the request to that object. The definition of an object reference provides for not only process location information, but an identity, or marker, for the runtime instance to specify it uniquely in the process.

When a request comes in, the object adapter needs to look up the marker in some internal table to find the runtime object. If it can't find the object, it throws an exception back to the client. Most vendors provide hooks into this process. If the marker for the object can be made to represent an *object identity* for the system entity (see the persistence discussion below, on the POA in particular), rather than just a reference for the runtime object, then the object adapter can implement more sophisticated activation policies. For instance, if the runtime object cannot be found, a new instance can be created and loaded with the information from the data store. Such object adapter policies are part of the internal management of the life cycle process.

Activation/deactivation policies

The policies you adopt for activation and deactivation affect your system. Ideally, you would not want an object deactivated while there are interested clients, and conversely, the object need not hang around when it is no longer wanted.

Activation Daemon: If you have an object activation daemon (OAD) to support the ORB, then it can implement a number of activation policies governing responses to client requests. The simplest policy is to start a process if one is not currently running, and to have all clients share that same process. The next step up is to start a new process for any new request. This induces high overhead, but works if the service does not maintain any session state. It is also workable if the objects are fully persistent.

A more intricate family of policies start a new process per client. These are complicated by having to establish what really defines a client. You can define a client as a username, or a client process, or something else completely. Other policy possibilities include creating a new process per object instance or per system entity. The OAD would make the decision to make a new process or reuse an existing one by looking at the object identity as well as the service identity in the object reference.

Object Adapter Policies: Assuming that we are using a shared service process, runtime instances cannot be kept in memory forever. But if instances are cleaned out too soon, some clients may be left with invalid object references. Some policy for cleaning up objects needs to be in place.

The client processes can share in the responsibility for this part of the intraprocess life cycle. You can provide a remote *remove()* method on the object which, when invoked, notifies the object adapter that it can clean up this runtime instance; or, if many clients share the same runtime instance, the method manages a remote reference count. However, there are many scenarios in which relying solely on the clients to call *remove()* is insufficient and far from robust. If a client dies unexpectedly, the reference count could be wrong. If a client passes a reference on, there can be confusion about who owns the reference, and again the count can become corrupted. A fundamental rule is that a service should be far more robust than the many clients which depend upon it. The reliability of the service, which involves such factors as memory management, should not hinge on external clients.

Clients: An object can be removed when it has no more clients. Distributed reference counts can try to give clues as to when this happens, but they're only as robust as the client processes, machines, and network connections. Another strategy is to look at system connections to the server process. Counting system client connections may not be sufficient, however, because clients connected to a service may be looking at disjoint or overlapping sets of objects, and it is nearly impossible to be sure which objects are matched to which clients. In addition, since CORBA object references can be externalized, they can be persisted or transferred without an explicit client connection. Or a client can close a socket as part of resource management, but expect to reopen and continue using the object reference. Or all the connections can be going through a single proxy bridge, as is the case in many Web or firewall access situations. Thus there is no sure method for exactly tracking clients in order to safely remove objects.

Timeouts: The outcome of all these complications is that to make a server robust, you must put a backup plan in place. One approach is to have an object in the server which is responsible for looking at the object adapter table and removing objects based on some criteria. Even if a given CORBA implementation does not allow full access to the object adapter, almost all implementations will provide hooks to instantiate objects from a data store. At this point objects can be placed in a list for tracking. There are also typically hooks to preprocess and postprocess calls going to specific objects or all objects (Figure 5-2). Using this pre/post processor it is possible to track calls to objects to implement timeout or "least recently

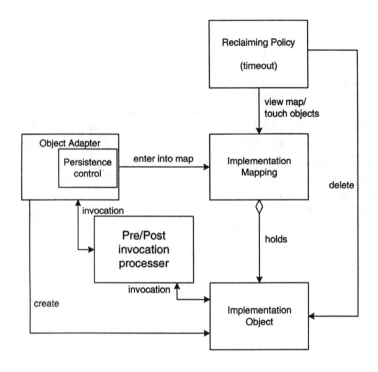

Figure 5-2. *Reclaiming objects*

used" mechanisms. As it is crucial to not remove objects while they are servicing client requests, such a deactivator list must be very thread safe, and should make good use of the pre/post processing hooks to prevent objects from being improperly eliminated.

Reused Instances: Another policy is becoming more popular with introductions of component models such as Enterprise Java Beans. Normally, when an object is activated, three related steps happen at once: the runtime object is instantiated, the data is pulled from the store, and the object is made available. This new policy separates the three steps. A goal of these component models is that by putting a layer of indirection on top of the implementation objects, the implementation objects can be very insulated from the ORB core, and from other basic services such as persistence.

Although we don't want to go deeply into a full component model, which is far beyond the scope of this chapter, the basic life cycle pattern involved is interesting. It requires the object identity to be reassignable. A pool of implementation instances can be instantiated, but not loaded from the store; in fact, with no identity preassigned (Figure 5-3). At request time the adapter chooses an instance and morphs it into the correct entity by initiating a data load. Before each data load, the object needs to be certain it is fully stored in the data store. This approach is most appropriate for a system that must handle large numbers of fairly fine-grained system entities, and a usage pattern in which each object is touched for a relatively short duration.

Shared Instances: Given a very fine-grained and large set of system entities, instantiating an object for each system entity is expensive in both number of objects (memory) and time needed to instantiate all the objects. A possible solution is to share the runtime instances between system entities (Figure 5-4).

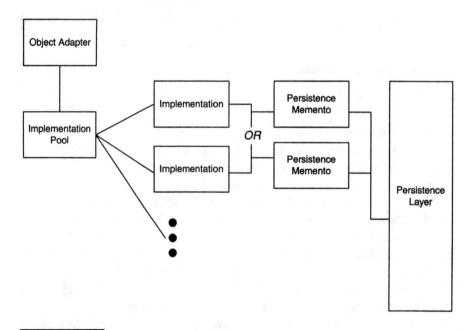

Figure 5-3. *Pool*

The object adapter can make many object references available, but map all references to the same runtime instance. This works best when the marker for the objects is that of the system entity. Then, during the processing of a request, the implementation object can ask for the marker of the object reference used to make the request. Interpreting the marker as a system entity identifier, the implementation can process the request as appropriate to that entity. Internally there can be either one implementation object or a set of objects that each handle a subset of the system entities.

A problem with this is that currently, only a few ORB vendors fully support this kind of feature. Many make the assumption that the object implementing the entity is the same instance that receives and processes an incoming request. Or at least they assume they are tied in a one to one relation. It may be necessary to build an indirection layer as in the component model approach, or at least use in a mapping object which will allow the implementation objects to view the mapping performed by the object adapter. Note that this situation is changing with the advent of the POA (discussed below).

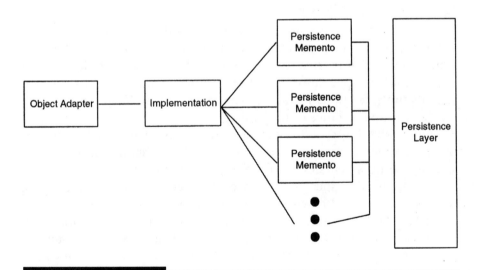

Figure 5-4. *Shared instance*

Distributed Object Life Cycle

In the wider distributed scope we want to consider what it means to manipulate system contexts. Trying to generalize operations on objects in contexts actually produces a small possibility set. We can *move* an object into a context or *remove* it from a context. We can *copy* the object and put the copy into a different context. If an object doesn't exist, we must *create* it before putting it into a system context; and likewise, if there is no place for an object to go, we need to *destroy* the object. Now, although to remove an object from a system context and to destroy it are two separate concepts and the distinction may be useful in many situations, in the realm of distributed objects, if an object is removed from a context, it must be moved elsewhere or it is lost. Thus either we move the object or we destroy the object. So even though there is some benefit in keeping the semantic difference between the two clear, for a generalized set of operations in distributed environments that supports the idea of complete server encapsulation, the semantics of *remove* cover those of *destroy*. So to sum up, combining *destroy* with *remove*, we have four operations: *create()*, *move()*, *copy()*, *remove()*.

Life cycle service

The CORBA life cycle service concerns itself with the issue of constructing interfaces to enable the above operations (see "Life cycle IDL" below) from remote clients. It does not define what these operations mean semantically to specific objects. For instance if an object lives longer than its runtime implementation, what does it mean if *remove()* is called on the runtime instance of that object?

The CORBA life cycle service defines how a client can "create" an object in a remote space. This of course requires a factory on the service side. It defines a generic factory interface, but still recognizes the need for an application-specific interface. This generic interface has the method *create_object()*, which takes an object identity and a list of name/value pairs (*Criteria*) to add application-specific information.

The other methods in the life cycle interface are directed at manipulating a particular object, and so are defined in an interface from which we expect to derive application interfaces. *Move()* and *copy()* both take a reference to a generic factory to move or copy to, in addition to a *Criteria* set for application particulars. The interface provides a very generic way of dealing with remote objects and their creation in a foreign process space. If the factory passed to the *move()* or *copy()* method can handle the same type of object, then the object can in effect move or copy itself, given some way to transfer runtime state.

Life cycle interpretation

When considering the semantics of the basic operations it is important to think about which system contexts we want to manipulate. If we consider life cycle for the system entities, *move()* could mean moving the data store. If we constrain our view to runtime, we are shuffling instances from process to process. If we consider where an object lives to be where its access point is, moving it may be relocating its directory entry. The following expands the discussion of each operation and what it might mean.

Runtime instance

Managing the life cycle of runtime instances beyond the scope of a single process can be extremely useful for managing resources. Exposing the life cycle control in explicit remote method invocations eases the complexity of load balancing and failover management.

Move()

Implementations can generally be summed up in terms of behavior and state. If a mechanism is put in place to move the current state of an object to another process that is capable of instantiating an implementation object with the correct behavior, you can effectively move the runtime object to another process. This requires that a copy of a class implementing the behavior be resident on the machine to which the object is being moved. Version control of the objects is an important issue. If the version of the receiving class is not the same as that of the original class, the state transfer may be incompatible and the system will crash. Far worse is if the versions differ by behavior. There will be nothing so obvious as a crash; just incorrect business logic being executed, which might not be detectable until the data store is corrupted. This is where using a technology like Java may be useful. Java allows the possible transfer of the behavior, via Java class files, along with the encapsulation of the state.

Moving the runtime object may be very nice for shuffling resources around, or for moving a heavily used object to collocate it near the calling process to speed up communications (a basic premise of mobile agents). Although moving an object may be useful for optimization and administration, moving an active runtime instance may cause client references to go stale. Ways of coping with this include vendor-provided interfaces for sending IIOP location forward responses, and "smart proxies" which can handle faults by performing a location forward.

Copy()

If we are copying the object implementation, then we can start with the same mechanism used for the move operation to copy the state and optionally behavior to another place. But consider that there are now two implementations that can be updated and modify the data store. Keeping the two copies in sync is vitally important; otherwise different parts of the system will have an incomplete and perhaps inconsistent view of the objects.

Inconsistency is usually unacceptable given most business requirements. So you must make some effort to be sure the copies do not overwrite each other in the data store. When all clients are touching the same object, it is easy to lock or to coordinate between clients through the single object instance. With multiple possible copies in existence, you will need a concurrency service of some sort to coordinate the copies. In many cases the concurrency controls inherent in the data store will be enough for update consistency. There are very different possible approaches to locking (e.g., optimistic vs. pessimistic); for some more involved discussion of locking, see Chapter 6, "Transactions."

However the transaction control is achieved, data consistency between the copies must still be maintained. When an update occurs, all copies should be aware of the change in order to reload or deal with it in the manner appropriate to the update control. If the data store provides some sort of call back, the persistence layer could handle this by forcing a behind-the-scenes reload. If not, then the persistence layer, or application layer, could generate events on an event channel. Another option is that if all instances are copies of a central original, the original can coordinate the central view. The copies would not draw from the data store, but would rely on the original to replicate the object state when needed. All updates to the state in this case would be delegated to the original object to be propagated to the data store.

Copy()—detached

Another option for copying the implementation object is to copy the object into a detached state. This means making a full copy of the implementation object, except that the object is not connected to the data store. Changes to true persistent objects should propagate to the data store; however there may be times when a client may want to manipulate an object in possible "what if" scenarios. This concept is most useful when a significant (as defined by the business) subset of the objects are copied into a detached state. Then a user, such as a financial analyst, can play with the object model to simulate changes in the system and view interactions in the model. This can be useful if there is a simulation aspect to the model, or even if the analyst just wants to play with the numbers and make all the correct changes at once.

This detachment can be implemented by duplicating (forking) the service process, then disconnecting the persistence layer from the actual data store. This would mean the implementation object would not have to know anything about the difference between the real implementation and the detached copy. An optional feature for this type of process would be for the persistence layer to collect the differences between the local model state and the state in the data store, and to merge the two when it came time to commit.

Remove()

From the runtime instance viewpoint the remove operation is an important method. CORBA does not define an automatic distributed reference count, so garbage collecting is problematic, even if we don't have concerns about sharing objects. If a client is given the ability to create an object through a factory and then pass that reference around, it should be the responsibility of that client to free or remove the instance it created. Developers with a C/C++ heritage know all too well the importance of proper management of instantiated objects.

Distributed reference counts

Since there is no concept in CORBA of distributed reference counts, allowing clients to share objects can be a tricky thing. The *copy()* operation can be used as the mechanism for incrementing the reference count. The *remove()* operation would then decrement the reference count. So each client that owns a reference, or in other words, calls *copy()* to increment the reference count, is thus responsible for calling *remove()* for each "copy" it owns. Cleanup is important, and clients (see above discussion of timeouts in life cycle transitions) may not be fully reliable. The *move()* operation could transfer the ownership of a reference, especially in cases when the server instance knows something about the clients holding references.

System entity

As the idea of life cycle can be applied to objects in general, and not just distributed objects, we want to consider a framework for managing the life cycle of domain entities rather than just implementation objects.

Move()

A possible view is that the concrete existence of a system entity lies in the data store of that object; so to move an object is to move the data store of the object, rather than just its runtime instance. This may be a business requirement, or may simply be desirable for managing data store space. After an object's store is moved, you may need to move the runtime instance to a process whose persistence layer has a connection to the new data store. This is in fact a good way to move the object altogether. The runtime object can be transferred to a new process, using a mechanism discussed above. Then the object can be handled by the persistence mechanism for that process. The persistence mechanism will store the object in its natural intraprocess life cycle, which should create a new entry in the appropriate data store for the object.

Copy()

In addition to the idea of copying an implementation instance, there is the idea of copying the object in the data store. This could have two meanings: copy for replication (fail-over protection and load balancing) purposes or cloning. Cloning is creating a new object with a different identity but the same state and behavior of the original. Copying for replication brings with it concurrency issues, some of which may be satisfied by the replication services of the underlying data store.

Directory access

Since the context of an object in a system can be considered the access point to that object, an alternate place to implement life cycle management is within the confines of the directory service. The directory service most often used is the CORBA Naming Service. This can be used to establish semantic contexts indicated by the directory tree structure. In such a system, changing the binding of an object can be quite significant.

Move()

Changing the context of an object, or moving the object, can mean simply reorganizing the name space where the object is registered, and thus the object's accessibility. When you are organizing a name space, often one branch of the naming service is for private objects and one for publicly published objects. The public name space might have multiple branches for different client audiences in the system. Thus, moving an object could mean making it public, or changing which clients and/or users can see it. For instance, if a printer is moved from floor A to floor B, that change could be reflected by moving the corresponding printer service in the name space. Or if a service is provided publicly from 9 a.m. to 5 p.m., it could be placed in the public branch, and moved to the private branch during off hours.

One system design strategy is that the security configuration (who is allowed to access which objects or classes) is indicated by the structure of the name space. Thus, an object's position in the directory tree defines which users are able to access it. This allows for a very dynamic control over accessibility on a per-object basis, rather than just the class level, as is typical of many security packages. Another example is having the name an object is bound to in the name space reflect some sort of ranking of objects, such as a crude measure of load or primary vs. secondary systems. In such a system, moving the object in the name space changes the ranking of the object.

Copy()
Most directory services allow objects to be bound more than once into the directory. Copying would be simply binding the object in multiple contexts, reflecting the accessibility of the object by multiple groups, or from multiple positions. If the name is a ranking, then, in given contexts or for different metrics, each object can have multiple rankings. If the structure represents security access of groups or users, an object could be made accessible to multiple users or groups by binding it multiple times.

Remove()
Removing the object from the name space, or removing one copy of it reflects the loss of access to that object from that context. If the object is destroyed, then during the process of destroying the object, every reference to the object in the name space should be removed.

Persistence

Although object instances have a finite lifetime, as we have discussed above, what they represent must often span instance and server lifetimes. A reliable long-term store is essential not only for many forms of application data, but for session data as well, in order to recover from failures. Almost every system that maintains any sort of state will need to persist that state. Persistent storage mechanisms come in a wide variety of flavors, ranging from file systems to relational databases, to object databases, and beyond. The flavor used in a particular system will vary according to its needs; from an architectural viewpoint, all are alike in that they require the use of some operations to save and load data, and some notion of identity to tie objects to the appropriate state. The true architectural issue lies in resolving where and how in the system such operations are used and tied to the business logic, and where and how such identity is defined.

Know when to save, know when to load

Persistence must be accomplished against the backdrop of object life cycle above and system failure, which will be explored in chapter 9. As objects flicker in and out of existence owing to invocation-induced activations and failure-induced recovery attempts, they must often retain the same state and/or identity. Loading and saving state might be performed at several points in the object life cycle.

In many systems persistent objects load their state upon creation. Thus, the load occurs when the objects are created, often via a factory. At some point the objects are destroyed until they are needed again. A rather different approach is to use a pool of objects that are loaded with state when needed, and then cleared instead of destroyed. The same objects are continually reused, serving as containers for a succession of identities and states.

A complication occurs when the information in the data store can change via some path independent of the objects that use that data. In this case, a notification mechanism is necessary so that a data store change triggers a forced reload of the relevant objects.

One approach to saving object state is to perform the save at the natural end of the object's life cycle, thus persisting the state between activations. To guarantee that an object's state can be recovered after an unnatural demise, however, it must be saved to a durable store upon any state change during its lifetime. An alternative to this is queuing up save requests to be handled in a background thread. Such an asynchronous approach improves response times, but should only be used if recovering up-to-date state is not deemed as important.

State must often be saved by using controlled transactions. Transactions are the subject of the next chapter and will not be explicitly discussed in this one. That said, it must be kept in mind that any references to saving state can be understood as implying the potential use of transaction handling. While this is a complication, it does not alter the basic issues regarding state saves that we will address.

Sometimes state should not be saved. Systems with implied commits or object copy support will require the ability to deal with some objects that should be persisted and some which should not. This requires the ability to differentiate between otherwise similar object instances based on life cycle status.

Knowing how to save and load

There are two primary aspects to the actual work of loading and saving objects: maintaining identity, and mapping between data in a store and object state.

The work required in mapping between objects and the data store depends on the nature of the store. An object database, for example, will require minimal work to integrate. Typically, however, the store will be a relational database. This necessitates an object-relational mapping (ORM). Such mapping is a large subject in its own right and will not be discussed here. There are many current ORM products and strategies, we will only briefly discuss how such a mechanism can be employed, rather than the details of any particular approach.

For an object to be persistent, it must have some long-lived identity which can be used to uniquely identify the information required to reconstitute it. This identity can be used as the basis for object IDs. Such an identity is generally a primary key for the information set the objects represent. This easily maps to relational keys.

The actual loading and/or saving of an object's state can be done in several ways. The simplest is for the objects themselves to interact with the store. This is a rather crude approach, as it entangles the object business logic with store-mapping–specific code. Such a design leads inevitably to development and maintenance problems. A more decoupled alternative is for factory type-mediators to handle the relationship between the business objects and the store. Separating an object and the entity that handles the associated persistence plumbing for it produces a clean design in which the persistence mechanism can be more smoothly changed. This leads to the notion of separate persistence handlers, layers or services, which we will explore further later.

If an object does not handle its own persistence, then another object must somehow have access to the first object's state in order to load or save it. Direct access to state, however, is a notable violation of the object-oriented principle of encapsulation. A standard object-oriented approach to controlled exposure of state is to use accessor (get) and mutator (set) methods. A more sophisticated possible solution to this is a variation on the classic "Gang of Four" Memento pattern for capturing and externalizing object state. A *Memento* implementation holds state externalized from an *Originator*, which creates and accept mementos (Figure 5-5). A memento has two effective interfaces, an all-revealing one for the originator, and a narrow one for a *Caretaker* which holds on to the memento. The variation is to open mementos up in a well-defined way so that the persistence mechanism can get what it needs. Note that there is no way to separate out the persistence function and not expose access to the state in some manner.

Exposing state by itself is usually insufficient for accomplishing persistence. Therefore, merely having accessors/mutators and/or accessible mementos is not enough. For example, if a relational database is used, then information concerning the tables involved and the SQL calls will have to reside somewhere. It is possible to create a generic system using introspection, but this is unusual. Instead, persistence code typically includes the information needed, often via code generation by a tool. This is the case with many of the approaches to be discussed.

Where to save and load

Persistence can occur in several places in distributed systems. Persistent storage can be deemed a server-side facility, thus obviating the need to examine client-side persistence. It is best if a system's persistence mech-

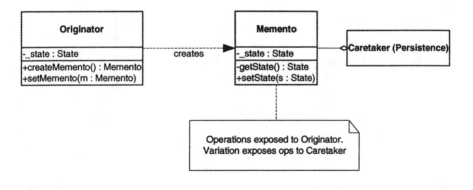

Figure 5-5. *Persistence with Memento*

anism is completely transparent to clients. This makes the clients simpler and cleaner and decouples them from the server. The persistence system on the back end can then be changed without any damage to the clients. This allows for some degree of flexibility. The one exception to this is systems in which clients require control of transaction processing.

There are various ways to structure the server for persistence. In particular, persistence could come into play at the object adapter level, within objects, as a layer below objects, or via a dedicated service. In the sections to follow we will examine these alternatives.

Persistence layers

One standard approach to persistence is to define a persistence layer below the business logic layer. If the interface to such a layer is well constructed it can be backed by different data stores and caching systems completely transparently to the higher level logic (Figure 5-6). Such layers can take many forms.

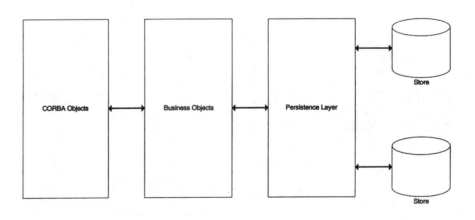

Figure 5-6. *Persistence layer*

A layer will often use an engine that runs the interaction with the data store. This can involve performing any object-store mapping, connections and transactions management, and error recovery and reporting. A sample design is one in which the domain objects to be persisted have corresponding data mapping objects that map from relational result sets to the domain objects. The mapping objects or separate interaction objects have the SQL and any specialized handling code. The mapping/interaction objects are fed to an engine that handles connection pooling and the like, and uses them to run transactions against relational databases.

A persistence layer can be more or less generic so that the information that it requires can vary from actual SQL or OQL to property lists that indicate mapping information to nothing but the domain objects themselves. A persistence engine could simply use hard-wired SQL, or make use of domain object metadata or introspection. While there is a wide spectrum of variations, good designs allow for a large degree of flexibility so that it is possible to change the data stores without affecting the higher-level application logic. It might be desirable to have a persistence layer back end that can deal with different data base types, so that it can front, for example, both relational and object databases. Flexibility can also be important with regards to allowing for customized object-data mapping logic to handle special cases, complex mappings, and optimizations.

Given the many ways in which persistence can be organized, and the complexities inherent in the problem, developers will often turn toward vendor-supplied solutions.

Vendor approaches

Persistence is a fundamental need, and as such has spurred a variety of vendor-specific solutions. Some of these have been point integrations between ORB and database products. These can take the form of specialized adapters that overlay particular database products. Other vendor products provide builder tools and middle-tier servers. Such tools can generate data objects from data schema and provide the developer with hooks for business logic. The finished system then runs in the specialized server, which provides runtime features such as transaction management. Such solutions impose their own frameworks on system architectures, locking systems into the products.

ORB vendors have also provided their own hooks for persistence by exposing ORB functionality. An example of this is IONA's loaders. Loaders can be defined at different levels of granularity (per class, process, or database) and are called when a target object cannot be found. A loader can use identifying object information, called a marker, to create the desired object from the data store. Loaders also have a save operation that can be called when the server process terminates, when the object is disposed of, or via an explicit invocation. This ability to instantiate the correct object given some identity is exactly what ORB Object Adapters are supposed to do, leading to the possibility of a more standardized solution.

POA possibilities

The Portable Object Adapter (POA) was approved by the OMG in mid-1997 and replaced the original Basic Object Adapter (BOA) in the CORBA 2.2 specification. Although the POA has thus far been the subject of more ink than full implementations, it is anticipated that the POA will be completely incorporated into the major CORBA offerings by the time this book is published[1]. In addition to providing server-side portability, the POA supports a wide spectrum of server types, including those with persistent state.

Like the BOA, the POA can activate servants in a variety of ways, but it is more flexible. A server can use many POAs that support different policies. Policy objects are used to specify key characteristics of a POA's behavior when it is created. Some key POA policy types related to persistent objects include *LifespanPolicy* (TRANSIENT, PERSISTENT), *IdAssignmentPolicy* (USER_ID, SYSTEM_ID), and *RequestProcessingPolicy* (USE_ACTIVE_OBJECT_MAP_ONLY, USE_DEFAULT_SERVANT, USE_SERVANT_MANAGER).

A PERSISTENT *LifespanPolicy* indicates that objects can outlive their creating process. ID assignment can be done by either the POA or the application, allowing for identity control. Application-assigned IDs can be based on a primary key for a data set. Object IDs are encapsulated within object references.

Request processing can be handled in several ways. The POA keeps an Active Object Map for mapping Object IDs to running servant objects.

This can be supplemented by specifying the use of a default servant to be used if an Object ID cannot be mapped. For more control, use of a servant manager can be specified.

Servant managers are user-developed objects that can control the full life cycle of servant objects: creation, activation, deactivation, and destruction. Servant managers are callback objects; they are registered with a POA within the same process and then are invoked by the POA when needed. There are two *ServantManager* interfaces that can be implemented; the interface meant for persistent objects is *ServantActivator*. This has an *incarnate()* operation called by the POA when it gets a request for a non-active object. The *etherialize()* operation is called when deactivating servants. Both operations are passed the object ID. Servant managers standardize some of the techniques used for persistence in the past, providing sufficient hooks for the use of key-based object IDs to load/save object state to a data store.

The above discussion focuses on how the POA can react when given an object reference for some request. In order for this to happen, the object reference must exist. Object references can be created in several ways. It is possible to have the POA create an object reference via factory methods without an active servant. Alternatively, a servant can be activated and associated with a given object ID to produce a reference. Other possible means also exist. Once a reference exists it can be used and exported to clients.

A much needed feature that can be discussed in the context of the POA is being able to handle large numbers of possibly fine-grained objects. A strategy for accomplishing this leverages Object IDs. The IDs can be created from two logical parts: one identifying a general object type, the other specifying a key for a particular instance. A servant manager can use the first ID part to map to a servant, which then uses the second part to create or fill the actual domain/data object. This allows for a smaller number of expensive distributed servants to support a larger number of domain/data objects.

The brief survey of POA abilities is just an outline of the rich set of object control mechanisms that the POA makes possible. The POA will no doubt be used for some persistence solutions. However, using the POA for persistence raises a basic architectural issue. Putting persistence at the object adapter level ties it into the system at the ORB level; it becomes part of the plumbing. A different approach is to make the functionality widely available at a higher level: the service level.

The service approach

The Persistent Object Service (POS) was one of the original Common Object Services. The POS has been deemed to be overly complex, poorly specified, and flawed. Lacking any real implementations, the POS was slated for termination under the OMG sunset policy and an RFP for a replacement was issued in mid 1997. This replacement is the Persistent State Service (PSS).

Persistence is a complex issue; the many views on how to structure persistence result in part from the multiplicity of software elements it affects. This has been reflected in the PSS specification process. The RFP resulted in two initial submissions. Instead of merging their submissions, the groups then splintered, producing three revised submissions. A PSS vote may be held before this book is published. (The only thing that takes longer to publish than a technology standard is a book that covers it.) As the final victor in this process is unknown at the time of this writing, it is worth exploring the salient features of the last round of submissions.

The goal of the PSS is to provide a bridge between the ORB domain of the POA and servant objects and the storage domain of the persistent store. Thus, the PSS is in some sense a specification of an interface internal to CORBA servers; it is not meant to be visible to clients. PSS is strictly a back-end service.

The PSS RFP specified several requirements that all the submissions have addressed. An example of this is generalized interfaces for datastores so that a wide variety of persistent stores can be used.

The RFP called for an IDL-compatible way of expressing schema for the state to be persisted. This has taken the form of language constructs to be added to or extracted from IDL to represent state. Such a representation makes it possible to generate data objects and/or access mechanisms. A benefit of this approach is increased clarity of design; schema information that was previously hidden in auxiliary classes or the data store is now part of the IDL design. A drawback is the possibility of brittle schema being elevated to a high level, potentially broadening the effects of any change.

A particularly interesting RFP requirement is the ability to support large numbers of fine-grained objects efficiently. This requirement appears to be indirectly addressed by the submissions; that is, this is deemed an outcome of the proposed PSS structures.

The component quest

The PSS is an attempt to make it possible to simply specify the state to be persisted and utilize a supporting infrastructure without too much additional coding. A further step in this direction is the current trend toward server side components.

The component vision is based on the notion of components with application-specific logic, and server containers in which the components run and that supply the components with persistence, transaction handling, and other infrastructure services. The point of this is to be able to buy a supporting server that handles all the plumbing and to have to write nothing more than the business logic. This has long been a holy grail of the development community. The current driving and emblematic force behind this concept is Enterprise Java Beans (EJB).

Inspired to a large extent by EJB, a CORBA Components proposal is in process at OMG and may be approved shortly after the writing of this chapter. Component persistence will be based on the PSS. A Component Implementation Definition Language (CIDL) is used to specify component implementation structure and state. In practice, CIDL's state specification should be the state/schema language of PSS; at the very least, it will map to it. Vendor tools will generate skeleton code from the CIDL. This code, and the server container the component runs in, are meant to then automatically manage persistence for the component state. Thus, the problem of arranging persistence becomes merely specifying the state to be persisted.

Persistent conclusions

Persistence is in some sense an artifact of the nature of computer memory. That said, all but the simplest architectures will require some form of persistence. Persistence can often be a deciding factor in choosing a software framework, as it can require a great deal of work and runtime expense if done poorly—and may still require a great deal of work if done well. We have discussed several approaches to persistence, of both the buy and build flavors. As I hope I've made clear, regardless of the approach taken, the persistence apparatus in a system can determine or be determined by the design of the whole system. It is therefore essential to consider persistence from the outset of the architecture process: it is truly a core architectural issue.

Life Cycle IDL (Partial)

Here is part of the IDL from the Life cycle Service discussed above.

```
typedef struct NVP {
    Naming::Istring name;
    any value;
} NameValuePair;

typedef sequence <NameValuePair> Criteria;

interface LifeCycleObject {
    LifeCycleObject copy(in FactoryFinder there, in Criteria
                    the_criteria)
            raises(NoFactory,NotCopyable,
                    InvalidCriteria,CannotMeetCriteria);
    void move(in FactoryFinder there, in Criteria the_criteria)
            raises(NoFactory, NotMovable,
                    InvalidCriteria,CannotMeetCriteria);
    void remove()
            raises(NotRemovable);
};

interface GenericFactory {
    boolean supports(in Key k);
    Object create_object(in Key k,in Criteria the_criteria)
            raises (NoFactory, InvalidCriteria,
                    CannotMeetCriteria);
};
```

Summary

In this chapter we examined the life cycle of a distributed object, both active and inactive. We discussed why it is critical to establish the responsibility for ensuring that the object is in the correct state at the right time. This is difficult because of the very nature of a distributed object system—we are referring to objects across process boundaries, reference counting and garbage collection is increasingly complicated, and there are no silver bullets. You need to design with this in mind and determine ahead of time how you will manage your distributed objects life cycle.

Notes

1. POA implementations are already available in some free ORBs, such as TAO (http://www.cs.wustl.edu/~schmidt/TAO.html) and MICO (http://diamant-atm.vsb.cs.uni-frankfurt.de/~mico/).

Chapter 6

Transactions

Every day we perform transactions. A transaction is an interaction that involves an exchange; this could be monetary, information, service requests or other information. In addition, all the steps in a transaction have to happen or none at all. Quite often the first thing that comes to mind when transactions are mentioned are monetary exchanges, like the transfer of funds from one account to another or the use of automatic teller machines. The one thing that all transactional systems have in common is the requirement to maintain the integrity of the information. You do not want to transfer funds from your bank account to another bank only to find that the money has been lost in the ether.

Information regarding business transactions used to be kept in written ledgers; this provided a form of indelible record which could be audited and easily (though painfully) accounted for. It also used to take some time to perform the transfer of funds—on the order of days. This was fine for relatively small volumes of transactions. Nowadays in the hectic bustle of the modern capitalist world, we can easily see millions of transactions taking place on a daily basis within just one institution. The information for these transactions is stored within databases and passed between systems electronically over networks. While this is more efficient than the written method, it is also more volatile. Therefore, developers have created mechanisms to help ensure the integrity of the information.

Database management products provide us with functionality to support transactions. They supply APIs that enable us to demarcate the beginning and end of a transaction (the transaction boundaries), and the means to store the record of the transaction in a persistent manner. With the growth of systems and electronic interbusiness communication, we are seeing the need for transactions that span multiple databases. Transaction monitors have been developed to coordinate transactions across multiple databases. The OMG has specified the Object Transaction Service (OTS) to be the transaction monitor for systems of distributed objects. Now we can purchase off-the-shelf products that implement the OTS for our CORBA-based systems.

In this chapter we will take a look at the workings of a transaction processing system and the role of the transaction monitor, its main components and how it coordinates transactions within a distributed system. Then we will look at the OTS as defined by the OMG and see how this is used within a system of distributed objects.

Transaction Processing

As I just mentioned, we need to record the effects of a transaction in a persistent manner, and computer systems are ideal for handling the large volume of transactions found in the modern business. We also need to be sure that transactions run to completion with all the results recorded. We do not want partial results. For example, when you make an airline reservation you do not want your account debited and then later to find you do not have a ticket. The system supporting the transaction needs to ensure the integrity of the information within all databases involved. We need a system that ensures that requests are completed, and in the case of a failure, no changes were made. These are all-or-nothing systems: Either the effects of all the work involved to perform a transaction happen or none of the effects happen.

Systems that handle transactions need to be responsive. We may have many travel agents making airline reservations at the same time; the client application making the reservation should still be responsive regardless of the volume of requests happening at the server. Therefore, these systems need to have the capability of running many transactions concurrently.

Transaction processing (TP) systems are usually part of a three-tier architecture: client, application server, and database. The infrastructure that supports the application server includes the Transaction Monitor. TP monitors are designed and developed to help support the construction of distributed systems. They help us realize better performance, handle large volumes of concurrent transactions, and support the requirements of a transaction.

Transactions

To ensure the integrity of a system a transaction has to be atomic, consistent, isolated, and durable. The acronym ACID is commonly used to refer to these properties:

- **Atomic**—for a transaction to be atomic it has to execute completely or not at all. The transaction is all-or-nothing; that is, all the changes of state to the system happen or none of them happen. For example, if you transfer funds from one bank account to another, and the update of the destination account fails for some reason, you do not want the debit of the source account to happen. For this transaction to be atomic, either both accounts are updated or none is.

- **Consistent**—it is important that the consistency of information within the data store is maintained as well as the application. A transaction should not leave the application in an undetermined state, and the integrity of the data store needs to be maintained. Both the application code and the transaction processing system share the responsibility of maintaining consistency. To maintain the consistency of the database means that referential integrity is preserved, all primary keys are unique, and the business rules are maintained.

- **Isolated**—a transaction should execute as if it were the only transaction on the system; that is, the effect of a set of transactions running concurrently is the same if they were run one at a time. Another name for this is to say that the transactions are serializable: the effect is the same as if the transactions were run in serial fashion.

  For example, two transactions try concurrently to reserve the last seat on a flight. If both determine availability of the seat before any updates, then each transaction will go ahead and both the customers will be charged. If we run each transaction in serial fashion, however, the first would succeed and the second would fail. Both of these transactions satisfy the requirement for atomicity but are not isolated.

For each of the airline reservation transactions to be isolated, they need to run as if there were no other transaction running on the system. This is achieved in database systems by acquiring a lock on the data that a transaction is accessing. This lock prevents other transactions from manipulating the same data until the holder of the lock is finished.

- **Durable**—for a transaction to be durable means that the results of a transaction are not lost. If a transaction completes, the results of the transaction are stored in a persistent store, usually a database. Even if the transaction processing system subsequently fails, the information pertaining to completed transactions will remain.

  This is usually achieved by the transaction processing system writing all changes that occur within a transaction to a log file. Upon the commit of the transaction, the transaction processing system ensures that the log file is on disk, then proceeds to update the database. Since failure can occur after the commit, but before all the updates occur, it becomes the responsibility of the transaction processing system, upon recovery, to go through the log files and apply the necessary changes. If a failure occurs before the commit then none of the changes will be made and the transaction is aborted.

Database systems and TP monitors

Modern database management systems (DBMSs) come with capabilities to handle transactions, logging, lock management, and recovery. Usually, the API for using a DBMS is vendor-specific, and applications that use such systems go through the API supplied by the vendor. Most DBMSs also allow a database to be distributed, using the vendor's own protocols and APIs.

Database systems provide the application programmer with the functionality to demarcate the boundaries of a transaction; that is, your application can use the API supplied with the database to indicate the start and end of a transaction. The DBMS takes care of ensuring that the results of the transaction are recorded within the database, and if necessary, handles the rollback of information in case a transaction is aborted.

TP monitors provide the functionality to manage transactions across heterogeneous databases. Most systems that provide distributed transaction processing will use some form of TP monitor. You can find TP monitor products on the market, such as Encina from Transarc, Top End from BEA, and so on. Such TP monitor products provide interfaces in standard programming languages such as C, C++ and COBOL. The functionality of database management is abstracted within the resource management component of a TP monitor; the resource manager can be a participant in a transaction. The TP monitor provides another component, the transaction manager, that coordinates a transaction across one or more participants.

Figure 6-1 illustrates a model for distributed transaction processing as defined by the X/Open Company Limited. The three main components of the model are the transactional application, transaction manager, and resource manager. The X/Open standard defines interfaces between each of these components. The application makes transaction demarcation

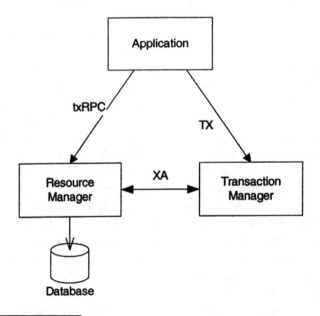

Figure 6-1. *X/Open model*

calls (start, commit, and abort) to the transaction manager and transactional remote procedure calls (txRPC) to the resource manager. Contextual information about the transaction is passed along with the txRPC communication. The resource manager is registered as a participant in the transaction with the transaction manager, which then communicates using the XA interface. The XA interface enables the resource manager to participate in the *two-phase commit* protocol. The two-phase commit protocol has been designed to help ensure the ACID properties of a distributed transaction.

Resource manager

The resource manager, as its name implies, is responsible for handling the interactions with a resource involved in a transaction. There will be one resource manager per resource, though many resource managers can participate in the transaction. These resources take the form of persistent store, such as databases, queues, and file systems. The resource manager works in conjunction with the resource to provide support to ensure that the transaction is atomic, durable and isolated.

Fortunately, you do not need to write a resource manager; most database vendors provide an implementation for their database system. Most of these also provide an XA interface, which allows their products to be used in conjunction with off-the-shelf transaction managers. In the jargon of the TP world, the terms *resource* and *database system* have become synonymous.

The resource manager ensures the durability of a transaction by managing the persistent storage (*resource*) for the transaction. It is responsible for ensuring the reliability in case of failure. The resource manager also makes use of durable logs during a transaction. These logs contain a record of the effects of a transaction and can be used to roll back the state of the persistent store in the case of failure. Information in the logs contain the before- and after-images of each operation in a transaction. This information can be used to roll back the effects of a transaction or to continue the commit of a transaction to the database. At the time of a transaction commit, the database stores all changes to a durable log before any actual write to the database. The commit has not completed until all changes have been put in durable storage. Saving the changes to durable storage happens during the prepare stage of a *two-phase commit*.

A transaction may have three states at the time of failure:

1. **Completed**—if the transaction completed, then there is no need to do anything upon recovery. The information is in the database.

2. **Prepared to commit**—a "prepare to commit" request will have been issued. The resource manager should have a log of all potential and actual database changes. If these database changes have not been applied, then the resource manager can "play" the log to complete the transaction.

3. **Not prepared**—again, the resource manager has a log of all database changes so far. However, since the transaction did not issue the "prepare to commit" request or the prepare was not completed, the resource manager can use the log to roll back the state of the database. If no writes happened to the database, we can just discard the log.

Using these mechanisms to recover from failure enables the resource manager to ensure the durability of the transaction. We can be confident that the transaction has been recorded.

Transaction manager

The transaction manager provides facilities for the coordination of all participants in the transaction. It keeps track of all transactions and their participants and ensures that a transaction is atomic when there is more than one resource involved.

When an application starts a transaction, the transaction manager issues a unique transaction identifier. This helps identify the context of the transaction: the context is passed along with each communication and tells each participant with what transaction it is involved.

Whenever a resource is involved in the transaction, the transaction manager is informed. This registration of resources is usually handled by the application when needed. The transaction manager then coordinates the registered resource managers (participants).

When the application finishes a transaction, it issues a commit to the transaction manager, which then uses the two-phase commit protocol to commit all the resources. If the transaction manager receives an abort from any of its participants, it informs all the resource managers to undo all the transaction updates.

The transaction manager works in conjunction with the lock manager for each resource to ensure transaction is isolated. The lock manger maintains a list of locks, for each transaction, on the associated resource; it grants, or denies, lock requests based on whether there is a conflict.

Locks

To achieve an isolated transaction, we need to ensure that two different transactions are not altering the same information in the database. The preferred mechanism to achieve this goal is through the use of locks. A lock is a "token" associated with data in the store that is being manipulated. If a lock is granted to a transaction, then subsequent requests by other transactions to manipulate the same data may be blocked (if the locks conflict).

Most database systems provide a lock manager. The lock manager is responsible for keeping a record of what information is locked, who requested the lock, and the type of lock. This information is kept within a lock table associated with the database.

Table 6-1 illustrates potential lock conflicts. If a transaction obtains a write lock on some data, then requests by other transactions to read the data will be blocked until the lock is released. Quite often, the underlying database system will apply the locks to the data in a transparent manner. The database system examines the query and the appropriate lock is applied as necessary. For example, if your query were to read a row from a table, then a read lock would be acquired, and if you were updating, then a write lock would be acquired. Usually, you do not need to be concerned with performing direct requests for locks.

Table 6-1: *Lock Conflicts*

	read	write
read		X
write	X	X

The sequence of lock acquisition by a transaction is also important to ensure that the transaction is serial. If a transaction releases a lock too early—that is, before all the work of the transaction is finished—there is the potential for a partial result to be used within another transaction.

A locking rule that guarantees that a transaction is serializable, and therefore isolated, is *two-phase locking*. This rule states that a transaction should obtain all its locks before releasing any of them; that is, a transaction may not obtain a new lock after it has released any locks. Therefore, there are two phases: the first phase is when the transaction obtains its locks; the second is when the transaction releases its locks, which is at the time of commit, or abort, of the transaction. By using this rule, the lock manager ensures that other transactions cannot see, or alter, any data being manipulated by another transaction until the transaction has ended.

All database systems provide mechanisms to lock information accessed during a transaction. However, the granularity of the information locked can vary between different database systems. The lock can be at the level of a database file, page, table, row, object and so on. The use of locks also affects performance and complexity of your application. Lock conflicts impose delays upon the execution of a transaction, and deadlocks can occur when there are application transaction interdependencies.

Lock granularity

The granularity of the locks that the database system provides can affect performance of your application. Coarse-grained locks can be at the level of a database file, table, or page; fine-gained locks at the level of individual records or fields. When using coarse-grained locks, the likelihood of conflict with other transactions is higher, though the lock management overhead is smaller. Conversely, with fine-grained locks the likelihood of lock conflict is reduced, but lock management overhead increases.

For example, if a transaction to update bank account information for a customer locks the whole account table, then no other customer account can be dealt with until that transaction is finished. Alternatively, if your transaction has to perform an update on thousands of accounts, each with fine-grained locks, then it needs to obtain thousands of locks.

It is preferable to use fine-grained locks to minimize potential lock contention in a system with a high volume of transactions. To solve some of the complexity of lock management, the lock manager maintains locks at multiple granularities. Here the lock manager utilizes *intention* locks at the coarser granularity. For example, if your transaction is going to read a record in a table, it will put an intention read lock on the table (or page), and then a read lock on the record. This would warn other transactions that want to update information within the table that there is a potential conflict.

Deadlock

When two or more concurrent transactions are manipulating the same information, it is possible to end up with deadlock. Deadlock occurs when transactions are competing for the same lock. For example, each transaction holds a write lock on some data that the other transaction requires a read lock on. This circular dependency is not resolvable without some system intervention.

Figure 6-2 illustrates such a situation where contention can arise. If Transaction 1 obtains a read lock on account 1, then Transaction 2 will block when it tries to obtain a write lock on account 1. In addition, if Transaction 2 got the read lock on account 2 before Transaction 1 request-

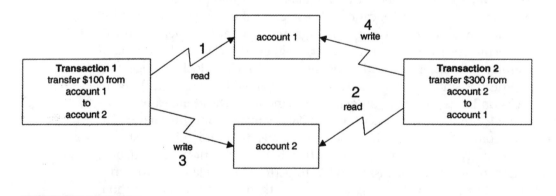

Figure 6-2. *Contention*

ed its write lock, then Transaction 1 is blocked. This is a deadlock situation. To maintain the two-phase locking rule, the system has to decide whether to abort one or both of the transactions. The decision may be based on some heuristic; for example, terminate the transaction with the shortest execution time or the one that uses the least system resources.

Deadlocks are detected either by using a time-out mechanism or by using a graph-based approach. In the time-out approach, if a transaction is taking too long, then it is aborted. The time-out mechanism can lead to situations where transactions that were not deadlocked are aborted, and deadlocks will not be detected until the time-out period is reached. In the graph-based approach, a graph of all transactions and the resources they have locked is maintained; if cycles are detected in the graph, then there is a deadlock and the transactions involved in the deadlock can be aborted.

Deadlocks can occur also in a distributed system. Here there are many data managers that do not know about each other. The time-out and the graph-based approaches can also be used; however, when using a graph-based approach you need to have one central server on the system responsible for maintaining information about all locks in all data managers. This can get complicated to manage, and so the preferred mechanism for deadlock detection in a distributed system is by using time-outs.

Two-phase commit

We shall now look at the mechanism used by a TP monitor to ensure that a distributed transaction is atomic. If two or more databases are involved in our transaction, then there is the added complexity of ensuring the ACID properties of the transaction across all databases. If there is a failure with one database, we need to ensure that the other databases involved in the same transaction do not commit.

For example, consider a funds transfer from your checking account to a savings account[1], and the information for each account is kept in separate databases. If the withdrawal from your checking account is successful, but the update of the savings account fails, then the transaction is not atomic (and you would be upset with the bank). To ensure the atomicity of the transaction and the happiness of the customer, the update of the checking account database needs to be reversed. You could write an application-specific solution, but such solutions will soon complicate your application code. The two-phase commit protocol was devised to solve these situations.

Two phase commit ensures that a transaction that updates data on two or more distributed systems is atomic and durable. Either both systems are updated or neither of them is updated. The two-phase commit protocol allows the transaction manager to coordinate all the participants in the transaction. The protocol takes into account that any of the participants in the transaction can independently fail and recover.

The transaction application starts the transaction by sending a "begin transaction" request to the transaction manager. The transaction manager is then responsible for coordinating the transaction; it generates a unique transaction context that is propagated to all transaction participants. All participants in requests associated with a particular transaction use the transaction context. Every resource manager involved in the transaction joins the transaction by being registered with the coordinator for that transaction at the time of an initial request to use the resource. Other transaction managers can also be participants in a transaction. Each of these transaction managers can be responsible for managing resources at their nodes.

So let's take a look at how the two-phase commit works. When the application finishes the transaction, it sends a commit message to the transaction manager. The transaction manager then coordinates a two-phase commit with all participants in the transaction. The two phases of the protocol are a *prepare* phase and a *commit* phase.

Phase 1: Prepare phase

The coordinator sends *request-to-prepare* to all participants. After each participant is prepared, it then "votes" by sending a message back to the coordinator:

- Prepared—the effects of the transaction are in stable storage, but have not yet been committed.

- No—this usually happens if there has been some form of local failure.

If the participant has suffered a catastrophic failure, or is overburdened, it may not send any message to the coordinator.

Phase 2: Commit phase

If the coordinator has received *prepared* messages back from all participants then it can then proceed to the commit phase.

- If any participant votes *no* or does not reply to the *prepare* message (the coordinator times out waiting for a reply), then the coordinator decides to abort the transaction.

- The coordinator sends the *commit* or *abort* message to all participants.

- Participants acknowledge receipt of the message by sending back *done*.

It is important that your distributed TP system is able to handle failure, especially with the increased opportunity for failures to occur due the distributed nature of the system. The two-phase commit protocol has been designed to handle the various failures that can occur.

To facilitate recovery, the transaction coordinator and the participants all maintain logs. These logs are durable records of the effects of a transaction. They can be used to roll back (return the state of all databases to that before the transaction), or to continue the commit transaction from the state at the time of failure.

During the prepare phase of the two-phase commit, all resource managers should ensure that their logs are in durable storage before voting. Even if one resource manager votes to commit, the eventual outcome of the transaction is not determined until the transaction coordinator hears from all participants. It just takes one resource manager to vote no, or to fail in communicating its decision, for the coordinator to decide to roll back the transaction.

Although the two-phase commit protocol helps handle failure and coordinates distributed transactions, there are still situations where participants in a transaction can block. Between the time of acknowledging a prepare message to the coordinator and the receipt of a commit (or abort) message, the participant is in an uncertain state. The participant is blocked from proceeding with further work while it is waiting to hear from the coordinator. If the coordinator fails and is down for a long time, then the blocked participant needs to decide what to do. It can make a heuristic decision, talk to other participants to see if anyone received a message from the coordinator, or time out.

The OMG Object Transaction Service

The Object Transaction Service (OTS) brings the capabilities of a transaction manager to the world of distributed objects. Nowadays you can find implementations of the Object Transaction Service (OTS) from many ORB vendors and third parties. The OTS includes the functionality discussed in the previous section: transaction control, two-phase commit, lock management, resource management and so on. We shall now spend some time looking at the OTS and getting an idea of how to use it to provide transactional semantics for our distributed objects.

As with most OMG specifications, the OTS is very flexible and provides users with a variety of programming models. We can let an implementation of the OTS take care of most of the work of managing a transaction, or we can be very explicit in how the transaction proceeds. We can use off-the-shelf resource managers with the OTS as well as plug in our own recoverable resources. Our applications can interact with other non-ORB transaction applications that use the X/Open standard. Our applications can also interact with other ORBs and other instances of the OTS. Being flexible, the OTS is empowering when it comes to implementing a transactional system. However, it can be easy to shoot yourself in the foot!

As you proceed through the rest of this chapter, you will obtain an idea of the flexibility and an understanding of the workings of the OTS. I will not cover all aspects of programming the OTS (this is a book in its own right), though you will get an idea of how the OTS works, the salient features, and what you need to do to use it. This should be enough information that will let you decide whether, and how, the OTS fits into you distributed object architecture.

As was mentioned in Chapter 2, every CORBA specification uses IDL to define the services, and the OTS is no exception. All the components for transaction management have their interfaces specified in IDL. You can find the complete interface definitions and a more detailed explanation within the OMG specification.

You should also note that the Concurrency Control Service (CCS) has been designed to work in conjunction with the OTS. The CCS provides mechanisms to implement and manage locks and thus help ensure the isolation property of individual transactions. If you are using the OTS with a compatible resource manager (usually one that supports the XA interface), then you will not need to use the CCS; however, if you implement your own recoverable resource or object cache and the application has any degree of complexity, then you will probably need to use the CCS.

As we proceed through this section, the example code is mostly in IDL. However, implementation examples have been provided in C++, though these should be understandable to readers familiar with Java. I have deliberately kept the implementations simple as a means to highlight the concepts; a full implementation would need more code to handle all the possible outcomes and exceptions.

Transaction model

The OTS provides an object-oriented model for a distributed transaction processing system. The essential underlying functionality is the same as discussed in the previous section on transaction.

In the OTS model, there are transactional clients, objects, and servers as well as recoverable objects and servers. Each of these entities participates with each other to provide the transactional properties of the system.

- **Transactional Client**—a transactional client is usually a user interface to the application. This client invokes operations on transactional objects, and usually is the originator of a transaction.

- **Transactional Objects**—transactional objects participate in the transaction and contain, or reference, data affected by the transaction. Non-transactional objects can also participate in the transaction, however you need to be aware of integrity considerations if these objects contain state.

  Transactional objects may inherit from the *TransactionalObject* interface; however, this does not guarantee that all methods in the implementation are transactional. You can provide transactional implementations and non-transactional implementations. A transactional object may contain state that is affected by the transaction but is not recoverable.

- **Recoverable Objects**—A recoverable object is also a transactional object; however, it directly contains state affected by the transaction. A recoverable object registers an associated *resource* with the transaction service. This resource stores the persistent state of the recoverable object and participates in the two-phase commit protocol.

The transactional client interacts with application servers. In the distributed transaction system, there are two types of application servers:

- **Transactional Servers**—contains one or more objects that are affected by the transaction. We say that a server is transactional if it contains one or more transactional objects. A transactional server interacts with resource managers or other transactional or recoverable servers.

- **Recoverable Servers**—like a transactional server, a recoverable server contains objects that are affected by the transaction. We say that a server is recoverable if it contains one or more recoverable objects. A recoverable server has an associated resource that contains persistent data and interacts with the protocols of the transaction service.

Basic OTS programming model

Usually the transaction client will also be the transaction originator. The transaction originator will use the *Current* object to start the transaction. The transaction originator will then make requests on transactional objects. The transaction context is passed along automatically to objects inherited from the *TransactionalObject* interface, with subsequent method invocations to transaction, and recoverable, servers. These servers become participants in the transaction.

Any of the transaction participants can rollback the transaction. This is achieved by their use of the *Current* object. They can also inquire as to the state of the transaction. If the transactional object is involved in more than one transaction at a time, it can distinguish between the transactions using a handle to the coordinator. This enables you to implement a transactional object so that the isolation requirement is met.

If the transactional object is also a recoverable object, it will have an associated resource. This resource is registered with the coordinator of the transaction. The coordinator can then communicate with the resource to perform the necessary actions for the two-phase commit protocol.

Once the transaction originator is finished issuing its requests, it can use the *Current* object to issue a commit or rollback. The transaction service will then use the coordinator to do the necessary work of committing the transaction with the two-phase commit protocol.

Interfaces

We will now review the interfaces of the OTS that are used in the "implicit indirect" programming model. This programming model is the simplest provided by the OTS, and it is probably the most commonly used. Additionally, it makes use of the major interfaces of the OTS and we can see how they interact to produce the functionality of a distributed transactional application. Figure 6-3 illustrates these interfaces and their methods.

- **Current**—The *Current* pseudo-object[2] provides the mechanisms to manage a transaction. An instance of the *Current* object is associated with the thread of execution. You use the *Current* object to begin, commit, and roll back transactions. If you need to manage or propagate a transaction context explicitly, then you would use the *Current* object to obtain a *Control* object, which would then be passed as a method parameter.

- **Control**—The *Control* object provides mechanisms to help with the explicit management or propagation of a transaction. Using the *get_terminator* method, we can get obtain a *Terminator* object, which can be used to end a transaction. We can also pass the *Control* object as a parameter to remote methods for explicit propagation of the transaction.

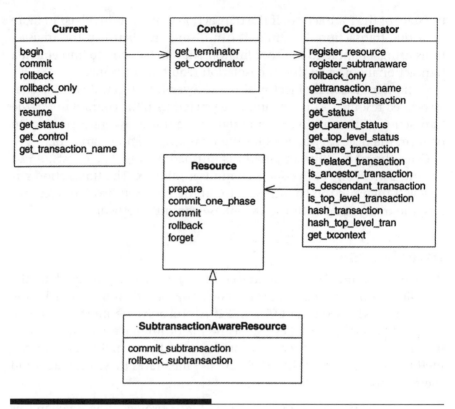

Figure 6-3. *Major Interfaces of the OTS*

- **Coordinator**—The *Coordinator* interface provides the mechanism to register participants in a transaction. A recoverable object registers its associated resource with the coordinator of the current transaction. One *Coordinator* instance is associated with each transaction.

- **Resource**—The *Resource* interface defines the operations invoked on each resource by the transaction service during a two-phase commit. This allows each resource to vote as part of the two-phase commit. Refer to the previous section for more information on the two-phase commit protocol.

- **SubtransactionAwareResource**—This is a specialization of the resource interface used for a resource that is part of a nested transaction.

- **TransactionalObject**—The *TransactionalObject* is an abstract interface with no methods, used to tell the ORB infrastructure that interfaces derived from it can be transactional. The transaction context is propagated with all method invocations on an object that inherits from the *TransactionalObject* interface.

Programming models

The OTS supports various programming models. Which of those models you use is determined by how decide to manage and propagate the transaction context. You can let the underlying infrastructure of the OTS take care of transaction management, or you can explicitly propagate the context and manage the transaction. You can also decide to mix these approaches depending on the needs of your application.

Transaction context propagation

Objects can support two mechanisms to receive information associated with the transaction.

- **Implicit Propagation**—If your object inherits from the *TransactionalObject* interface, then a transaction context will be propagated with each method that is invoked. You will also need to link in the libraries corresponding to the ORB vendor's OTS implementation.

- **Explicit Propagation**—The transaction context is propagated by passing the *Control* object as an explicit parameter to methods being invoked.

An advantage of implicit propagation is that you do not need to change the signature of existing methods. You just inherit from the *TransactionalObject* interface.

Explicit propagation allows you to mix transactional and non-transactional methods within the same object. Also use explicit propagation if you need to give other distributed objects the ability to terminate the transaction.

A disadvantage of explicit propagation is that the OTS does not have the ability to keep track of all objects that are involved in the transaction. This prevents the OTS from providing "checked" behavior for the transaction. "Checked" behavior allows the transaction manager to provide an extra level of integrity. A transaction is "checked" when the transaction coordinator ensures that commits from all participants complete. The coordinator builds a tree of all objects in the transaction; this is used to ensure that an object has received replies for all of its requests. This is useful if any of the transactional method invocations are deferred synchronous (for a description of deferred synchronous, see the discussion of DII in Chapter 4).

Context management

Client programs may use direct or indirect context management to manage a transaction.

- **Indirect Context Management**—The *Current* object is associated with the current thread of control and is used to manage the transaction.

- **Direct Context Management**—An application uses the *Control* and associated objects to manipulate the transaction directly.

Indirect context management simplifies your code and enables the application to use any optimizations within the ORB infrastructure. However, if you are using explicit propagation, then you may find it more convenient to manage the transaction directly.

Exceptions

As with any application, you should be aware of the possible exceptions and program accordingly. The OTS extends the exceptions included as part of the standard ORB infrastructure. These exceptions inform you if a method is called as part of an invalid transaction, if a transaction is required, and if the transaction has been rolled back.

Recall that in the discussion of two-phase commit, we talked about the possibility of a resource manager being in an indeterminate state. At this point, the resource manager may make a heuristic decision about the transaction. This can lead to a situation where some resources have made a decision to commit while others have rolled back. This can lead to a problem with data integrity. The OTS specification defines a set of heuristic exceptions that will be thrown in the case where a participant makes a heuristic decision. You need to handle these exceptions when they do occur and perform integrity checks as needed. For example, if one of the resources made the decision to commit, but the transaction was rolled back (or vice versa), then the data integrity has been compromised. If this happened during a transfer of funds between accounts, we could end up injecting more money into the system!

Though some resource managers will attempt to communicate with other resources involved in the transaction before making their heuristic decision, the final decision may not be appropriate. Also, recall that if the transaction coordinator does not hear from a resource manager as a result of the prepare stage, then the coordinator usually assumes that the resource will vote "no" to the transaction and a rollback will proceed. It is not uncommon for manual intervention to be necessary to resolve the effects of incomplete transactions.

Recoverable resources

With hope, you are using a database, or other form of persistent store, for which there is a resource manager compatible with your OTS. However, if you're not, then you can implement your own recoverable resource. This may be a wrapper around another off-the-shelf persistence mechanism, or completely homegrown; though before you do decide to go down this path, you should be aware that in the current climate of rapid development, you are potentially diverting development resources from the actual business problem.

The OTS specification provides support for XA-compatible resource managers. This covers the majority of relational databases. If your data store falls into this category, you can avoid implementing your own recoverable resource. You should refer to the documentation supplied with your OTS implementation as to what steps need to be taken to register your XA compatible resource manager with the OTS.

The *Resource* interface defined by the OTS specification allows you to implement your own recoverable resource. Listing 6-1 shows the IDL for a resource object. You can see that this interface supports the functionality for the underlying resource to participate in the two-phase-commit protocol.

Listing 6-1: *IDL for a resource object*

```
interface Resource {
    Vote prepare()
        raises(HeuristicMixed,HeuristicHazard);
    void rollback()
        raises(HeuristicCommit,HeuristicMixed,HeuristicHazard);
    void commit()
        raises(NotPrepared,HeuristicRollback,
                HeuristicMixed,HeuristicHazard);
    void commit_one_phase()
        raises(HeuristicHazard);
    void forget();
};
```

Here is a brief description of the methods:

- *prepare*—This method is invoked as part of the two-phase commit protocol. The resource prepares the results of the transaction, and it can vote. If the transaction does not change any persistent information, the resource would vote *VoteReadOnly*. If all the information for the transaction has been put into stable store, then we would receive a *VoteCommit*. You should note that the resource could still be asked to roll back the results of the transaction. If there were a problem, then the resource would vote *VoteRollback*.

- *rollback*—The resource should roll back all changes due to the transaction.

- *commit*—All changes that are part of the transaction are committed to the data store.

- *commit_one_phase*—The resource should commit all changes.

This optimization is used in cases where there is only one resource involved in the transaction.

- *forget*—If the resource causes a heuristic exception (see the section on exceptions), then it is required to remember that the exception has occurred. Once the coordinator has determined that the exception has been addressed, the resource will receive a *forget* message.

Your resource is registered with the OTS using the *register_resource* method of the transaction coordinator. As an example, Listing 6-2 illustrates part of the IDL for a document store. This is used as a resource to store documents.

Listing 6-2: *Partial IDL for a document store*

```
interface DocumentStore :
   CosTransactions::TransactionalObject,
   CosTransactions::Resource
{
...
   boolean save(in Document doc) raises(DBError);
   Vote prepare()
      raises(HeuristicMixed,HeuristicHazard);
   void rollback()
      raises(HeuristicCommit,HeuristicMixed,HeuristicHazard);
   void commit()
      raises(NotPrepared,HeuristicRollback,
            HeuristicMixed,HeuristicHazard);...
};
```

Now if we look at the implementation of the *save* method we can see how the resource is registered with the transaction coordinator.

I have factored out the code for the resource registration into the *register* method (Listing 6-3). This method is responsible for ensuring that the resource is not already registered with the coordinator for this transaction. This is achieved because the implementation of the document store keeps track of the resource with which it has been registered. It is important that you store the object reference to the recovery coordinator.

Listing 6-3: *The register method*

```
void
DocumentStore::register(CosTransaction::Current* current)
{
    CosTransactions::Control control;
    CosTransactions::Coordinator coord;
    control = current.get_control();
    coord = control->get_coordinator();
    // make sure that the resource is only registered once
    if ( myTransaction != 0 ) {
    // this resource is already associated with a transaction
    // check to ensure that it is the same transaction
        if ( myTransaction != coord->hash_transaction()) ) {
            // throw an exception ...
        }
    } else {
        myTransaction = coord->hash_transction();
    }
    ...
    RecoveryCoordinator recCoord;
    recCoord = coord->register_resource (this);
    ...
    // do the work to store the recovery object
    ...
};

boolean
DocumentStore::save (Document doc)
{
    // use OTS specific call to get a handle to the Current
    // object
    register( current ); // register this resource for this
        transaction
    // now save the document
    // it may be necessary to obtain a write lock ...
    ...
```

```
    // end of transactional operation
};

Vote prepare()
        raises(HeuristicMixed,HeuristicHazard)
{
    // places all changes in durable storage
    // if successful then return a Vote of VoteCommit
    // else return VoteRollback, VoteReadOnly etc.
};

void
DocumentStore::rollback()
        raises(HeuristicCommit,HeuristicMixed,HeuristicHazard)
{
    // rollback changes from the log
};

void
DocumentStore::commit()
        raises(NotPrepared,HeuristicRollback,
            HeuristicMixed,HeuristicHazard)
{
    // commit any changes to the store
};
```

It is the responsibility of the resource to maintain a persistent log of the transaction; the object reference to the recovery coordinator can be put into the log associated with this transaction.

If a failure occurs within the process containing the document store object then the recovery coordinator is used to recover the state of the transaction. This is only necessary if the resource has gone through the prepare phase of the commit protocol and voted *VoteCommit*. If the resource has not prepared for the transaction at the time of failure then the transaction coordinator will assume a *VoteRollback* when it fails to get a vote from the resource.

The OTS specification does not say how the transaction manager restarts the recoverable resource, though it does say the recovery coordinator's *replay_completion* method should be called upon restart if the resource has been prepared. How this is done is implementation dependent and you should refer to the specific manual for your OTS implementation.

In general, when a server is restarted it needs to reinstantiate all the recoverable resources that were associated with that server. It is your responsibility to store the necessary information so that the server can recreate the resource objects. When a resource object is recreated it needs to look through its transaction log so that it can return to the state it was in at the time of failure. Once this has happened, the *recovery* method is called.

The implementation of the recovery method will need to perform the following steps to recover each resource:

1. rebind to the recovery coordinator

2. invoke *replay_completion*

If there is no recovery coordinator, or the resource was not prepared, the resource can be rolled back.

Synchronization objects

There may be situations where you wish to be notified just before the start, and/or after the completion, of a two-phase commit. For example, for optimization purposes you may decide to implement a cache mechanism and only make use of the underlying resource when a transaction commits. In this case, you will want to be notified that the application has initiated a commit so that the cache is flushed to persistent storage.

The OTS provides the synchronization interface for just this purpose. This interface provides methods where an object can be notified before the start of a two-phase commit and after the end of the two-phase commit. You should note, however, that the OTS specification does not require this interface to be supported by all implementations. You should consult the documentation of the specific OTS that you are using to see if the synchronization interface is supported.

Listing 6-4 shows the IDL for the synchronization interface. Objects that implement this interface are registered with the transaction coordinator using the *register_synchronization* method. The coordinator invokes the *before_completion* method before the start of the two-phase commit, and the *after_completion* after the two-phase commit.

Listing 6-4: *IDL for the synchronization interface*

```
interface Synchronization : TransactionalObject {
    void before_completion();
    void after_completion(in Status status);
};
```

Having an object notified before the two-phase commit enables you to write application-specific code. If you implement a cache, then as an optimization you can flush changes of the objects within the cache to the database. You can put trace information into the method, and implement code to ensure the integrity of the object before it is committed to the database.

When your object is notified after the completion of the two-phase commit, you may want to perform some application-specific cleanup. For example, if the status says that the transaction failed, you may want to remove the relevant objects from your cache. In addition, you may want to trace the activity of the transaction.

Listing 6-5 shows IDL for a simple document cache. For performance reasons, we want to cache documents as they are found, rather than return to the database every time.

Listing 6-5: *IDL for a simple document cache*

```
interface DocumentCache : Synchronization {
    Document getDocument(string query) raises(NotFound);
    void SaveDocument(Document);
};
```

This can raise other problems. You may have two servers that allow applications to read and update documents; each server has an instance of the document cache. When it's time to save a document, the server will need logic to ensure that the document in the database has not been changed by another application; this integrity check can be performed in the *before_completion* method. Other solutions would be to have one cache shared among all the servers, or, at the time of change, to broadcast to all caches the fact that there has been a change.

Nested transactions

Nested transactions are transactions that are embedded within other transactions. The OTS specification refers to the nested transaction as a subtransaction. Nested transactions can be used in a system where the effect of a failure of a subtransaction does not require the rollback of the whole transaction.

Subtransactions can be used to isolate failure and when parallelism is needed. If a subtransaction fails, we may not need to abort the parent transaction. Instead, the parent can execute code to compensate for the failure of the subtransaction. This, of course, also complicates the implementation of the system. The parent transaction can not commit until all the subtransactions have completed. If the parent transaction does abort, then all the subtransactions may need to be rolled back; in other words, the effect of a commit in a subtransaction may not happen unless the parent transaction commits.

The OTS does support nested transactions, and so do some resource manager implementations; but, if you do decide that you need to use nested transactions within your application, you should consult the documentation for your OTS and choose a compatible resource manager. You should be aware, however, that no relational database currently supports nested transactions, and neither does the XA protocol.

Example: transactional document management

To help illustrate the previous discussions we'll return to the document management example. Here we want to make the retrieval and storage of documents transactional. To do this, we can alter the *ContentProvider* interface and provide a new *DocumentManager* interface to inherit from *TransactionalObject*.

Listing 6-6 illustrates IDL for both the *DocumentManager* and *ContentProvider* interfaces. The *DocumentManager* interface replaces the pervious *DocumentLocator* interface. I have also added a *create* method to the document manager; this enables us to create new document instances. The parameter to *create* indicates the name of the new document. You should also be aware that since the *ContentProvider* interface is transactional, all derived interfaces will also be transactional.

Listing 6-6: *DocumentManager and ContentProvider interfaces*

```
exception DBError { string reason };

interface ContentProvider : CosTransactions::TransactionalObject {
    Content getContent() raises(NoContent);
};

interface DocumentManager : CosTransactions::TransactionalObject {
    Document create(in string name) raises(DBError);
    Document find(in string query) raises(NotFound);
};
```

Listing 6-7 illustrates an altered Document interface that enables us to change the contents of the document and add new sections.

Listing 6-7: *Document interface*

```
interface Document : ContentProvider {
    attribute boolean isSection;
    Documents getSubDocuments() raises(NoDocument);

    SectionNames getSectionNames() raises(NoDocument);
    Document getSection(in string name) raises(NoDocument);

    // editing capabilities
    Boolean addSection(in Document section) raises(DBError);
    Boolean removeSection(in String sectionName)
        raises(DBError);
    Boolean setContent(in Content) raises(DBError);
};
```

As you can see, this IDL does not restrict the location of all document parts to the same database. It could be perfectly reasonable to have some of the sections of a document located in another database, and for documents to share sections. An example of this would be a series of documents that describe funds; some funds may share the same prospectus. Rather than have two copies of the same prospectus with each fund, we have all the appropriate funds refer to the same prospectus document. We can rely on the OTS to ensure that an alteration to a document that is itself distributed will occur within the one transaction.

Listing 6-8 illustrates some client code in which we create a new section and then add it to an existing document. This code uses the indirect-implicit model.

Listing 6-8: *Client code creating new section to a document*

```
try {
    current->begin();
    Document_var newSection = docMgr->create("Fund Description");
    newSection->setContent( newContent);
    document->addSection( newSection );
    current->commit();
} catch (CORBA::TRANSACTION_ROLLEDBACK) {
    // transaction was rolled back ...
} catch (const DBError ex) {
    current->rollback();
}
```

Whenever any of the above methods are invoked from within a transaction, the transaction context will be propagated. If the implementation makes use of an XA-compatible resource, then the OTS will coordinate the transaction. The application just needs to register the resource with the OTS. The process of registration, however, is implementation-specific. For example, IONA's OTS implementation takes a handle to the XA "switch" structure, which contains pointers to all the underlying resource managers' XA functions.

Concurrency Control Service

The Concurrency Control Service (CCS) provides interfaces that enable you to implement your own lock management. The CCS was designed to work in conjunction with the OTS. If you do write your own shared resource and you wish to ensure the isolated property of transactions, you will also need to use a mechanism to manage locks; then you need to use the CCS. I would advise, however, that you use the locking mechanism of the underlying database when possible.

You should be aware that off-the-shelf resource managers, especially XA-compliant ones, provide their own lock management. If you are using a resource manager that is compatible with the OTS, then you do not need to concern yourself with the CCS.

The CCS does not define a resource or the granularity of the locks. For example, in a document, each component could be a separate resource or the whole underlying document database could be a resource. The CCS allows you to provide a locking mechanism at a suitable level of granularity for your service.

Model

Locks are used to control concurrent transactions accessing the same resource. Before any access can occur, the current transaction needs to acquire the appropriate lock on the resource. If a conflicting lock is requested, then the request will either receive an exception or will block until the lock request can be satisfied.

The CCS defines several modes of locks. Table 6-2 illustrates these locks and their conflicts. The Upgrade lock is provided as a means to avoid a common form of deadlock. For example, if two clients have a read lock on the resource and both want to update the resource (and therefore obtain a write lock), deadlock can occur as soon as one of the clients asks for a write lock. However, if each client obtains an upgrade lock first, then the conflict can be avoided.

Table 6-2: *Lock Conflicts*

Granted mode	Requested Mode				
	Intention Read	Read	Upgrade	Intention Write	Write
Intention Read					X
Read				X	X
Upgrade			X	X	X
Intention Write		X	X		X
Write	X	X	X	X	X

I mentioned in the previous discussion on locks that the intention lock is used to manage mixed-granularity locks. An intention lock is obtained at a higher granularity, and informs other requests that there could be a potential conflict. For example, we can have a resource containing documents, and a document can be hierarchical with sections and chapters. To read a section, the client would obtain an intention read lock on the document and then a read lock on the section.

Because it is possible for multiple locks on a resource to exist, the CCS defines a lock set. You associate each resource with a lock set. This lock set is a collection of all locks associated with the resource. The CCS defines an IDL interface to the lock set; this interface is used to manage the locks within the lock set. Related lock sets can be managed as a group through the use of a lock set coordinator.

Two types of lock set can be associated with a resource: implicit and explicit. This is analogous to the propagation types of a transaction context. Operations on the implicit lock set are done as part of the current transaction, whereas operations performed on the explicit lock set require a reference to the transaction coordinator associated with the transaction that is requesting the lock.

The CCS also allows a transaction to obtain multiple locks on the same resource. These locks can be in the same or different modes. Other clients trying to access the resource will only be granted a lock that is compatible with all the modes of the first client. This means that the lock set maintains a count for each lock type for each transaction.

Because of this interdependency between the child and parent transactions, the rules for locks of conflicting modes can be relaxed. When a nested transaction requests a lock, the request is successful if all the potentially conflicting locks that exist were granted on behalf of the parent transaction or one of its subtransactions. However, a subtransaction cannot drop a lock that was acquired by the parent or another subtransaction.

Using the CCS

Lock sets are created using a lock set factory. The IDL for a lock set factory is shown in Listing 6-9. This interface provides the ability to create two types of lock sets. The first is an implicit lock set, using the create method: the lock set is implicitly associated with the current transaction. The second is an explicit lock set, using the create_transactional method: the transaction coordinator has to be passed to the lock set with each request.

Listing 6-9: *IDL for lock set factory*

```
interface LockSetFactory
{
    LockSet create();
    LockSet create_related(in LockSet which);
    TransactionalLockSet create_transactional();
    TransactionalLockSet create_transactional_related(in
        TransactionalLockSet which);
};
```

Figure 6-4 illustrates the relationship between the resource and the lock set. Each resource has an associated lock set. The resource uses a lock set factory to obtain a lock set, this lock set is then used during the lifetime of the resource. If the resource itself is inherited from TransactionalObject, then it can use an implicit lock set; otherwise, the transaction context is explicitly propagated and an explicit lock set will be required.

When you implement a resource it is your responsibility to call the necessary methods on the lock set appropriate to your method. For example, if the the method reads information from the resource, then a read lock should be set; similarly, if the method writes, then the appropriate

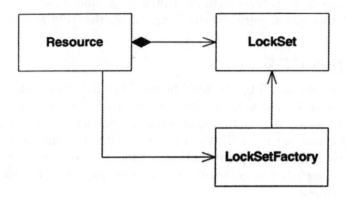

Figure 6-4. *Resource and lock set*

intention write and write locks should be set. The associated lock set will manage these locks and return success or failure.

Listing 6.10 illustrates the interface to the lock set. The methods to the transactional lock set are the same, only the first parameter is a *CosTransactions::Coordinator* which allows the lock set to associate the lock request with the appropriate transaction. The lock request will block until the request can be satisfied, however if you require a non-blocking request then use the *try_lock* method.

Listing 6-10: *LockSet interface*

```
interface LockSet
{
    void lock(in lock_mode mode);
    boolean try_lock(in lock_mode mode);
    void unlock(in lock_mode mode) raises(LockNotHeld);
    void change_mode(in lock_mode held_mode,in lock_mode
        new_mode) raises(LockNotHeld);
```

```
LockCoordinator get_coordinator
        (in CosTransactions::Coordinator which);
};
```

To facilitate the two-phase locking model, the CCS provides a lock coordinator. A lock set involved in a transaction can return an appropriate lock coordinator. The lock coordinator provides the *drop_locks* method, which drops all locks within a transaction family. You need to tell the *get_coordinator* method to return a coordinator for a specific transaction; you can do this by passing the transaction coordinator as a parameter to the method.

Summary

No large computing system is complete without some form of transaction management. The integrity of your information is important, and with distributed systems, the management of that information is much more complex. Fortunately, many people have spent years tackling the problems that arise in such systems, and solutions are reasonably well understood. We looked at what is involved and learned what ACID transactions means for your system. The principles are the same, regardless of whether your system is based on DCOM, EJB, or CORBA.

We have saw how the CORBA standard defines a transaction service (the OTS). We saw that it can be relatively straightforward to turn your distributed system into a transactional system. We also looked at the flexibility of the OTS, which provides extensive control, enabling you to integrate your own persistence mechanism.

References

Bernstein, Philip A., Newcomer, Eric. *Principles of Transaction Processing.* San Francisco, California: Morgan Kaufmann, 1997.

OrbixOTS Programmer's Guide and Administrator's Guide, IONA Technologies, 1998.

Gray, Jim and Reuter, Andreas. *Transaction Processing: Concepts and Techniques.* San Francisco, California: Morgan Kaufman, 1993.

Object Management Group. *Concurrency Control Service*, OMG document 97-12-14. Available at http://www.omg.org

Object Management Group. *Transaction Service Specification*, OMG document 97-12-17. Available at http://www.omg.org

X/Open DTP. *X/Open Guide Distributed Transaction Processing: Reference Model.* Version 3. Reading, Berkshire, UK: X/Open Ltd., 1996.

Notes

1. In Britain, these are referred to as the current account and a deposit account.

2. A CORBA pseudo-object is one that is specified using IDL, is implemented by the ORB vendor, and is not a distributed object.

Chapter 7

Security

Any system you build can become a potential target for misuse and attack by either the curious or the malicious. Regardless of the reason for the intruders' invasion, you will want to provide some measures to protect the system. To be realistic, rather than paranoid, your security policy and implementation will depend very much on the nature of your business and its associated risks. For this very reason, security is a term whose meaning changes dependent to whom you are speaking.

As well as security for business reasons, there is also the need for security for social reasons. Most respectable business will want to protect the privacy of their customers; it is difficult to give privacy assurances to potential customers if you have not implemented any security mechanisms. This goes beyond securing a transaction for an online purchase. For example, you may want to run an ethical online business and assure that information collected about your customers will not be used for nefarious marketing purposes.

In this chapter, we will be looking at what it means for a system of distributed objects to be secure. First, we look at what security is and what you need to consider when determining your security policy. Next we will review the salient features of the CORBA security service; this will help you gain an understanding of how the security service works. Then we will take a quick look at the integration of SSL with CORBA to provide security for distributed objects over the Internet. Finally, we will discuss the management issues that arise when dealing with a secure system. After reading this chapter you will have an understanding of the features provided by the security service and where it fits into a distributed object architecture.

Security Principles

To many people, security equates to encryption and authentication; that is, the ability to keep information and the identification of your users private. As you proceed through this chapter, however, you will see that for many organizations security means more than encryption and authentication.

Before we can look at how to implement a secure system, we need to describe what we mean by security and discover how secure we need to be. When you look at the literature describing secure systems, you find security described in terms of the potential threats to the system and how these can be averted.

The identification of security threats is the first step in determining the security policy for your organization. Once these threats have been identified you then devise mechanisms whereby the security problems can either be stopped or avoided. It is important to be able to show how these mechanisms prevent the perceived security risks. For example, if you provide a mechanism for nonrepudiation—the ability to identify without doubt the participants of a transaction—you may have to show how this prevents a customer from denying a purchase.

The aim of the security component of your architecture is to restrict access to information and resources; however, before you can demonstrate that the security implementation meets your needs, you need to classify the potential threats to the system and determine how those threats can be perpetrated.

Elements of security

Implementations of security services commonly address these requirements:

- **Confidentiality**—Information, (messages) transmitted between distributed components of the system should be private; that is, an unauthorized user or component should not be able to decipher the contents of a message.

- **Integrity**—Information needs to be protected from unauthorized alteration. This includes ensuring the integrity of information transmitted over the network.

- **Availability**—A system needs to be available when authorized users need to use it. As well as the technical infrastructure taking care of load balancing, failover and so on, mechanisms must be in place to detect and prevent denial-of-service attacks.

- **Accountability**—Users of the system should be accountable for their actions. You need to be able to trace the actions and the results of those actions.

- **Non-repudiation**—In addition to accountability, you may need to store nonrefutable proof of who the participants were in an action. This is to stop either side from denying involvement in a transaction.

You should be aware of which subset of the above requirements your application will need. For example, you may not care who sees the content of messages, but do care that the message is delivered intact. You will find, though, that most security products will provide functionality to satisfy at least the first four requirements.

Security threats

Security threats to any system can originate from inside as well as outside the organization. A disgruntled employee can wreak havoc, or someone with the wrong access privileges may unintentionally erase information. Hackers can break into the system out of curiosity, or competitors may infiltrate to perform industrial espionage. The reasons why your system may become a target are varied.

Methods of attack on a distributed system are either through access to the communications or being able to masquerade as an authorized user (or other component of the system). We can classify threats to a system within the following categories:

- **Acquisition of Information**—unauthorized access to information. This may be achieved via eavesdropping of communications, access to unprotected stored information, masquerading as a valid user and so on.

- **Alteration of Information**—alteration of the content of messages communicated between components of the system, or alteration of stored information.

- **Resource stealing**—use of computing facilities, such as components, objects, services, computers without authorization.

- **Vandalism**—malicious damage to the system that prevents normal operations; information in the system may be altered, or the system hindered, making it unusable. This also includes denial-of-service attacks, in which the system receives a saturation of requests from one source to prevent any other valid access.

- **Repudiation**—denial of participation in a transaction; for example, a customer may deny participation in an electronic transaction, or a merchant may claim a valid transaction that did not actually occur.

Before anyone can attack your system, they need to gain access. Networked systems by their very nature are more vulnerable to unwanted attention. These attacks are usually done by use of existing communication mechanisms, or masquerading as users with authorized access. You should be aware that when your applications use a standard protocol, it becomes easier to intercept and understand on-the-wire communications[1]. Some of the methods that may be utilized to attack your system include:

- **Masquerading**—using the identity of another user. The user name and password may have been stolen, or the attacker may have obtained the access token generated for an authenticated user.

- **Message tampering**—altering the content of intercepted messages.

- **Replaying**—recording messages sent between systems and replaying them at a later date. A previously privileged user may use this after their privilege is revoked. This mechanism may also be used to implement a denial of service attack.

Large systems composed of distributed objects introduce extra security problems. How much trust is there between the different objects, what happens when the implementations are changed (version problems?). Interactions between each of the objects is less predictable, and the administration of security policies per object can become complicated and error-prone.

Unfortunately, there is no silver bullet when it comes to the security of a system of distributed objects. The foundation of a secure system is to be aware of potential security problems and to implement procedures to deal with them. Products like the OMG security service help with the implementation, but not with the identification of problems and the development of policies.

Security functionality (features)

To meet the requirements mentioned above and alleviate the risks, a security system would implement the follow functionality:

- **Authentication**—provides a mechanism to verify the identity of every user of the system. All principals, users and other components should be authenticated before they are allowed to proceed with interaction with the rest of the system.

- **Encryption**—prevents the interception of communications between users and components. The degree of privacy this provides depends on the algorithm used and the security of the cryptographic keys.

- **Checksums**—provides a mechanism to ensure the integrity of the message. If we are not concerned with privacy, then we could just encrypt the checksum to ensure that the message is not tampered with; this has a lower computational cost than encrypting the whole message.

- **Authorization**—provides assurance that the user, or entity, accessing a service, object, or method is allowed to do so. Once a user has been authenticated, they should receive a set of one or more credentials that can be used by any of the services to check the validity of a request. The credentials can be checked with access control lists (ACLs) to determine whether the request is valid.

- **Auditing**—provides a mechanism for accountability. The security system should give you a means to log all requests. This log should include a time stamp, proof of identity of the requester, and the nature of the request. The information should also be stored in a secure manner to prevent tampering.

- **Nonrepudiation service**—generates proof of the identity all parties involved and records the request. This also needs to be stored in a secure manner so that neither party can tamper with it. For settlement of disputes an arbitrator (preferably a trusted third party) should be used.

You can get an idea of how some of the above functionality may be implemented from the sidebar on encryption technologies. The actual implementation will depend on the vendor of the security product that you purchase. You should also be aware of any legal requirements that may be in force at the time you are implementing your system. For example, there are export rules regarding encryption technology that originates in the USA and the size of cryptographic keys that may be used.

Developing a security policy

We have just covered a description of what security is, what functionality can be provided by a security service, and the types of threats to a system. We shall now take a look at what is involved in determining a security policy for your system.

You need to determine what threats actually apply to your system before you can implement effective security mechanisms. To do this you need to perform a risk analysis. Your risk analysis should look at the actual security threats to your system along with the cost of any threat actually happening. For example, if your system publishes news stories, you may be more concerned with ensuring that the content of a story is not changed without proper authority than who gets to read the final story. The cost to the business is higher if news stories are altered without the proper authority.

To justify the investment in the security infrastructure, it helps to express the risks in terms of the business. A mechanism to determine risk is to look at the cost to the business if the security breach happens. There will be a threshold that will help you determine what risks are more

Encryption Technologies and Digital Signatures

We will now take a quick look at current encryption technologies and their mechanisms. For the more inquisitive of you I recommend the book "Applied Cryptography" by Bruce Schneier.

The encryption of messages plays an important, usually central, role in the implementation of a secure system. Encryption is used to secure the lines of communication; that is to ensure that no eavesdropper is able to decipher the message. Additionally, techniques based on encryption can be used to assist with authentication. For example, encryption technology is used to implement digital signatures. These are the digital analog to a written signature; digital signatures are used to verify the identity of users.

The goal of cryptography is to transform the message into a form that cannot be understood by a third party, such that the only person able to reverse the transform is the intended recipient. Encryption is said to transform the message from "plain text" to "cipher text." There are two broad categories of computer cryptography: secret-key and public-key. The technology used to implement the security service can make use of either approach.

Secret-Key Encryption (Symmetric)

Encryption mechanisms based on shared knowledge between the sender and receiver have been used for centuries. With the advent of the computer, the realm of encryption techniques has expanded. Secret-key, or symmetric, encryption is based on the fact that both the sender and receiver of the message must know the encryption function (or its inverse) and a shared secret key. The same key is used to encrypt the message as is used to decrypt the message.

For this mechanism to work and ensure security, the secret keys need to be distributed in a secure manner. That is, each pair of users that wish to communicate need to gain knowledge of a shared secret key. For example, if Watson wishes to send an encrypted message to Holmes, Watson needs to communicate his secret key to Holmes using a secure mechanism (maybe meeting at Baker Street and writing down the key). This can become cumbersome if Watson needs to send an encrypted message to the whole of Scotland Yard. Each pair of users of the system needs to share a secret key. For systems with large numbers of users the number of keys rapidly increases.

Public-Key Encryption (Asymmetric)

Public-key, or asymmetric, cryptography was invented in the 1970's (this was first proposed by Diffie and Hellman 1976). This eliminates the need for trust between both communicating parties. Here one key is used to encrypt the message while another is used to decrypt the message.

Each user has two keys, one public and the other private. A message encrypted with one key can only be decrypted by use of the other key; that is, any message encrypted with the public key can only be decrypted with the private key, and vice versa. Using the previous example, when Watson wants to send a message to Holmes he encrypts the message using Holmes' public key. Holmes is then able to decrypt the message using his corresponding private key. Key management here is more manageable than secret key encryption, since the number of keys needed increases linearly with the number of users.

important. You can look at each of the security risks and the cost to the business if they are realized, then determine the appropriate action.

To determine your security policy you would do the following.

1. Identify your assets and determine their value.

2. Identify potential methods of attack.

3. Identify where your system is vulnerable.

4. Estimate potential loss and how much that loss may cost.

5. Identify countermeasures and how much it would cost to implement them.

6. Compare the cost of implementation with the cost of loss.

This may be achieved using formal or informal approaches. Regardless of how you approach your risk analysis, you will probably not think of all possible security holes. The process of performing this analysis, however, will help you create a security infrastructure that can later be tweaked.

After you have performed your analysis, you need to find products that will help you implement your security policies. You should also look at the mechanisms provided by the security products for administration and maintenance. You also need to assign responsibility to one or more human administrators; a security mechanism that detects unauthorized access is not effective if a responsible person is not notified so that appropriate action can be taken.

As well as the above considerations, you should take into account the physical security of your computer systems. If the machine on which you keep your certificates is easily accessed by anyone entering your organization, then you may have a problem. Access to important machines should be restricted. For example, besides ensuring that the access is by authenticated users, you may want to restrict physical access to the machine room. It is often a good idea to have a specialist perform a security audit.

Review of the OMG Security Service

Probably one of the most complicated pieces of infrastructure for a distributed system is provided by the security service. It took the OMG a couple of years to produce the security specification, which is one of the

Digital Signatures

Public-key encryption can be used to provide digital signatures. A simple example is that Holmes wishes to send a message and assure his colleagues that the message is from him. He can encrypt the message using his private key. Anyone receiving the message can then decrypt it using Holmes' public key. Since Holmes is the only person who could have produced the message, his colleagues can be sure that the message came from him. This relies on the fact that each key pair is unique.

So now, we have a mechanism to sign a message and provide the functionality for nonrepudiation of the originator. Holmes cannot deny that he generated the message because he is the only person with the corresponding private key. But anyone with access to Holmes's public key is able to read the message.

What if Holmes wants to send a private signed message to Watson? This can be achieved by combining two methods. First Holmes encrypts the message with his private key (hence signing it) and then encrypts the result with Watson's public key. Only Watson can read the resultant cipher text, and he knows that Holmes was the originator based on the digital signature.

For public-key encryption and digital signatures to work, we need to distribute the public keys. Holmes could send out an email with his public key, or it can be placed in a publicly accessible database of keys. Your confidence that the public key you retrieve for Holmes is correct depends on the amount of trust you have in the mechanism of key distribution. A solution is to only accept keys from trusted sources; this is dealt with in the section below on digital certificates.

Hybrid Mechanisms

Public-key encryption is considerably slower than secret-key methods (about 1000 times slower, according to Schneier). As a result, hybrid mechanisms have been developed. Here public-key encryption is used to facilitate the distribution of "session" keys that are then used with secret key algorithms. The message is encrypted using secret-key cryptography, and then the associated secret key is encrypted using public-key cryptography.

For example, Watson wishes to send a message to Holmes using a hybrid approach. First, a random key is generated for the session; this "session" key is used to encrypt the message using a secret-key algorithm. Next, the session key is encrypted using Holmes's public key. Both the encrypted message and the encrypted session key are then sent to Holmes. Holmes can then decrypt the session key using his corresponding private key and then use the session key to decrypt the rest of the message.

Message Digests

Message digests are one-way hash functions. These operate on an arbitrary-length message and produce a fixed-length value. They are one-way because they are not reversible: you cannot deduce the message from the value. It should not be possible to find two messages that produce the same message digest. Several message digest algorithms have been devised; the most popular are MD4, MD5, and MD2, designed by Ron Rivest of RSA; and Secure Hash Algorithm (SHA) created by the U.S. National Institute of Standards and Technology (NIST).

Message digests can be used to help protect the integrity of the message and the nonrepudiation largest chapters of the CORBA services specification. This reflects the complexity and importance of security for any serious application.

The OMG specification defines a framework rather than a specific implementation. An advantage of this is that a variety of underlying security technologies can be used to implement the security service, allowing a vendor to pick a technology appropriate to their market and political constraints. For example, a security service implementation produced in the USA would be constrained by the legislation regarding exports of cryptography[2]. This does, however, add complications for inter-ORB interoperability when the underlying security technologies differ.

The features of the security service are available to your applications with minimal programmatic intrusion. Most of you providing security in your distributed applications using the security service will find that the majority of the work will be determining the degree of security you require, your policies, and administration.

When you look at the security specification, you will see that that it has been divided into various features and interoperability "packages," some of which are optional. When you look at various implementations of the CORBA security service, you will see varying support for the packages from different vendors. You should be aware of what functionality you need from the security service before making your purchasing decision.

Two packages provide the main functionality of the security service. An ORB has to supply these packages to be compliant with the specification:

- **Level 1**—Security is provided by the ORB infrastructure. There is minimal to no programmatic intrusion; existing CORBA applications can be made secure using the provided infrastructure. There are some, though minimal, interfaces that a programmer can use to interface with the security service.

- **Level 2**—In addition to supporting the features of a level 1 implementation, there are a set of interfaces (specified in IDL, of course) that the application programmer can utilize to interact with features of the security service. More fine-grained control of security features can be applied by the application, such as the quality of protection, mechanisms for delegation of credentials, options for audit, and so on.

of the sender. For example, Watson wishes to send a message to Holmes. Watson generates a message digest of the message and then encrypts it with his private key (effectively the message digest is then signed by Watson). He then sends the message along with the encrypted message digest to Holmes. Holmes can then calculate the message digest for the message, decrypt the encrypted message digest using Watson's public key and compare the two, if they are the same, Holmes can be sure that the message has not been tampered with. Furthermore, because the message digest was encrypted using Watson's private key, Holmes can be certain that only Watson could have originated the message.

By combining message digests with the hybrid encryption mechanism, we can ensure the privacy of the message through encryption, the integrity through message digests, and the nonrepudiation of origin through the digital signature. The algorithms used may vary with the security software that you purchase, though the principles will be similar.

Certificates

For digital signatures to work, you must have the public key of the signer. Your assurance of the identity of the signer can only be as good as your confidence in the ownership of the public key. If Moriarty wishes to forge electronic documents from Holmes, then he would create a private/public key pair and publish the public key as belonging to Holmes. Messages then sent to Watson by Moriarty would then appear to be signed by Holmes! One solution is for Holmes and Watson to exchange public keys when they meet; unfortunately, this is not possible when the two cannot meet or there may be many people with which to communicate.

A scaleable solution to this problem is the use of certificates and certificate authorities. A certificate is a digital document containing identification information and a public key. A Certificate Authority (CA) then signs the certificate to vouch for the validity of the certificate. Now we have the problem of publishing the public key of the certificate authority in a way that is trusted. One mechanism is to ensure that the certificate authority is well known (the U.S. Post Office and VeriSign are two examples) and that its public key is widely advertised. Trust may also be achieved through the CA having its own certificate signed by another CA known to the recipient.

For Holmes to obtain a certificate, he needs to present his public key to the CA with evidence as to his identity. The requirements that each CA has for proof of identity may vary; the validity of the certificate depends on the trustworthiness of the CA. (Watson needs to trust that the CA has done its job before accepting a certificate from "Holmes.")

The ISO authentication framework (X.509) makes use of digital certificates. Besides the CA's signature, an X.509 certificate contains a version number, unique serial number, user's name, public key, encryption algorithm identifier, and period of validity. This information may be stored in, and obtained from, public databases. If the private key is compromised, the CA will issue a certificate revocation. ∎

One of the goals of the security service is to provide security for applications and users in a transparent manner. The Level 1 package of the security specification supports applications composed of distributed objects running in a secure environment without further modification. This secure environment is provided by the infrastructure inherent in the ORB with a security service implementation; however, if you do wish to implement security aware objects, then you will need to use the interfaces defined as part of Level 2 of the specification.

In addition to the two main functionality packages, there are also optional packages to define additional security functionality, replaceability, interoperability, and security mechanisms. Currently there is only one optional security feature package; the functionality required for nonrepudiation is optional. While the OMG has defined the interfaces, not all implementations are required to provide it.

An ORB implementation that provides one of the two replaceablity packages allows you to alter the underlying security technology; an ORB vendor can provide one of the replaceability packages (with no security implementation) and thus allow third party security implementations. An ORB that provides the replaceabilty package is said to be "security ready"; it is ready for a third party to add security functionality.

Different levels of interoperability are achieved by the various Common Secure Interoperability (CSI) feature packages. The Secure Inter-ORB Protocol (SECIOP) package also defines how security information is contained in the IOR, and the necessary negotiations to agree on a security protocol so that requests can be transmitted securely between different ORBs.

The revised security specification provides four mechanism packages. A security service implementation that interoperates must do so using one of the four security mechanisms. These mechanisms provide support for the major security protocols (SPKM, GSS Kerberos, CSI-ECMA, and SSL).

Security model

The features provided by the OMG security service can be added to an ORB in a non-intrusive manner. Existing distributed object applications that make use of a CORBA ORB can run without alteration using a secure ORB. The security service also provides interfaces that can be used by security-aware applications; you may wish to provide more fine-grained control of access or audit to your objects.

For the more adventurous the security service provides replaceability interfaces. You can insert the new mechanisms for encryption, authentication and so on. It is not mandatory for an ORB vendor to provide these interfaces, and not all implementations give you access to replace the implementation of these interfaces. This is achieved using interceptors (see sidebar).

Figure 7-1 provides a simple view of the security model as provided within the OMG specification.

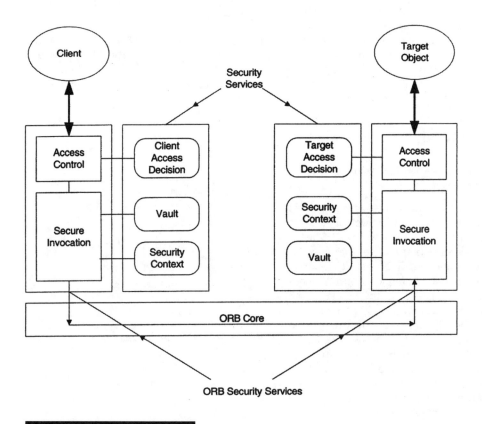

Figure 7-1. *OMG security model*

Interceptors

Interceptors were first introduced in the Security Specification as a mechanism to provide security in a nonobtrusive manner. Since their introduction they have become part of the CORBA infrastructure, and have been incorporated into the revised security specification as one of the optional replaceability packages.

By intercepting the communications before the application deals with the request, or sends the request on the wire, it is possible to add the necessary extra work to perform security functions. For example, you will want to encrypt the message just before it is transmitted and decrypt it just after it is received; this is achieved by intercepting the message at these points in the ORB infrastructure. There are two types of interceptors, with their interfaces defined using IDL:

- **request-level**—performs transforms on a structured request
- **message-level**—performs transforms on an unstructured buffer

Request-level interceptors are used regardless of whether the client and target objects are collocated or in separate processes. When a request-level interceptor receives the message, it is in a structured form; it is possible to extract information about the request and optionally add extra information to the request. The interceptor may also invoke other methods on remote objects before (and after) reinvoking the original request. For example, the access control interceptor is implemented so that the *client_invoke* method can be used to check client access control with the access decision object and the *target_invoke* method can do the same at the target side.

Message-level interceptors are only used when the message has to go over the wire. By the time that the message-level interceptor is used, the request is in a form ready for transmittal over the wire. The interceptor can do further transformations of the message. For example, the secure invocation interceptor is implemented where the *send_message* method can invoke the encrypt method on the security interface to turn messages into cipher-text and the *receive_message* method can decrypt incoming messages.

It is the responsibility of the ORB to maintain a list of interceptors and when they should be invoked.

```
module Interceptor {
    native Message;
    interface Interceptor {};

    interface RequestInterceptor: Interceptor {
        void client_invoke(inout CORBA::Request
request);
        void target_invoke(inout
CORBA::ServerRequest
                    request);
    };

    interface MessageInterceptor: Interceptor {
        void send_message(
                    in Object target,
                    in Message msg
                    );
        void receive_message(
                    in Object target,
                    in Message msg
                    );
    };
};
```

Principals, authentication, and credentials

You will come across the term "principal" in most documents about security. In this the CORBA security specification is not unique, and defines a principal as follows:

> *A principal is a human user or system entity that is registered in and authentic to the system.*

A necessary feature of any secure system is the ability to identify the users and other entities, principals, that make use of the system's services. The system needs reasonable assurance that the principal accessing the system is whom they claim to be. A mechanism to achieve this is to authenticate principals and provide them with a set of credentials.

Typically, a user initiates actions within the system, and this initiating principal needs to be authenticated with the system; that is, the security system has to be satisfied that the principal is a valid user or system entity. The mechanism used to authenticate a principal depends on the underlying technology used to implement the security service. Though commonly authentication requires that the principal provide some proof of identity, this is achieved through the use of secret information know only to the principal and the authentication system. For example, the information could be the user name and password or a cryptographic key.

By allowing the authentication mechanism to be supplied by the underlying security technology, the OMG Security Service can support practically any authentication mechanism. These include simple user name/password, symmetric secret keys, asymmetric public keys, or a combination. The underlying security services used are not visible to the users of the security model.

In the case of a Level 1 implementation, the authentication mechanism is usually supplied by the underlying security technology. For example, IONA's security service implementation uses DCE Security as the underlying technology and users would be authenticated as part of the DCE Cell. Security-aware applications, using interfaces supplied with Level 2 of the CORBA security service, could ask the user for identification and proceed to authenticate the user with the principal authenticator.

The security service replaceability package requires that the ORB implement two interceptors:

- **Secure invocation interceptor**—A message-level interceptor used to establish the security context. This interceptor uses cryptographic services to provide message protection and verification.
- **Access control interceptor**—A request-level interceptor that determines whether a method invocation should be allowed by asking the Access Decision object. This inter-

ceptor also handles the auditing functionality.

These are illustrated in Figure 7-2.

You should note that not all ORB implementations provide an interceptor mechansim. Though some products do provide similar functionality with propriety implementations. For example, IONA's Orbix3 implements "filters" and "transformers"; these provide similar functionality to the request-level and message-level interceptors respectively. ■

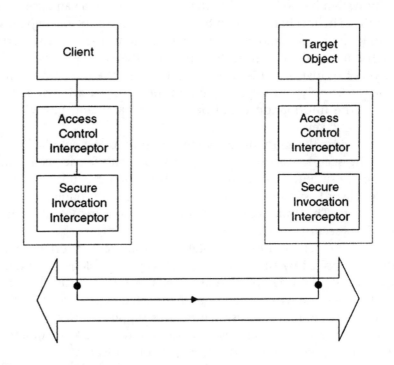

Figure 7-2. *Interceptors*

DCE

Distributed Computing Environment (DCE) is an open standard promoted by the Open Software Foundation (OSF). DCE provides a procedural model for the construction of distributed systems. At its core, DCE provides a mechanism to support remote procedure calls (RPCs). You can view DCE as the procedural predecessor to CORBA.

Construction of two-tier and multi-tier distributed systems using DCE is achieved in a similar manner to CORBA. You use DCE IDL to define the interfaces to your "remote procedures." DCE IDL is based on the C programming language and is easily understood. You compile the IDL to produce client stubs and a sever skeleton, which you use to provide an implementation. You use the client stubs to invoke the remote procedure.

DCE provides services to support a distributed computing environment; these include directory, time, and security services. Alongside these services is a threads library that provides a platform-neutral API for multi-threaded programs. In addition to these base services there are extended services. The distributed file system (DFS) and a management environment.

Unlike the OMG CORBA specification, the OSF also provides a reference implementation as part of the DCE standard. Like CORBA, there are many vendors that supply DCE products, such as Transarc and Gradient. Additionally, Transarcs's transaction management product was first developed for DCE; they have since provided an implementation of the OMG transaction service by leveraging the underlying technology previously used (IONA's OTS product incorporates Transarcs technology).

The crucial difference between DCE and CORBA is the programming model: DCE provides a "traditional" procedural programming model, whereas CORBA provides an object-oriented model. For more information on DCE, you can visit the Web site of the OSF at www.osf.org.   ∎

Once a principal has been authenticated with the security system, the principal is given evidence of authentication that cannot be forged. This evidence is known as the principal's credentials. Credentials are used to provide proof that the principal has been authenticated with the system and are used to validate actions that are initiated by, or done on behalf of, the principal.

Figure 7-3 illustrates the activity of authentication used by the ORB. The user sponsor is the code, or program, responsible for communicating with the principal authenticator and creating a credentials object. The principal authenticator returns an authenticated credentials object for the principal; this credential object contains authenticated identifiers and privileges. The user sponsor then sets the credentials with the *Current* pseudo-object. This *Current* object represents the current execution context (thread of execution) at both the client and the server.

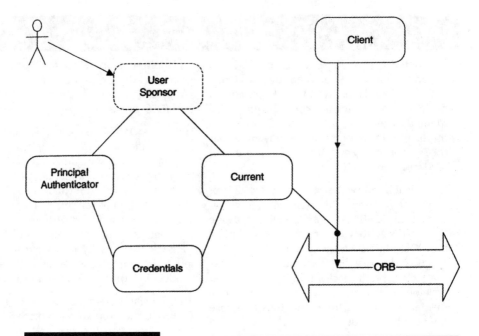

Figure 7-3. *Authentication*

Let's take a closer look at the credentials object as define in the CORBA specification. Figure 7-4 illustrates the credentials object and its contents. The credentials object contains security attributes for the associated principal. The security attributes consist of both identity and privilege attributes. It is possible for a principal to have more than one identity, for example different identities may be assigned for audit, access control, and accounting of system usage.

Privilege attributes are used to determine what the principal may access. These attributes depend on the access policies that have been determined for the system (see the "Authentication/access control" section). Examples of such privilege attributes would be the principal's role, group affiliation, security clearance, and so on.

Usually the credential object is only valid for a set time, the precise amount of time is determined by your security policy. Once the credentials have expired, the principal needs to be reauthenticated.

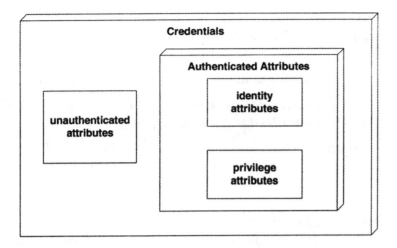

Figure 7-4. *Security credentials*

Security context

Once trust has been established between the client and target the principal's attributes are passed to the target. These attributes are used for access control, auditing, and so on. This creates an association between the client and the target object and in OMG parlance is called a binding. Each binding has an associated security context.

For the binding the ORB creates a security context at both the target and the client. The information contained within these contexts is specific for that binding and is derived from the credentials of the client, its identity and privilege attributes, and the policies associated with the target object.

Both the client and the target can check the state associated with the binding through the *Current* object. It is useful to note that for each binding a new security context is generated. This is transparent to the client and target.

Domains

For a large distributed object system, the management and administration of each individual object can rapidly become unwieldy. Domains provide us with a mechanism to group objects with similar security requirements. A domain provides us with more coarse-grained control of the security of our distributed objects.

The security specification mentions various types of domains:

- **Security policy domain**—defines the scope of security policy.

- **Security environment domain**—defines the scope of the local mechanisms of enforcement for a policy.

- **Security technology domain**—defines the scope of the underlying security mechanisms.

Security policy domains

The security policy domain, otherwise known as the security domain, provides a mechanism to enforce a common security policy over a group of objects. A security authority defines policies for the domain, such as access control, authentication, secure invocation, and so on. The domain management utilities provided by your ORB vendor should provide you with functionality to define the security domain, its policies, and member objects.

You can add "objects" from security-unaware applications to a security policy domain. The policies defined by the domain are then enforced by the ORB infrastructure in a transparent manner, though you should note that the unit of management is at the level of interfaces rather than instances; specific interfaces are associated with a domain.

As an aside, it would be nice to make entries in the namespace specific to a domain and provide management of security for specific instances. This could be achieved by having federated name servers; each associated with a different domain; each name server could be "secure" and have associated access policies.

A domain may have subdomains. You can organize these subdomains to represent different parts of your organization such as business units. Additionally you can have a federation of security domains, though it adds complexity as to how to map the privileges and roles between the different domains.

You need to determine how pervasive the security mechanism is going to be throughout your organization; then decide whether you need to provide subdomains, or federations of domains, and how they are going to be managed. You will also need to determine to what extent your security service implementation provides support for such domain structure and management.

Security environment domains

A security environment domain defines the scope where the enforcement of security policies can be achieved by means local to the environment and not part of the object system.

This can provide mechanisms for optimizing the implementation of security policies. For example, a valid environment domain could be the execution environment for a set of objects on one machine. It may be safe to assume that communications between objects on the local machine is safe and therefore a requirement to encrypt messages can be relaxed.

The security environment domain is not visible to the application or security services. Environment domains are implementation-specific and the responsibility of the security service vendor.

Security technology domains

Usually there is a one-to-one mapping between the security service implementation and the technology domain. The term *security technology domain* refers to the objects using the same underlying implementation of the security technology: for example, if one ORB makes use of Kerberos for its underlying technology while another uses SSL, then they are in different technology domains.

Objects residing in different technology domains would have a problem communicating with each other, for obvious reasons. To facilitate communication between technology domains would require the implementation of bridges (or gateways). The construction of such bridges at this time is problematic. Such problems include the mechanisms to deal with encrypted messages; sharing credentials and policies between domains; management of credentials; and so on.

The underlying security technology may support multiple protocols; in this case, there can be a negotiation between the different security implementations as to the protocol used for interdomain communication. The technology for this is currently immature.

Kerberos

Kerberos was originally developed at MIT as part of the Athena project. It was designed to be suitable for the TCP/IP protocol, which makes it a suitable candidate encryption technology for modern systems (the DCE Security Service utilizes Kerberos). Kerberos is based on symmetric (secret-key) cryptography.

The Kerberos model is illustrated in Figure 7-5. The Key Distribution Center (KDC) has an Authentication Service and a Ticket Granting Service (TGS). The KDC maintains a database of clients and their secret keys. If a user or other principal wishes to use a service, there are three steps as illustrated in Figure 7-5.

1. The client is authenticated by the Authentication Service and is given a ticket-granting

ticket. The client can the use this ticket to obtain tickets and session keys for specific services from the TGS.

2. The client requests a ticket for a specific server. The ticket is issued by the Ticket Granting Service.

3. Client then makes requests to the Server.

In Kerberos, tickets include a session key and an expiration time. This enables the client to continue to communicate with the server without repeating step 1 and 2. Once the ticket has expired, the client needs to obtain a new ticket if it needs to communicate further. A client will need to obtain a ticket (with a valid session key) for each server with which it wishes to communicate. ∎

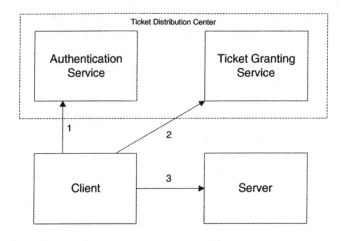

Figure 7-5. *The Kerberos model*

Different security technology domains are a problem for very large-scale networks such as the Internet, where many security technology domains exist. The easier solution for the Internet is to make use of protocols developed for the Web such as SSL (see the SSL section later in this chapter).

Interoperability

Whether distributed objects can interoperate depends on whether they are in the same policy and technology domains. For obvious reasons, objects in two different technology domains would have a problem communicating unless there were a gateway that bridged both security technologies. Interoperability between security policy domains is only possible if the security attributes from one domain are understood and trusted in the other domain. This adds complications if you define your own roles and privilege attributes within a domain.

Delegation

In a system of distributed objects, many objects working in unison may perform a task. This results in a series of interobject method invocations. How do you determine if the initiating principal has the authority to invoke any of the methods of the remote objects? In addition, each of the intermediate objects may have their own credentials and privileges; how does this affect the task at hand? We may need to confer extra privileges to the principal so that a task can be completed.

Access decisions need to be made at each object within the chain. The access model becomes complex, as the authority of a principal to perform the type of access must be tested at each object in the call chain. Access control rules may differ for each object in the chain, and authorization schemes can also differ.

The solution is to provide mechanisms for delegation of the principal's privileges. The initiating principal's security attributes are passed along to objects in the call chain. This gives each of the objects the ability to act on behalf of the initiating principal. This also provides the security system a mechanism to track the actions of any principal.

Rules for how the intermediate object uses the delegated credentials are determined by the policy of the security domain, though it is possible for a security-aware application to impose additional rules. When an intermediate object is invoking a method on another remote object, it may use its own credentials, the delegated credentials, or a combination of credentials. The mechanism used is determined by the security policies for the domain, though a security aware application can influence this.

It is possible for the initiating principal to restrict the delegation of privileges. For example, the credentials may contain more privileges than needed for a specific operation, so it may choose just to delegate the privileges needed to get the work done. Additionally a client may impose limits on the amount of time, or the maximum number of method invocations, for which delegated credentials are valid.

The security service defines five types of delegation:

- **No delegation**—the intermediate object uses the client's privileges for access control, but the privileges are not delegated. The intermediate object can not use the client's privileges when invoking another object.

- **Simple delegation**—the intermediate object assumes the client's privileges. The intermediate object impersonates the client when invoking other objects in the series. The intermediate object may further delegate the client's credentials.

- **Composite delegation**—the intermediate object uses both its own credentials and the client's credentials when invoking other objects. The subsequent target object can then individually check the credentials of the intermediate object and client.

- **Combined privileges delegation**—this is similar to composite delegation except that the target object is unable to tell whether the privileges originated with the intermediate or the client.

- **Traced delegation**—a chain of credentials is created. Each intermediate object adds its credentials to the chain that is then delegated. It is then possible for the target to go through the chain of credentials and trace all participating objects and their privileges.

The specification does not require implementations of the security service to supply the last two types of delegation. If these are required as part of your security policies, then you should check the documentation of your security service.

You can specify the type of delegation through the utilities supplied with your security service. Additionally, target objects can extract received privileges and use them to make local access decisions, use credentials for further method invocations, or build new credentials with different attributes., Only security-aware applications can select delegation schemes, however.

Authorization/access control

The security system ensures that authenticated clients only perform actions for which they are authorized. Authorization can be controlled through the use of access control lists (ACLs), capability lists, and role-based access control. The security service provides administration functionality to assign privileges to principals. As was mentioned above, the privileges for a principal are contained within the associated credentials objects. The ORB can obtain the privileges for the principal through the associated security context, which is obtained via the *Current* object.

Access control is built into the ORB infrastructure. The ORB uses an access control interceptor (for a description of interceptors see the sidebar) to ask the access decision object whether the requested access is allowed. Access control can occur both at the client and at the target. Client-side decisions are whether the client can invoke the operation on the target. Target-side access decisions define whether the target is allowed to accept the request.

A security-aware application can make explicit use of the security service interfaces to determine access control. The application can ask the domain manager whether the requested access is allowed; the domain manager would then use the privileges from the *Current* object and the information within policy objects to determine whether the invocation is valid. You may want make use of this mechanism for control of access to more fine-grained objects that are not exposed through IDL.

The ORB bases its access decisions on the following:

- **Privilege attributes of the principal**—such as identity, role, group, and so on.

- **Controls on the privilege attributes**—such as the time for which they are valid.

- **The method to be invoked**—such as who is allowed to invoke the method.

- **Control attributes of the target object**—such as the access control list.

Access control policies for each object are maintained using ACLs. For practical purposes it is useful to use groups and roles for access control. In a large organization it can be difficult to manage the privileges for every individual user.

Privacy and integrity of messages

Communications send across a network can be intercepted and tampered with. An important part of security is ensuring the privacy and integrity of messages. This is achieved using encryption techniques.

- **Integrity**—we need to prevent the modification of the message. Encrypted checksums can help ensure message integrity and sequence numbers can be used to ensure that messages arrive in the correct order.

- **Confidentiality**—encrypting a message ensures the privacy of the content and that the message is not read in transit.

While the mechanisms used are transparent to the user and applications, some implementations of the security service allow you to specify the strength of encryption and confidentiality. As you require higher quality of protection (QoP) then you also need better encryption algorithms supplied by the underlying security infrastructure. It is also possible to specify different QoP for the request and response. For further discussion of encryption techniques see the encryption sidebar.

Audit

Sometimes you need to be able to tell who did what and when. To facilitate this, the security system must be able to audit actions taken. If you recall, we mentioned that identity attributes are part of the principal's credentials; the principal's identity is used for auditing. It is possible to use a specific audit identity.

Auditing can be used to detect actual or attempted security violations. Information gathered for purposes of audit are sent to Audit Channels, which in turn store the information in a persistent store. It is possible to monitor this information and trigger actions based on suspicious activity. For example, if a principal has failed to authenticate for more than a predetermined number of times, there may be someone trying to break in by guessing passwords.

Because there may be many potential events, and your system can rapidly become overwhelmed dealing with all of them, you need to select some criteria on which to base your choice of what gets audited. Audit policies can be set at both the system level and the application level; audit policies enable you to determine the criteria for the type of events to be audited. Your ability to automate triggers depends on the implementation of the security service. The types of information captured and used to determine audit policies are:

- attributes of the principal, such as audit ID, group, or role

- target method

- object or object type

- time

- success or failure of the operation

Once your audit policies are set, then the audit information is sent to audit channels. An audit channel is responsible for storing the gathered information in a persistent manner. However, the CORBA specification does not determine how the messages can be filtered, how to secure the channel, or how the results can be analyzed. This is the responsibility of the implementers of the Security service, and it is advisable that you check the documentation for your security service.

Nonrepudiation

The nonrepudiation service is based on the ISO nonrepudiation model. This service provides mechanisms to generate irrefutable evidence of events (or actions) within the system. The ORB needs to provide proof of receipt (that the information was delivered) and proof of origin (who sent the information). This service can only be provided as part of a Level 2 implementation, as the application objects need to interact directly with the interface to the non-repudiation service.

Figure 7-6 illustrates the components of the nonrepudiation service. It is important to note that the CORBA specification only supplies the interfaces for evidence generation and verification. Neither evidence delivery nor evidence storage/retrieval are specified by CORBA; the implementation is determined totally by your security service provider.

To provide proof of origin the client calls the *generate_evidence* method of the *NRCredentials* object. This information is then sent along with the

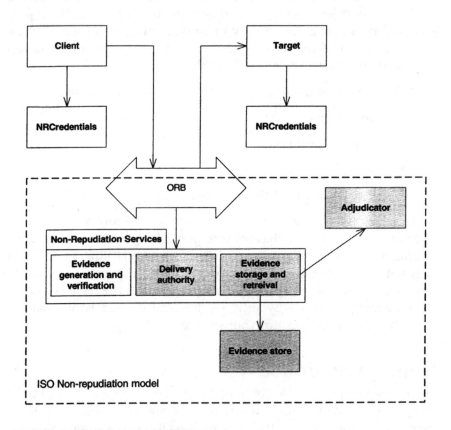

Figure 7-6. *Nonrepudiation components*

request to the target. The target can then verify the credentials by asking its *NRCredentials* object. Proof of receipt is achieved in a similar manner, the target asks its *NRCredentials* object to generate evidence and the resultant evidence is attached to the reply to the client. The client can then verify the evidence via its *NRCredentials* object. A time stamp may be included in the generated evidence; this prevents recording and play-back of the communications.

Security interoperability

The CORBA security service specifies how two secure ORBs can interop-erate. Common Secure Interoperability (CSI) defines three levels of inter-operability. However, you should be aware that while the specification describes the mechanisms for interoperability further work in this area is currently under way within the OMG.

There are three levels to CSI and the Security specification defines them as follows:

- **CSI Level 0**—identity-based policies without delegation

- **CSI Level 1**—identity-based policies with or without unrestrict-ed delegation

- **CSI Level 2**—identity- and privilege-based policies with con-trolled delegation

The inter-ORB communications protocol has been modified to sup-port the transfer of security related information, this has been called Secure Inter-ORB Protocol (SECIOP). Currently, for this to work, both ORBs need to support the same underlying security technology, at least for the encryption of communication. The CSI is under revision, and we hope to see interoperability between security service implementations with different underlying security technologies.

SECIOP provides a mechanism by which the ORBs can negotiate the level of security required and the policies supported. This information will indicate the level of protection for messages, whether the client should be authenticated, and so on. For interoperability to succeed on a practical level, however, not only do the ORBs need to speak the same wire protocol, they also need to have consistent security policies.

SSL and CORBA

Secure Socket Layer is a security protocol that is usually layered between an application and TCP/IP. The use of SSL from a programming perspective is relatively straightforward. If you have written an application that makes use of TCP/IP sockets, then there is minimal code change; you may need to add some initialization calls to set up the use of digital certificates, though the socket API is the same. Because of its relative simplicity and the use of TCP/IP, SSL has become the mechanism of choice for security on the Web, with support in most major browsers.

SSL makes use of a hybrid approach to secure communications. Public-key encryption is used to share a private session key between the client and server. The server can also authenticate the client by requesting the client's certificate. See the sidebar on encryption technologies for more information on the underlying principles.

Since IIOP is the application protocol for CORBA and sits on top of TCP/IP, it would seem a natural fit to place SSL between the two as a security mechanism; in fact, various ORB vendors support the use of SSL in this manner. In response, the OMG incorporated SSL into the security specification; SSL provides functionality for CSI level 0.

For SSL to be used, an IOR will contain a tag indicating that the object accepts SSL communication and the associated TCP/IP port number. The ORB infrastructure then passes IIOP communications through the SSL port. This provides a mechanism to encrypt messages using SSL. SSL also supports client certificates, which can also be used for authentication, though client authentication can only be achieved if the SSL option to exchange certificates is enabled.

For secure communications to work, an X.509 certificate must be associated with the server. This certificate contains the public key of the server. It is important that the corresponding private key is kept in a secure manner by the underlying ORB infrastructure. If this private key is compromised all future communication is suspect. In one implementation of CORBA SSL (from IONA), the private keys are kept in an encrypted form; an application can retrieve its private key by use of a pass phrase.

The specification does not mention how you initialize you client and target applications to use SSL, nor does it handle how you mange X.509 certificates. These details have been left to the implementation.

Summary

An advantage of the CORBA Security Service is its nonintrusive nature. The OMG security service is probably not a perfect solution, though it does provide many of the features you require to make your distributed system secure.

While the security service specification provides IDL interfaces to create and manage security policies for your distributed objects, you do not really want to write management utilities. Most implementations will give you utilities to do just that, though the level of sophistication of these interfaces varies with each vendor. In addition, while it is possible to affect the policies of the secure system from an application, this also opens potential security holes.

The creation and management of domains has been left to the facilities specification and is not part of the security service specification. This is a serious lag between the two specifications and means that this functionality is vendor-specific. I suggest that you pick a implementation that suits the scale of the security service you are deploying; more sophisticated management tools will be necessary for enterprise security than for small departments. Tools for managing the security service should be provided by your vendor. It was beyond the scope of the security specification to say what tools are used; however, a set of management interfaces are provided that management applications can use (I strongly advise that you buy rather than implement these tools).

References

Schneir, Bruce. *Applied Cryptography*, 2nd ed. New York: John Wiley and Sons, 1996.

Orbix Security Guide, IONA Technologies, 1997.

Object Management Group. *Security Service v1.5*, OMG document formal/98-12-03. Available at http://www.omg.org

OSF DCE Application Development Guide, Rev 1.0. Englewood Cliffs, New Jersey: Prentice-Hall, 1993

OSF DCE Application Development Reference, Rev 1.0. Englewood Cliffs, New Jersey: Prentice-Hall, 1993

SSL 3.0 Specification. Available at http://home.netscape.com/eng/ssl3

Schiller, Jeffrey I., *Toward A Safe and Secure Distributed Computing Environment*. MIT I/T Integration Team. Available at http://big-screw.mit.edu:8001/~jis/mitsec/

Stiener, J., Neumann, C., and Schiller, J. *Kerberos: an authentication service for open network systems*. Proceedings Usenix Winter Conference, Berkeley, California, 1998.

Notes

1. This is not to be taken as advocating the use of proprietary protocols for your communications.

2. Crytographic products are considered by governments as munitions, and as such are subject to import and export restrictions. The most publicized example is the restriction placed on the size of keys used in security products for export by the government of the USA.

3. Plans for the next generation of IONA's Orbix include support for interceptors.

Chapter 8

CORBA and the Internet

Use of the Internet has exploded since the first Web servers and browsers were introduced to the public in 1993. Everyone is producing Web-enabled versions of their applications. Companies are using the Web to provide services to their clients and employees. Almost every new project ends up having some Web component. Applications that make use of distributed objects are not unique in this respect; in fact, technologies like CORBA that provide the "universal object bus" are a good marriage with Web technologies that provide the "universal user interface."

In this chapter, we take a look at distributed object architectures for the Internet. How to integrate CORBA with Web technologies and the interaction of CORBA with Internet security mechanisms. We will then also look at upcoming standards and how these can be integrated with CORBA—specifically, the use of Extensible Markup Language (XML) and the next generation of HTTP (HTTP-NG).

Architectures

Two types of CORBA-based architectures exist for the Web. The first is when your applications speak IIOP over the Internet: the client application can communicate directly with your CORBA objects. The second is an architecture in which a gateway is built that translates from the standard

193

Web protocols to CORBA: an indirect communication exists between the client application and the CORBA objects.

Your decision on which architecture to implement will depend on various factors. How much influence do you have over the end user's environment? What are your security considerations? What are the characteristics of the network? To help you make an informed decision, we will now take a quick tour of these architectures. For each architecture, we will look at why you would use it, how it is implemented, and what you need to be aware of when you make your decision.

CORBA Web clients

You may decide to expose your distributed objects directly to the Internet. After all, CORBA does speak IIOP, which uses TCP, the lingua franca of the Internet. However, before you do so there are a few considerations. What is the nature of the CORBA client that you will provide to your users, and how will you distribute it? Does your design take into account the higher latency of a wide area network? Have you produced an infrastructure suitable for twenty-four hour use? Finally, are there any "firewall" issues to be addressed?

We could decide to distribute the same CORBA client applications to our global users that we have given to the users on our internal local network. How do we deliver this and how much control, or influence, do we have over the end user's environment? Even within a large global corporation there are issues with distribution of software to internal users distributed over a large geographic base.

The advantage of using standards like CORBA is the support across heterogeneous environments: machines, operating systems, and programming languages. But we do not necessarily want to implement and support a client application for different operating systems (or even different languages). We could publish our objects and say to a sophisticated, ORB savvy user, "Write your own client application." For the system to be widely adopted and used, however, we need to distribute a client application that can run anywhere. To achieve this goal the obvious target language and environment these days is Java.

Since its introduction in 1995 by Sun Microsystems, Java has become not only ubiquitous but also associated with the Web. Any machine capable of running a Java virtual machine can execute a Java application. Because of Java's platform-neutral nature, we can be reasonably assured that our application can run on any user's machine. Additionally, since Java virtual machines can be embedded within other applications, such as Web browsers, we can use already familiar tools to deliver our functionality.

Java gains its portability from being compiled into "byte code." Byte code is a file format that can be interpreted by the Java virtual machine (JVM). The JVM is responsible for translating the byte code at run time into code that the local machine understands and can execute. However, because the byte code is interpreted, your application will run slower than native applications for the same operating system and hardware. Just-in-time (JIT) compilers, which transform the byte code into the native machine code, can help to make the performance of a Java application comparable with native applications.

Java applications executing within the context of a Web browser have been termed applets. Applets are downloaded at run time, so code is distributed only on demand. The JVM enforces a security model on the applet that helps to protect the user's local machine from unauthorized access and ensures that the applet only speaks back to the machine that served it—although if an applet is signed (has a digital signature that is certified by a certificate authority), then it can be granted permission to perform actions that would otherwise normally be denied.

The OMG has defined a mapping from IDL to Java. An implementation of this mapping is supplied as part of Java 2 (Java IDL). This means that all Java applications and applets have access to CORBA functionality as a standard! Even if you decide not to use Java IDL there are implementations of the IDL to Java mapping from various ORB vendors.

Figure 8-1 illustrates the Web client architecture, written in Java. We can implement the client in Java, and distribute it as an application, or as an applet that is downloaded when needed. This is similar to your "standard" CORBA architecture, although part of the network will reside in the public domain (and outside of your control).

One of the problems with this architecture is the amount of time it takes to download the applet. We can minimize the download time for our applet by using technology that allows the applet to be cached on the user's machine and only updated when there is new code. We can

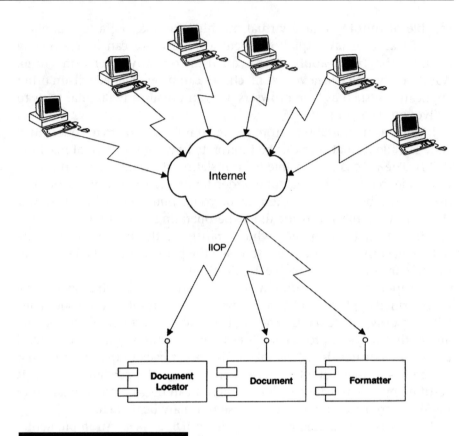

Figure 8-1. *CORBA and the Web*

obtain tools that help with the distribution of our applications, such as Castanet from Marimba.

Web server/ORB gateway

You may want to provide the functionality of your distributed objects to users on the Internet; however, the world outside is unknown. You may have little or no influence on the user's environment. For instance, you cannot require that the user install any special software, though it would be nice if we can leverage the knowledge and skill that the user already has by using the ubiquitous Web browser. To do so requires that we provide a gateway that does the work to translate from the protocol of the Web to the protocol of the ORB. To understand how to achieved this, we will take a quick look at Web servers, their protocol, and API.

Web browsers talk to Web servers using the HyperText Transfer Protocol (HTTP). Browsers find resources on the Web by using a Uniform Resource Identifier (URI); the commonly used form of URI is the Uniform Resource Locator (URL). Figure 8-2 illustrates the structure of a URL. A URL contains information on the location of a resource and associated parameters. The Common Gateway Interface (CGI) is part of the HTTP protocol that defines how external programs and scripts interact with the Web server.

In the early days of the Web, you would have written a CGI script using an interpreted language such as Perl. Since then Web servers have become more sophisticated; most now provide hooks for that allow you to write server-side programs in a variety of programming languages. For example, the Web servers from Netscape and Microsoft provide application programming interfaces (APIs) that enable you to use programming languages such as C++, C, and Visual Basic. With the popularity of Java, there is support for modules implemented in Java (known as "servlets") to run within the Web server.

Using one of these approaches, we can write a CGI program that is also a CORBA client. The responsibility of this program is to translate Web requests into method invocations on your distributed objects and to transform the response back into a form suitable for the Web. This CGI program is a gateway between the Web and CORBA.

Figure 8-3 illustrates the architecture for such a Web server/ORB gateway. Web clients communicate using the standard HTTP mechanisms;

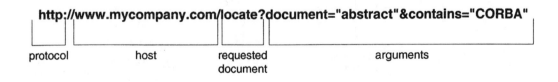

Figure 8-2. *URL structure*

that is, they use a Web page provided in HTML and interact with the system using URLs and HTML forms. Then the gateway moderates the communication with the various distributed objects. In effect, the gateway maps URLs to method invocations on CORBA objects.

We shall now look at a specific example: providing a Web/ORB gateway for part of our Web publishing system. In this example we will look at the locate functionality. We will not be changing the any of the distributed objects that we have already implemented; we will just provide another type of ORB client.

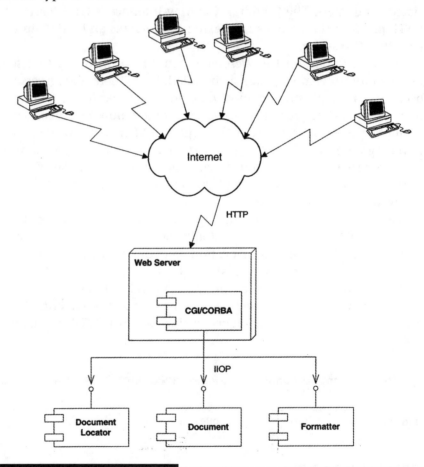

Figure 8-3. *Web server/ORB gateway.*

How does the Web browser communicate with our gateway? The URL for a locate request will take the following form:

http://www.library.com/servlets/locate

Now we add the parameter for the query:

http://www.library.com/servlets/locate?query="document=test"

Finally, we can also specify the format as part of the URL.

http://www.library.com/servlets/locate?query="document=test"&format=" HTML"

The URL now contains all the information necessary to locate the document of interest and specify the format of the result. This request can also be formulated as an HTML form. Listing 8-1 illustrates part of the HTML for such a form.

Listing 8-1: *Partial HTML for document location form*

```
<FORM action=http://www.library.com/servlets/locate method=POST>
    <br>Locate document matching the criteria:
    <INPUT TYPE="text" NAME="query" SIZE="30">
    <INPUT TYPE="hidden" NAME="format" VALUE="html">
    <INPUT TYPE="submit" NAME="locate" VALUE="Submit">
    <INPUT TYPE="reset" NAME="reset">
    <br>
</FORM>
```

Listing 8-2 illustrates the code for a CGI program to process the above input. This has been written using Java and utilizing the Java Servlet API. This code has been simplified for ease of illustration (more error-handling code would be in the actual implementation).

Listing 8-2: *CGI to process input from Listing 8-1*

```
//
// Simplified servlet example for Document locator
//
```

```
public class Locator extends HttpServlet
{
    NameServiceProxy NS; // wrapper round Name service - see chapter 4
    public void init(ServletConfig config) throws ServletException
    {
        try {
            super.init(config);
            // get a handle to the name service
            org.omg.CORBA.Object initNCRef =
                    ORB.init().resolve_initial_references("NameService");
            NamingContextRef rootContext =
                    NamingContextHelper.narrow(initNCRef);
            NS = new NameServiceProxy(NS);
        } catch () { // Put error handling in here
        }
    }

    public void doGet (HttpServletRequest req, HttpServletResponse res)
                        throws ServletException, IOException
    {
        processRequest(req,res);
    }

    public void doPost(HttpServletRequest req, HttpServletResponse res)
                        throws ServletException, IOException
    {
        processRequest(req,res);
    }

    void processRequest(HttpServletRequest req, HttpServletResponse res)
                        throws ServletException, IOException
    {
        // use the document locator
        String query = req.getParameterValues("query")[0];
        String format = req.getParameterValues("format")[0];

        try {
```

```
Document doc = locator.find(query); // TODO - test for error

// get the formatter corresponding to format requested
if ( content.format == "HTML" )
{
    org.omg.CORBA.Object objRef =
      NS.resolve("Formatters/" + content.format);
    Formatter formatter =
      FormatterHelper.narrow(objRef);
    Content content = formatter.format( doc );

    res.setContentType("text/html");
    PrintWriter out = res.getWriter();
    out.write ( content.data.extract_string() );
}
out.close();
} catch () { // put error handling in here
}
}
}
}
```

The above example provides an application-specific gateway between the Web and CORBA objects. The code in the above servlet maps from the "locate" request to the method invocations on both the document locator and formatter objects. First, it uses the locator to find the document and then uses the formatter to produce the result as HTML. The resultant gateway is a very thin CORBA client.

If, however, you decide to implement a generic Web/CORBA bridge, you should first consider several issues. You will need to provide a generic mapping from HTTP requests to CORBA method invocations. This means formulating a way to specify generic requests—that is, specify object instance, method, and arguments—as part of the URL. This gets even more complicated if more than one CORBA object needs to be involved to satisfy the request. Also, devising a generic mechanism to map from the results of method invocations on CORBA objects to HTML may not fit the style of the sites you are going to support. Finally, to justify such effort, you need to ask yourself, "On how many projects am I going to use this gateway?" You will find that since application-specific gateways are relatively simple, it is not necessary to provide such a generic approach.

A mixed blessing of the Web/ORB gateway approach is that no special requirements are imposed on the user of the system. The look and feel, capabilities, and vagaries of your user interface are at the mercy of the user's Web browser and its configuration. To reach the widest audience, you may want to limit the capabilities of your HTML interface to the lowest common denominator or write code to detect the browser version before generating any HTML. Additionally, HTML is not ideal for an interactive application; it can become quite cumbersome to navigate through a dozen pages to perform a simple task.

A benefit you can realize from this approach is that you can use standard Web-based mechanisms for security. Communications between the user's Web browser and the Web server can use secure HTTP. You can use digital signatures to verify and authenticate the identity of your users. You can also use a security service approach (see chapter 7) and pass the security context as part of an HTTP cookie.

IIOP and Firewalls

Whenever you deal with the World Wide Web (WWW), you need to be concerned with security. The Internet is a public place and any computer attached to the Internet can be a target of unwanted access. A firewall provides a degree of security. Almost every company, institution, and school uses a mechanism to protect their internal network from unwanted access. The degree of protection will vary according to the needs, awareness, and budget of the organization.

The computing term *firewall* derives its name from the buffer created around a forest to stop the spread of fire. In an analogous manner, a firewall controls the communications into (and out of) a site attached to the Internet and provides a mechanism to protect data on a private local area network from uncontrolled access. The use of a firewall has an impact on the use of IIOP, the preferred protocol of your CORBA components.

While this is not a book about Internet security, you will need to understand the implications of firewalls for a system of distributed objects. In this section, we will take a brief look at the mechanisms that can be used to construct a firewall. We will then see how distributed objects using IIOP can communicate when a firewall is present, and take a brief look at the proposed OMG standard to do this.

Firewall technology

You can implement a firewall using hardware, or software, or a combination of both. A firewall controls both inbound and outbound communication. It enforces rules that the communication must satisfy before proceeding. All applications communicating across the firewall will have to follow these rules. Using tools or configuration files, you can configure the firewall to allow communication between a set of known computers, individuals, or services. A firewall is also a control point between a trusted network and an untrusted network (like the Internet). Firewalls are a central point of control and can become a potential bottleneck if not administered properly.

Two categories of technology are used within a firewall: filters and proxies. Typically, a firewall will make use of both. Filters work at the level of the network transport, whereas proxies work with the communication protocol of your application.

Filters

A filter may be implemented as a program running on a gateway machine or within the hardware of the router. The mechanics of the filter is similar in either case. Usually, you will find that the router used by your network has filtering capabilities. A router is often installed on the connection between your internal network and the outside (Internet), and is used to route the network traffic.

Filters work at the level of the network protocol. The majority of applications communicating over the Internet use TCP (sometimes UDP) as their network protocol. Both TCP and UDP make use of "ports" to identify the destination on a machine. These ports allow multiple client connections to an application on a single machine. Each connection to an application is bound to a network port on the machine. Well-known application protocols such as telnet, SMTP, DNS, and HTTP use well-known port numbers; for example, telnet uses port 23, SMTP port 25, and HTTP port 80. These numbers can be found in the IETF RFC 1700, which can be obtained from their Web site (see References for the URL).

A packet-filtering router is a simple form of firewall. It directs network traffic from the outside to the required destination. This filter is only concerned with the addresses of the source of the network packets and their destination; there is no need for the packet filter to understand any application-specific information.

You configure the packet filter to direct the network traffic according to a set of rules. These rules would define a set of allowed network addresses and ports. When your router receives a communications packet, the filter would decide whether to forward, drop, or reject the packet. This is achieved by comparing the information within the packet header and applying the rules accordingly. Each packet is screened based on the network address and port of the source and destination. For example, you can configure the router not to let through any network traffic for telnet by restricting port 23, but allow SMTP traffic, which uses port 25. Figure 8-4 illustrates such a router with a filter configured to allow SMTP but not *telnet*.

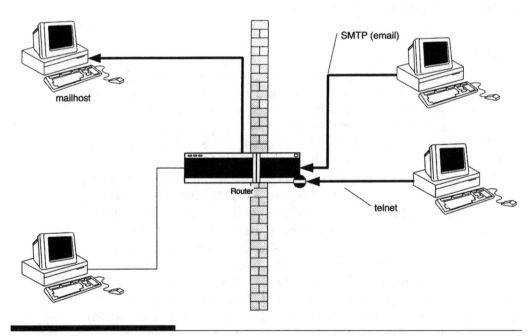

Figure 8-4. *Router configuration*

Proxies

There are two types of proxies: application proxies and network proxies. Application proxies are sometime referred to as application gateways, and network proxies are sometimes referred to as circuit gateways. Proxies act as relays, usually for a single service or protocol. For example, there are proxies available for most common network applications such as FTP and telnet. Proxies have the advantage of understanding the application-specific communication protocol, and can therefore be a bit more intelligent in ensuring that messages do not contain harmful information. Normally, an off-the-shelf firewall product will come supplied with various proxies for most of the standard Internet applications.

An application proxy acts as an intermediary between the application server and client. It understands the application specific protocol; for example, an FTP proxy understands the FTP protocol. Figure 8-5 illustrates the use of an application proxy. All telnet communication is routed

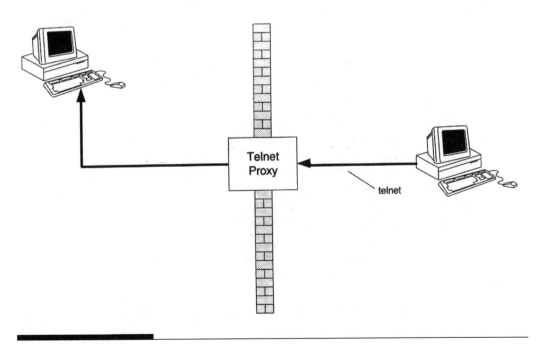

Figure 8-5. *Firewall proxy*

through the proxy. The proxy will then use its rules to determine whether to allow the communication to proceed.

Network proxies consist of a process running on a gateway machine, a machine through which all communication is routed. The most popular example of a network proxy is one that implements the SOCKS standard, defined by the Internet Engineering Task Force (IETF). For applications to communicate using a network proxy, they need to use the protocol defined by the proxy. For example, when using SOCKS, both the server and client are linked with the SOCKS libraries, which substitute for the standard TCP functions.

There is no application logic within a circuit gateway. The gateway does not understand the application-specific protocol, such as IIOP, but does speak a specific communications protocol such as SOCKS. The gateway behaves in a manner similar to the filters mentioned above, in that it routes packets between the two networks. However, the SOCKS protocol includes a negotiation between the client application and the gateway regarding security. The communication can be encrypted, and you can define access control based on network address and user information.

HTTP tunneling

If our firewall uses a filter and our distributed object has been configured to always use a well-known network port, then we can configure the filter to route communications for that network port. However, as we add more distributed objects or produce a more dynamic system, this solution will not work. It will become infeasible to maintain the integrity of the firewall and support a dynamic system of distributed objects. If there is also a firewall at the user's site, then we do not have any control as to its configuration. This means that we need to find another way for our application to communicate through the firewalls.

"Tunneling" refers to a mechanism to bypass the standard firewall security. (If all else fails then dig a tunnel under the wall!) When a firewall does not understand the communication protocol used by our applications, a solution is to convince each firewall traversed by our communication that we are speaking a protocol, on a known port, that they allow. The protocol of choice is HTTP, as it unlikely to be blocked, and the mechanism is called tunneling—hence the term HTTP tunneling.

Figure 8-6 illustrates communication using HTTP tunneling. Here a proxy is used that looks like a Web server—it speaks HTTP—but it examines incoming requests and translates from HTTP to the application protocol. For this to work, the client application also must translate from the application protocol to HTTP.

The proxy, which implements the tunneling mechanism, may also allow you to implement further access control. For example, you may be able to configure it to restrict communications to certain clients and instances of the application. In the case of distributed objects, you may be able to determine visibility and access control to the distributed objects.

IIOP proxies

Now that we have taken a brief look at firewall technology, let's have a look at the implications for IIOP. Currently, IIOP is not a communication protocol understood by firewalls. However, the recently adopted OMG Firewall submission defines how IIOP and firewalls will interact.

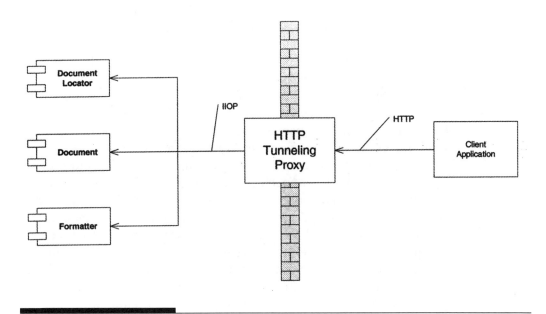

Figure 8-6. *Firewall tunneling*

We can expect to see the first commercial products that conform to this standard in the summer of 1999.

The OMG firewall submission defines an IIOP proxy—one that understands the communication protocol of CORBA. This is an application proxy and operates in a similar manner to the application proxies we discussed in the previous section.

Now let's take a look at how the IIOP proxy works. The object reference (IOR) that the client receives contains the network address of the distributed object. In the case of an inbound firewall—the firewall on the system that hosts the server objects—the IOR of the server object is altered to contain the address of the IIOP proxy. A client application will then talk to the IIOP proxy, which then talks to the requested object. In the case of an outbound firewall—the firewall installed on the client's system—information about the outbound firewall is part of the client-side ORB's configuration. All IIOP requests that are for the outside system will then go through the proxy on the outbound firewall.

Additionally, the firewall proposal recommends a change to GIOP to allow for bidirectional communication. This is useful for situations where your client provides callback objects. In this case the client creates a CORBA object and passes the IOR to the object back to the server. Thus, the server can communicate directly with the callback object (the server has become the client and the callback object is a server). Currently the CORBA standard specifies that a new connection on a new port is created for the callback object. This is problematic with firewalls, as they will block the new connection. The proposed solution is to reuse the existing connection between the client and server for bidirectional communication, so there is no need to create a new port.

The Internet standard for secure communications is Secure Socket Layer (SSL). SSL defines a mechanism to encrypt TCP communications and the use of digital certificates for the purpose of identification and encryption. The OMG firewall proposal incorporates SSL technology. The GIOP proxies need to handle digital certificates and either pass through IIOP/SSL or have the ability to participate in the SSL communication. Digital certificates can be used to verify the identity of clients and servers and access control can then be based on these.

You can find more information about the OMG firewall proposal from the documentation at the OMG Web site; the details can be found in the references at the end of the chapter. We can expect the first commercial products that conform to the proposal to be available late 1999. Currently there are two products available, WonderWall from IONA and Gatekeeper from Visigenic, that the proposal is based on.

HTTP-NG

The World Wide Web is not a static place. There are continual improvements, innovation, and new products emerging. The standards and technology that form the Web are defined by the World Wide Web Consortium (W3C), and this organization is continually seeking to improve the underlying technology. One of these improvements is the proposed next generation of HTTP, which has been aptly named HTTP-NG.

The architecture of HTTP-NG consists of three levels: message transport, remote invocation, and Web application. The message transport layer provides a mechanism to transport HTTP-NG messages; this layer can be built using a variety of message transports, it may also include components that deal with encryption, connection management, and compression. The remote invocation layer is a generic object-oriented messaging layer, which, like GIOP, provides a mechanism to invoke methods on remote objects. This layer does not provide any application-specific logic, such as caching or security. The top layer is the Web application, which includes Web browsers, servers, and other Web-enabled applications.

New Web applications will provide public interfaces that contain invokable methods. These interfaces will be defined using a "network definition language." It is the responsibility of the middle layer to broker communications to the application through this interface. Although this is similar to the mechanisms defined by the CORBA standard, the W3C has decided not to adopt any existing standard. It has stated that "It is not a viable solution to simply adopt CORBA, DCOM, or Java RMI for this layer, because each—in its current form—has technical and/or political liabilities for Web use" (HTTP-NG Overview, W3C). Rather, the W3C sees the protocol defined for the middle layer to be "a force for unification" and "The hope is that HTTP-NG's invocation protocol is eventually adopted by those other systems."

The W3C has not yet defined the "network definition language," although they do suggest that many different interface languages could be used to define the applications. We may see the use of OMG IDL, or an approach based on a markup language (such as eXtensible Markup Language, XML), used for the "network definition language."

HTTP-NG is designed to provide an efficient protocol for invocations over the Web. Given that the CORBA standard allows ORBs to support multiple protocols (using an ESIOP), we may in the future see an ORB using HTTP-NG as its Web-based protocol.

It is still early to see if the goals for HTTP-NG will be achieved. If HTTP-NG does provide "a force for unification," we can expect to see a convergence of distributed object technology, at least at the protocol level.

XML and CORBA

It would be difficult to avoid talking about eXtensible Markup Language (XML) in a section on CORBA and the Web. A lot of interest has been generated in XML since the autumn of 1997; it has been gaining momentum almost as fast as the Java "revolution" of 1995. So what is XML, what is the hype about, and how can it work with CORBA? To give a full answer to these questions would require another book; I shall present an overview here of XML and some pointers as to where you can go for further information. Then we shall look at how XML complements CORBA.

Quick tour of XML

XML, like HTML, is a subset of Standard Generalized Markup Language (SGML). However, unlike HTML, in XML the term *extensible* means that you can define your own tags and hence your own markup language. You can define your own document types and the rules used for document construction. In fact, lots of organizations and consortiums are doing just that: using XML to define markup languages for everything from electronic commerce to portable handheld devices.

XML is ideal for providing structure for information that you want to transmit over the Internet, and is now a W3C recommendation (a recommendation is a W3C standard). The best way to get a flavor of XML is by example. Listing 8-3 illustrates part of an XML document that represents an invoice. You will notice the lack of formatting information within the document; in fact, the document's content is just information specific to the transaction.

Listing 8-3: *Partial XML for generating an invoice*

```
<?xml version="1.0" encoding="ISO-8859-1"?>
<!DOCTYPE invoice SYSTEM "invoice.dtd">
<invoice>
  <date>
    <day>1</day>
    <month>December</month>
    <year> 1998 </month>
  </date>
  <due>
    <day>1</day>
    <month>January</month>
    <year> 1999 </month>
  </due>
  <amount>
    <currency>USD</currency>
    <value>450</value>
  </amount>
  <Customer>
    <Contact>
      <forename>John</forename>
      <surname>Brown</surname>
    </Contact>
    <Company>Bits and Bobs</Company>
    <address>
      <street>1 Wall Street</street>
      <city>New York</city>
      <state>NY</state>
      <zip>10005</zip>
      <country> USA </country>
    </address>
  </Customer>
</invoice>
```

Within a well-designed XML document, it is relatively easy for us to tell what each of the individual document elements represents. In addition, the document is structured to be easily parsed by a program. Plenty of parsers are available that you can use within your application.

We define the type of a document using a Document Type Definition (DTD). In XML, a DTD is similar to the concept of class in an object-oriented language. The DTD is referenced within the DOCTYPE element of the above example, it has a value invoice and can be obtained from a file on the system called "invoice.dtd". If the parser has access, or can gain access, to the DTD, then it can use the DTD to validate the document.

DTDs are being defined for multiple applications, from financial transactions to markup languages for handheld devices. Examples of these include the Resource Definition Format (RDF), which is used to express meta-information about documents, and the Open Finance eXchange (OFX) standard for the exchange of financial information over the Internet. There are also plans to incorporate more XML capabilities into the next generation of Web browsers.

Alongside XML, the W3C is defining the Document Object Model (DOM). This is an object model into which all XML (and HTML) documents can be translated. The model has been defined in both Java interfaces and OMG IDL. Once an XML document has been translated into an instance of the DOM, it can be manipulated, either within a Java program or from within the Web browser, using ECMA script.

So if XML just conveys the content of the document, how do we tell a browser or other application how the document is to look? The answer to this is the use of stylesheets. A stylesheet coveys formating information—how each of the elements within an XML document are to look when displayed (or printed). The eXtensible Stylesheet language (XSL) provides this functionality. XSL is similar to XML in syntax, with the addition of a scripting capability. You can write stylesheets that define how XML is to be displayed within a browser or on the printed page.

Part 2 of the XML specification deals with a richer linking model. It will be possible to create two-way links and links to parts of documents without requiring the equivalent of an HTML anchor. This helps with the construction of a more interactive and richer Web-based application for the browsers of the future. At the time of this writing, this is still undergoing some changes; I recommend that you look at the current specification to obtain more details.

To get started using XML, you will need an XML parser. The *de facto* standard is a "Simple API to XML" (SAX) compliant parser. SAX provides an event driven model, where you can implement your own handlers to take care of events such as "start element." You can find many implementations of XML parsers on the Web (I have listed some of the URLs in the reference section later), each complying to the SAX standard. You can also find implementations using SAX that will take your XML document and produce an instance of the DOM model. Both IBM and SUN have made available SAX-compliant XML parsers. With these tools you can be well on the way to implementing your first application—of course, you need to design your DTD!

How XML fits in with CORBA

XML adds value to CORBA-based architectures. CORBA provides us an open standard to represent and implement systems of distributed objects. XML provides us an open standard to represent information in a human- and machine-accessible form. We can use XML both for information shared between applications and for the output of our system.

Part of any distributed system is the transfer and sharing of information. We can use XML for the representation of this information. For instance, in the "document publishing" example we can use XML to represent our content. Listing 8-4 illustrates the IDL for such a construct.

Listing 8-4: *IDL for XML construct*

```
struct content {
    string dtd;
    string data;
};
```

Note that the content structure provides both the DTD and the XML data. We could alter this to make the DTD optional, as the destination application may have another means to acquire the DTD if necessary. The system can use the DTD to validate the information, while the data within the content contains only the information in which the application is interested.

We will now take a brief look at how XML affects the two CORBA Web architectures mentioned in the previous section. In the case of the Web

Server/ORB gateway we can use XML for the format of information passed between the CORBA services. We can also pass the XML back to the CGI/servlet, which can then format the result into HTML using an appropriate stylesheet. An alternative, if the user has a browser that understands XML, or a Java application/applet, would be to pass the XML back to the user's browser.

For the CORBA Web client we can use XML to pass information from our distributed objects residing within our site to the clients. The client application would be equipped with an XML parser. We can also use XML as a streaming mechanism to transfer the state of our objects, regardless of the programming language. This can be richer than using a CORBA *any*, because we can convey more information about the data than just its type.

In addition to devising your own application-specific DTD, you may wish to make use of DTDs developed, and being developed, for other applications and industries. You can find XML developments and the latest status at Robin Cover's Web page (see References for the URL). Work in XML varies from financial applications to healthcare, from markup languages for vector-based graphics to markup languages for handheld devices.

The OMG is even getting involved with the XML scene. XML Meta-information Interchange (XMI) format is an XML DTD adopted by the OMG. XMI is a standard markup language to exchange meta-information between repositories like the MOF, applications, and design tools. Other uses of XMI include the publication of meta-information on the Web and the use of the meta-information by occasionally (or disconnected) clients of a MOF. DTDs are being specified for both UML and the MOF; we will be able to obtain an XML description of our distributed system.

There are some obvious trends for the use of XML and CORBA. We will soon see tools based on the open standards (of XML and CORBA) that integrate with our repositories. We will be able to take our UML models and transform them to XML. We will also be able to represent our distributed objects in XML, though we have yet to see if people will use XML editors rather than IDL to define distributed objects.

Summary

We have now looked at various aspects of CORBA and the Internet, from the types of architectures used by CORBA-based Internet applications to the relationship of Internet technologies and CORBA. We have seen how firewalls and the security implications of the Internet affect CORBA.

The next few years will be interesting, as architectures using CORBA will increase for Web-based applications. We are seeing CORBA products being embedded within application servers and electronic commerce products, such as BEA's Tengha and Broadvision's e-commerce suite. Web sites are already being deployed using the "Web Server/ORB Gateway" approach (American Airlines and CNN Interactive).

In the next generation of CORBA-based Internet applications, we can expect to see the inclusion of XML-based technologies. One constant about the Web is that it is always changing. I have included in the References some URLs to Web sites that will contain the latest information.

References

Bray, Tim, Jean Paoli, and C. M. Sperberg-McQueen. *Extensible Markup Language (XML) 1.0*. February10, 1998. Available at http://www.w3.org/TR/REC-xml

Cover, Robin. The SGML/XML Web Page. Available at http://www.oasis-open.org/cover/sgml-xml.html

HTTP-NG information. Available at http://www.w3.org/Protocols/HTTP-NG

IETF RFC1928 (SOCKS). Available at http://www.ietf.org/rfc/rfc1928.txt

Internet RFC 1700. Available at http://www.ietf.org/rfc/rfc1700.txt

Iona Technologies. *WonderWall Administrators Guide*. IONA Technologies, 1997. Available at http://www.iona.com.

Luotonen, Ari. *Web Proxy Servers*. Englewood Cliffs, New Jersey: Prentice Hall, 1998.

Mowbary, T. *CORBA Design Patterns*. New York: John Wiley and Sons, 1997.

OMG Firewall Proposal. Available at http://www.omg.org/cgi-bin/doc?orbos/98-05-04

OMG Firewall Erratum. Available at http://www.omg.org/cgi-bin/doc?orbos/98-07-04

XML resources and parser information from IBM. Available at http://alphaworks.ibm.com/tech/xml

XML parser from Sun Microsystems. Available at http://developer.java.sun.com/developer/products/xml/

XML Parsers and tools, other. Available at http://www.xmlsoftware.com

XML information, general. Available at http://www.xml.com and http://www.xml.org

Yaeger, Nancy J, and Robert E. McGarth. *Web Server Technology*. San Francisco, California: Morgan Kaufman, 1996.

Chapter 9

Architecture Considerations for Deployment

Like people, real systems suffer from the vicissitudes of a whimsical reality. An architecture built according to the basic precepts discussed thus far would doubtless be flexible, scaleable, and able to handle the desired business functions with panache—but when actually deployed, it would probably fail in some way. Like people, real systems suffer. Your system might freeze at 12:17 AM every Saturday, slow to a crawl during a critical usage period, crash only when the project sponsor's boss logs in, or simply be hit by a power failure during a critical transaction. Above and beyond the dictates of good theoretical system design, systems architectures in the real world must be designed (and constructed) with an eye for the uncertain world of deployment.

Required Characteristics

Distributed systems must possess certain characteristics to function reliably after deployment. Several of these characteristics pertain to maintenance of quality of service, which is essential in the face of unforeseen interruptions in the flow of operations.

- **Stability.** When one part of a system fails, it can cause other parts of the system to fail. Even if a failed subsystem restarts, it may not be able to initialize itself properly if it depends upon other system elements that have also failed. Thus, the system may thrash as the failure cascades through the system in a chaotic manner. Dependable systems must be stable.

- **Continuity of service during failures.** In some traditional systems, if part of the system goes down and it takes an hour, or even a day, to come back up, very little is lost. A distributed system constantly exporting a service to clients, however, should have no perceivable interruptions. Forcing a client to re-login after a minute's delay may be acceptable for some systems, but automatically resubmitting login information and switching to a contingency server, causing a 60-second delay in data transfer, is far preferable. This is especially so with Web-based systems.

- **Continuity of service during upgrades.** Many traditional systems must be brought down during upgrades. Ideally, upgrades should not result in interruptions.

- **Awareness of fault severity.** There are some things that man cannot do alone; there are many more that machines cannot do alone. Systems are prone to both little problems that can be handled internally and bigger problems that cannot. It is important for a system to distinguish between the two, and suspend service and seek human mediation when required.

- **Implementation transparency.** As with security and transactions, it would be ideal if the runtime environment that a system lived in took care of fail-over and load balancing without having to code for such functionality explicitly in the business logic.

- **Optimization.** If a thousand users access a system during the middle of the day, a machine doing batch processing might be better used to handle some of the user load. Load balancing is related to fail-over: unacceptable response times can be considered failure and need to be addressed. Keep in mind that memory faults are seldom trapped and are very likely to kill processes in which they occur, making lessening the load on any single process an important prophylactic measure. In addition, many load balancing techniques are useful for synching and switching over to contingency servers for fail-over.

- **Trackability.** A system cannot be managed properly unless it and/or its administrators know what it is doing. Tracking can take many forms, from auditing pure business functions to following distributed stack traces. Collected information can feed notification and escalation mechanisms or provide metrics for load balancing. Tracking mechanisms are essential not only for development and testing, but for production as well.

An architecture built on the preceding precepts will probably be flexible and scaleable, and solve many technological issues to support the business domain; but once it is implemented and meets the real world, like so many people, it will crumble in some way. Systems suffer, subjected to elements outside of their control. Just because a system has the ability to be scaleable, that doesn't mean it has the wisdom to actually scale when it meets a strange usage pattern. Achieving these characteristics will be the goal of the mechanisms and patterns discussed in this chapter.

Keeping Track

Knowing what's going on at any given time in a system is the first step in managing the system. Orwellian as it may appear, most system entities can be monitored — and most should be. Trackable entities range from processes to users, from implementation objects to messages between services. However, it is usually not feasible to track everything all the time. The overhead of generating tracking messages can bog down a system during normal operations. You can reduce this overhead and make tracking feasible in several ways, notably by keeping the tracking dormant or functioning at a low level until you need to inspect a specific aspect of your system.

There are three major forms of tracking:

- **Logging** captures runtime data and control flow information, is typically archived, and often centers on one service at a time.

- **Monitoring** provides runtime information that is dealt with at run time (although it may also be archived) and that captures the state of the system as a whole. Information about entities that affect multiple services, such as users, can be captured only if a global monitoring mechanism is in place.

- **Auditing** records purely business-related information throughout the system.

Before discussing the various tracking mechanisms in detail, it is valuable to examine a key pattern that can be used to implement most of them. The base case is to have a single service where all information is gathered. At the life cycle points of any entity to be tracked (creation, destruction, state change, or other event), a message is sent to the central information-gathering service. In a more sophisticated, distributed version, local gatherers (one per machine) can be federated, feeding to the central gatherer, which can provide a centralized archive and user interface. Messages should be pushed from services to the local gatherer; the communication between these gatherers and the central monitor can then take a variety of forms. A variation of this is to archive logs at the local gatherer level and have a central monitoring service access the archives. One can also provide hooks to push messages up within the services. This can be useful for capturing exception information in context. Another possibility is to use multiple channels with different message priority levels. In fact, there are many variations and decorations possible, making for a great deal of flexibility.

Logging

Logging, at its simplest, captures the messages that the developers found useful to send to standard output while debugging. A slightly more sophisticated approach sends messages to the syslog (UNIX) or to the event log (Windows NT). This allows messages to be captured in a system-standard place, and in a slightly more scaleable fashion.

Regardless of how and where messages are captured, they are most useful when they can be searched, parsed, or browsed to find information of particular interest. This requires a common format. This also works best when all messages contain the same basic information in addition to the data specific to the message. Such basic information should include the context in which the event happened and where it happened in the system. The context includes information such as (in no particular order):

- the transaction being processed

- the security context, including the user ID for which the request was made (exercising care not to include any sensitive information, even if it is transient)

- the event type. Examples are life cycle (creation, deletion), business logic (calculations), communications protocol (servlet or ORB overhead), and data access (SQL generation or execution)

- the implementation context, described by thread names and the like

- whether the message represents an exception, and if it is recoverable

- a priority gauge of the "importance" of the information (for sorting or filtering)

- a date and time stamp

The notion of where in the system an event happened refers firstly to the class, the object instance, and the service name. Code references (line/file) may be desirable, but they are not sufficient. Local and distributed stack traces can also be helpful for tracing purposes.

Since logs tend to be local captures, each service—in fact, each instance of a service—will most probably have its own log, preserving indication of locality. Local stack traces can be useful for understanding exceptions. A fully distributed stack trace should be captured by a global system and does not really impact local logging, except as a possible source of request origin. Determining the originator of a request , usually via a security context, can be very useful, particularly when analyzing a service which is itself used by many other services.

Depending upon developer discipline to format all logging information consistently is rather chancy. In addition, it is practically impossible to change all the logging calls in a system if the log format has to be altered. For these reasons, and as a matter of good software design practice, it makes sense to have a system-standard logging class that is used everywhere and supplants standard output for developer usage. Such a class typically has a few static methods for performing logging and logging control and is a very simple but powerful mechanism. Consider the benefits of forcing all debugging tracing calls to look like the following:

```
Log.msg(this,1,"CTR:BusinessObject","Starting to build
relations");
```

The first parameter in the call above is the object reference itself, not simply its class, making it possible to track individual instances. The second parameter is a priority level, allowing for message ranking. This also makes it possible to turn off logging for messages below a certain level in production. The third parameter is a set of predefined tags to describe the action involved. The sample message could pass through filters for object construction, or for business object implementations. The last parameter is the message-specific text. The *msg()* method can internally add information such as the date and time, the thread name (if you have conventions for naming threads), the process ID, etc.

The logging output generated by such a method can take any form desired. A very useful format is XML, which is readily parsed:

Listing 9-1: *Example XML log*

```
<LOGMSG>
 <DateTime date="1/1/1999" time="3:45:04 pm"/>
 <Service name="fundsservice" host="hostid" pid="111" />
 <Priority level="1"/>
 <Thread name="pricerthread"/>
 <Object class="com.xenotrope.CalcEngine">objinstdesc</Object>
 <Type> <tag name="CTR"/> <tag name="BusinessObject"/> </Type>
 <MSG> Starting to build relations </MSG>
</LOGMSG>
```

The above example illustrates the wealth of filtering and tracing techniques this approach makes possible. Particular objects or object types can be watched, life cycles can be followed, and service activity can be tracked.

Another key benefit of this technique is that a Log object can implement a remote interface or call another remote interface. This means that the same logging calls can be used to print to standard output, write to a local log, write to a distributed logging service, or do any combination of these.

In the distributed case, however, a problem arises in the form of time stamp differences. If messages are time-stamped locally, it will be hard to interpret the messages at the logging service endpoint because of machine clock time disparities; however, if the Log object sends the message to a remote service, that service can have the responsibility for synching the messages. Such a remote service sequences the messages so that they have time stamps that have meaning relative to each other. This provides a particularly good way to log a service that is balanced among different processes.

A standard first cut of the Log class mechanism allows the calls to the remote logging service to be asynchronous or pseudo-asynchronous (one-way). This is appropriate if the goal is just to generate a central archive. But if the goal is to track interdependencies of threads or processes, it may not work. Messages from different services to the central logging service could be processed out of sequence, as the source services continue processing while the messages suffer various IO lags. This observation also applies if the logging service is multi-threaded.

The way to avoid the sequencing problem is to set up a single pipeline that all logging calls block on. With synchronous calls and a single-threaded logging service, messages will be logged in order of receipt, and services cannot proceed until a message has been processed. The downside is that the logging mechanism could become a bottleneck; thus, the design of such a system requires a tradeoff analysis and care in implementation.

Monitoring

Monitoring captures the global state of a system. While this can be archived, its power lies in delivering real-time performance metrics. An overall real-time view makes it possible to trace system entities and make administrative changes to the system. This makes monitoring a key component of system management. You must address two key questions in order to perform monitoring: what elements in the system constitute the state of the system, and what metrics are possible? These questions will drive much of the exploration below.

The granularity of the possible responses varies greatly. Monitoring can be done as low as the instruction level, although this requires great overhead and yields little insight. Clearly, you must capture higher-level aspects, but it is possible to veer off the scale at the high end as well. Entities to be monitored can also be implicit in the system, rather than explicit; an example is the contexts of service requests. Metrics are often established based on the numbers and types of objects in a system. As will be discussed, however, you can use many interesting metrics. While exploring the spectrum of possibilities below, it is important to remember that different systems will benefit from different forms of monitoring; each approach has its place.

Processes

Perhaps the most obvious metric for a running system is the number of processes it has running. The notion of processes as system entities is not new in OO programming; many ways of tracking and managing processes have been developed. One of the best-known ways is via SNMP (Simple Network Management Protocol), which has been in use for many years. Vendors have become fairly comfortable with SNMP and a few products integrate SNMP with server processes, while some even provide a partial view of the objects in services as SNMP entities. Since there is a one-to-one relationship between service and process in most simple systems, such an approach may suffice for many, particularly as a tried-and-true standard is an easier route to take than providing a homegrown mechanism.

Most ORB vendors still supply proprietary products to track and manage processes, usually on a service-by-service level, and almost always tied to their proprietary object location (naming) services. The OADs (object activation daemons) supplied with almost every ORB all work in the same basic way. In a data store (typically file-based) the OADs keep a mapping from service name to an executable with command-line parameters. When the object location service receives a request for a service, it asks the OAD if the process for that service is running, and if it isn't, to please start that process. Thus, the OAD needs to know which processes are running and how to start them, and since the information is already centralized, many vendors offer an API or a GUI interface to the information so it is possible to start and stop services by hand. In point of fact, the OAD and the object location service are usually very tightly coupled. The OAD often doesn't know if a process is up, but relies on the process registering itself with the location service, from which the OAD gets the information.

A downside to such services is that they are almost never federated. The OAD by necessity has to be a local daemon, living on the machine on which it will start processes. It is rare to find a vendor who also supplies a service that ties all the local OADs together, although as the need has become more obvious in deployed systems, vendors have started to show interest in addressing it.

As matters stand now, the products that come with ORBs to monitor processes are often not fully featured enough to really do what they need to do, or to measure up to the many pre-existing systems that already support protocols like SNMP. The lack of systemwide federalization, as well as the lack of any finer control than just bringing services up or down, means that in many situations, roll-your-own solutions are still necessary.

Services and objects

As just noted, OADs can be used to monitor the existence of services. While they often support a few ways of starting new processes, which will be explored while discussing load balancing, these ways typically lack sophistication and boil down to the same simple ability to bring whole processes up or down. This is insufficient for dealing with the complexities of monitoring services and objects. Standard OAD failings include a paucity of support for service properties and reinitialization policies and the fundamental limitation of only going into action upon a client request and of having that action constrained to a single machine. Once again, this means that a roll-your-own approach may be necessary. In order to facilitate this, you'll find it helpful to investigate several issues and strategies.

Unlike a process, a service itself can be distributed across multiple locations. This can occur when a service is balanced across machines. A more interesting case is that of a federated service composed of slightly different, but conceptually singular, subservices such as a query service or a printing service.

Another issue pertains to how services are represented and referenced. Consider the strategy of using a central monitor to track service activity. This monitor may group services in various ways such as logical function or process space. When a service registers with the monitor, it must provide some information about itself in order to be tracked correctly. Having an object that lives in a service's process and represents the service is often useful for resolving this issue. This object instance may or may not be connected to the object that implements the service interface; what it supports are the interfaces that the monitoring and management services need.

Monitoring objects occasions similar representation issues and adds the additional thorny issue of scale. Finer-grained monitoring, if done poorly, can lead to an unacceptable amount of overhead in code complexity and runtime memory and performance, as in a system in which every one of a great many objects must register with the monitor and expose administrative support. Fortunately, you can obviate these problems by simply centralizing the administrative representation within the service, creating a facade-like structure.

An example of this approach (Figure 9-1) can be applied as follows: Consider a service that generates a new object for each user session—a common design. Such a non-singleton service will use a factory mechanism. The factory entity can be set up to support monitoring also, as it already knows about all the objects it is generating. Instead of forcing the monitor to query each of the many individual objects, the monitor now needs to communicate only with the factory/administration entity, which can readily supply information tracked internally within the confines of the service.

Users

The ability to capture the interactions of a particular user with a system is a common design goal. This can be done by tracking the objects that have been allocated for a user. Given a factory mechanism for generating a session object for every new client, all that is required is that the factory maintain a user identification and pass it on to the objects it creates; then, by inspecting the objects, the monitor can get a view of the state the user is maintaining across the system.

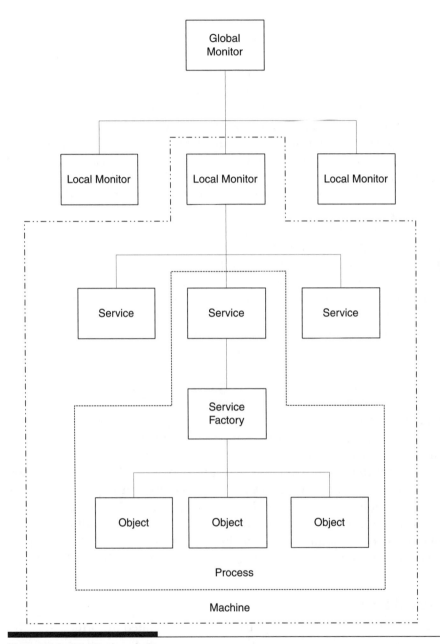

Figure 9-1. *Monitoring chain*

What this strategy does not yield is a view of what a user is currently doing. Such a view requires tracking method requests and associating them with a user. If a security service that allows delegation of user identification (i.e., a service can make a request to another service, not with its own security context but with the one from the user) is being used, then simply requiring all services in the system to require the security context allows access to the user information.

Requiring every service to generate a log message every time a user makes a request can be lot to ask of large and/or diverse development teams. This is why a transparent mechanism is highly desirable. Most ORB vendors have long provided API hooks called interceptors or filters that can accomplish this transparency. Such hooks have now been standardized by the OMG under the name of *interceptors*. Interceptors allow a process to globally interrupt and inspect the requests coming into the process before (or just after) they reach the object adapter. Using an interceptor that identifies the user from whom a request originates, and logs the user and the request, frees service developers from having to cope with the problem.

Another issue arises in multi-threaded environments in which a user can make more than one request at a time. The problem is evaluating whether a call to a service was ultimately made in response to one request from the user, or another request from the user. To deal with this, you need to put in place a tagging mechanism; this is often beyond the ken of most security services. Every time a request is made, you must put into the message an identifier, either marking the request's origin or marking it as a response to a previous request. This identifier also needs to be put into the context being sent to the next service, or piggybacked on to the request, so that the service receiving the request can know what it should log. It may also be valuable if the whole apparatus can be enabled or disabled as needed. All of this does add complexity and some overhead to a system, but it can be a powerful tool for debugging in development, and for monitoring user access patterns in production.

Auditing

Auditing is the capture of purely business-related information. The information archived is highly specialized and is usually a business requirement in its own right. Although auditing uses most of the same techniques as system logging and monitoring, the information is distinctly different, and the communications channels for auditing often need to be of a much higher reliability. An auditing system should not be part of a monitoring system, because the monitoring system is often the first line of defense for fail-over, and as a business requirement, the audit trail needs to be protected.

Achieving Fail-over

Discussing fail-over as an architectural issue means discussing it at the service level. While we are interested to some degree in how faults percolate through a service, as architects we will focus on how to restart entire services cleanly after a failure has become serious enough to bring them down.

Issues of state

A key issue in the resurrection of a service is maintenance of state—in particular, session state. As far as ease of recovery goes, the less state there is, the better. A stateless service is pure process; it can go down and be brought back up with a simple restart and no regrets. Many services, however, are stateful.

The impact of state on fail-over complexity varies. Some state may not need to be restored. A prime example of this is a service cache for reading that can be built back up over time. Session state, in contrast, must be fully restored in a consistent manner if the session itself is not to appear to die. This requires a persistence mechanism.

Although persistence was explored in depth in Chapter 5, a few relevant points are worth noting here. Systems will often use persistence layers so that state changes are written to a store such as a relational database. In addition, some CORBA implementations provide loader mechanisms, which are activation hooks for saving and loading objects. For the purposes of recovery, it is key that the saved state always be consistent. This can be done via regular transaction management approaches, such as using the OTS. If a system cannot guarantee that the data in its store is consistent, it will need a means of detecting and dealing with any inconsistency—a complexity best avoided.

A stateful server can maintain a cache or log of ongoing session state. Such a log can itself be replicated for additional safety. For the purposes of recovery, clients must have proxy object IDs that can be mapped to particular state points in the log. IDs or markers can be used with Object Adaptors (BOA/POA), and passed to the servers to recover the correct state.

It is worth remembering that not only can services fail, but that the persistent stores holding their state can fail as well. In distributed systems as in other systems, it can be desirable to maintain copies of the data stores. You can generally handle this by either duplication or replication. A system can use duplicate stores and each transaction/operation can be done on all the stores at once, thus giving the responsibility for data back-up to the persistence/transaction layers. Alternatively, all operations can be done against the primary store, which then uses a store-specific mechanism to synchronize the backup store. You can implement this via the replication features supported by all current major databases.

The act of failure

To state the obvious, services fail when some internal operation goes wrong. The details of internal failures are not relevant here, but how those failures percolate up to the service level are. Any service will need some way to deal with errors that occur in the course of processing. Major programming languages today, such as C++ and Java, have exception-handling features for trapping and signaling errors. Several points are worth making about ways in which exception handling plays into architecture.

Exceptions can be typed and grouped into strata that match levels of program structure; that is, each level of the system will have its own family of exceptions based on what can go wrong at that level. Each level in general knows best what errors to trap and how to recover from them. Exceptions are often mapped from level to level by trapping for an exception at the current level, trying to recover, and failing that, by throwing an exception of the next higher level up to that level. In such a system, the original causative exception can be conveyed as part of the new exception. If multiple errors are possible and can be usefully sorted out, then their matching exceptions can be chained together. This mapping pattern can be applied up to the system level where it can be decided how critical a given error is, and whether that error warrants shutting down the service.

Once a failure signal has reached the top level of a service and is trapped, the service can shut down cleanly if recovery is not possible. Death can be either quiet or involved; which is better depends on the complexity of the overall architecture. If services have no interdependencies, and are activated and accessed via an OAD, then a service could simply be allowed to down itself and be brought back up by the OAD upon the next attempted access. A more active system would have the service notify a central service monitor before shutting down. The service monitor could then take action with regard to not only the deceased service, but also services that depend on it—a possibility that will be explored more below. Notifying administrators via email, paging gateways, or the like is also then possible if the system deems human mediation necessary.

A last important detail is the question of partial failure. Services do things because clients have asked them to do things, so if something goes wrong in a service, it is almost always in the context of a client invocation. Many systems are designed to indicate the degree of completion of operations, for which the possibilities are *yes*, *no*, and *maybe*. By providing this information to clients, services can signal their degree of failure and give the clients the option of deciding how to proceed next. For some applications, it may be possible for clients to work with partial data, perhaps while trying to retrieve the rest. Clients must be able to deal with both communication and service failures so they must trap exceptions and respond appropriately. Client recovery from faults is just as necessary as resuscitating the services themselves.

The switch

Once a service is down, it must be restarted or replaced. There are several issues to discuss with regard to this: notably, how and where services are restarted, and how dependencies among services are to be handled so that the system remains stable in the face of the failure.

Systems that use OADs to bring up server processes will normally support various activation modes. You can choose different modes to enhance stability. For example, many CORBA systems support per-client activation, in which different processes are spun up for different clients or client processes. This isolates each server process so that if one dies, only its client is affected. It is also possible for distributed objects to share or not share the same server process, another isolation control. When evaluating activation policies, it is important to remember that they also affect the scalability of the system.

When a service goes down and is brought back up, entities publishing references to that service may have to be alerted. OADs, Naming services, Trading services, and the like fall into this category. OADs, which add a layer of indirection by publishing references to themselves, take care of this automatically; but it is important to remember to maintain any information that is exported by Naming, Trading, and other services correctly.

One key area of weakness in current CORBA products is support for handling service dependencies. This means that if an architecture does have non-trivial dependencies between services, it will also need its own dependency-handling mechanism. You can implement this in several possible ways. A central service monitor that has OAD functionality could have the responsibility for controlling restarts. Alternatively, the services themselves could be given some restart responsibilities. The central service monitor makes for a cleaner, more scaleable system, however, and is more readily generalized. Such a monitor can be empowered to send shut down messages to services, and to activate them by process invocation or OAD access.

Whoever has the responsibility for taking action needs to know two pieces of information: what the dependencies are and what action to take based on the dependencies. The dependency map can either be internalized or externalized by the services; that is, each service could maintain its own dependency information, which could be opaque or not, or the central monitor could hold all dependency information. Dependency information could be preconfigured, or, in a more dynamic system, discovered at run time by keeping track of other services used.

Issues of state also have an impact on dependency maintenance. If a service depends on another, stateless, service, then it can use any instance of the second service at any location. If the second service had some session state related to or required by the first service, then the first service would depend on the particular instance it had been using, and would have to be put back in contact with a fully restored version of that service instance after a failure.

Much of the above applies to the actions that should be taken after a failure. These could be notifications of services to re-establish references and information, or full stop and start signals. One approach is for each service to be aware of its dependencies. Services could then notify the service monitor and/or each other about impending failures. Services could indicate their intended course of action to the service monitor and request additional action; for example, a service could inform the monitor that it is reinitializing in some fashion and then request that the monitor restart another service.

Load Balancing

Load is some quantified description of how busy a computer is. There is no standard for this metric. Performance meters on nearly every current OS desktop measure load in various forms. But what do they mean? If the CPU utilization reads 30%, is the OS really sending 7 no-ops for every 3 instructions? You must choose a proper metric for load on a system-by-system basis.

Load balancing is about resource management. A load-balancing system analyzes the load on all available resources to determine the optimal allocation of those resources. Computing what the "best" performance is, however, depends on what aspects of the system are targeted for optimization. Before discussing load balancing, we must explore the subject of possible load metrics.

Metrics on requests

In order to determine a good load metric, the first question to ask concerns what work the services do that actually consumes resources. If the work is I/O-intensive, involving processing large files or making many short calls to a database, the bandwidth and number of connections might be a good measure for the load. If work is very compute-intensive, such as calculating transforms or solving differential equations, then a good measure might be CPU utilization.

The tough part of computing a metric lies in assigning a reasonable load number to each method that processes a request. You must examine the load for a method in two ways: how much load the method can be expected to generate in general, and how much load it actually generates for a particular request at run time. A load-balancing system will need at least a general estimate in order to make intelligent decisions for routing requests, and will benefit from actual runtime checks to increase the system's accuracy. Sometimes load may not be estimable with any accuracy until processing is underway. In other cases, you can estimate the load of an incoming request based on the request parameters. In simple cases you can perform an estimation based on knowledge of the implementation.

If all the requests to a particular service have the same characteristics, then a good measure of load is simply how many requests that service is handling at the moment. Since the characteristics (in terms of resources used) are exclusive, even if there are multiple categories of request types, each can be considered separately. For example, the best place to run a compute-intensive process may be on a machine that is currently I/O bound.

If processing requests uses a varying set of resources, strictly categorizing methods may not have much meaning. In such cases, you may need a more complicated optimizing routine. Take care, however, that the overhead of load calculation and optimization does not itself offset the gain from doing the load balancing. A sophisticated balancing system may prove worthwhile for a system with long jobs, such as a scientific model processor, and quite a detriment for a system with short jobs, such as one that does short data queries.

Metrics on machines

Another element to consider when evaluating metrics for load is the amount of load an individual machine is able to handle. A slow machine with a fast network card may be able to handle nearly the same I/O load as a fast machine with the same card, but not half the compute load. Accurately computing the amount of load a particular machine can handle can be tricky. If all the machines are equivalent, then this measure can be ignored, but if they differ, it is vitally important for proper balancing. In addition, the load a machine can handle is always relative to the performance criteria for a given system.

What you must determine is how many requests a machine can handle before performance becomes unacceptable. Accurate measure of the capacity of a machine may involve running performance tests on the machine, measuring completion time for average runs of each method. It is also important to run tests in parallel on the same machine to allow for the cost of process and thread switching. Resulting numbers can yield an estimate of how machines compare to each other. This is an area, however, where it is important to decide in advance how accurate the tests must be versus the amount of work they will require. It should also be remembered that the average run of a set of methods depends highly on the user's usage patterns, which may very well not be evident in a brand-new system, or which may change drastically as more features are added to the system.

Usage metrics

As truly accurate load metrics can become overly complex, common simplified estimations are often used. A core factor in making many such estimations is that of user usage patterns. If usage patterns are consistent from user to user, then the load can be estimated from the current number of users and the point in the pattern, rather than having to be calculated based on every method. If usage tends to fall into one of a few patterns, a client application or user preferences module can build up usage profiles so that when a particular user logs on, the system can ask the client application for a description of the expected load for the session. Even if a system's usage patterns are not exactly uniform or cannot be categorized, the number of users being serviced per process is a simple metric that can suffice for many systems.

Global metrics

Every running process adds to the load on a machine; thus, the load of a single service is not meaningful as a measure of load on a machine. The load of all services running on that machine must be considered to make meaningful decisions about balancing load between machines. This is why a global monitoring system is vital to coordinate service metrics across machines to support load balancing.

The balancing act

Deciding how the gross balancing will work depends highly on the resources available. You could simply divide up a given set of dedicated resources among the given services. Depending on the expected usage patterns and the characteristics of the requests handled by each service, services that use different resources can be placed on the same machines and services that use the same kind of resource split among different machines. This requires a static evaluation of the load each service will produce, given regular user usage patterns. The main benefit of this is that little or no runtime intelligence is needed. The main drawback is that there is no dynamic adjustment of load for unexpected usage, or optimization based on current processing; thus, the performance of the system hinges on the accuracy of the initial estimates.

A more common and much more dynamic technique is to more or less copy the system onto each resource. For every request the balancer then simply checks the appropriate load metric on all the machines and sends the request to the best-fit choice. This method tries to secure the best performance possible at the time of the request, but is dependent on the accuracy of runtime load estimates.

The approach usually taken is somewhere between the two above. Certain services, such as one backed by a local database, run on their own machines and the rest of the system is balanced among the machines remaining.

Another alternative is to try to assure some minimum level of performance, as opposed to the best performance. Given a very limited set of resources, you can set a minimum performance level for the system. If performance on the main application server machine for the system drops below the threshold, you can press another machine into service. This machine may not be determined beforehand; it can be the machine from a specific set with the lowest current load. Thus, the resources can be allocated to different systems, each resource ready to catch the overflow.

What to balance

There are really two general ways of balancing load: balancing sessions and balancing work. Balancing sessions is basically done by finding the least-loaded server when an initial request comes through, either via the Naming Service or a service factory. Balancing the work means deciding, for every request to the service, where the work can be handled with the best performance. The first approach is generally done on the global level, outside of the service implementation as much as possible. The latter is done almost solely within the implementation of a particular service, although it often uses monitoring, naming, and client code for support.

Balancing by Naming Service

If the load metrics chosen center around client sessions, then an effective place to handle balancing is when the client connects to a new server, or more preferably, when the client tries to locate the server for the first time using a Naming Service. As always in distributed systems, a client can itself be a service.

The OMG Naming Service defines the *NamingContext* as a core interface; therefore, even if a vendor-supplied implementation of the Naming Service doesn't support any load-balancing features, it is possible to implement the *NamingContext* interface to perform balancing and bind such contexts in the appropriate places in a naming hierarchy. This *NamingContext* implementation works by not simply binding a name to a single object reference, but rather to a list of references. When resolving a name, the context picks the best fit for balancing purposes and returns that reference.

To find the best balance, the context can ask the monitoring service for current load metrics and choose accordingly, as illustrated in Figure 9-2. However if the usage patterns and session length for the specific service are fairly consistent across sessions, then a simple cycling selection method works quite well. This may not always yield the best performance, but the average load of each service instance should be fairly even. If session lengths vary significantly, a randomized selection from the service instance list might tend to produce a slightly better average performance.

Sometimes it is more important to maintain a minimum performance level than to provide a service at all. If the loads on all the service instances are at their maximum, then the naming service has the ability to refuse a client access to the service. This forces the client to cancel or postpone its request, allowing the current jobs to run in a reasonable time.

With more information, the Naming Service can make better decisions. It can be useful to extend the *NamingContext* interface. CORBA connections are basically anonymous, so any information about the specific user or type of client application must be sent from the client, by

either a security context or an explicit call in the interface. The interface
can take usage hints, such as expected functions or subapplications to be

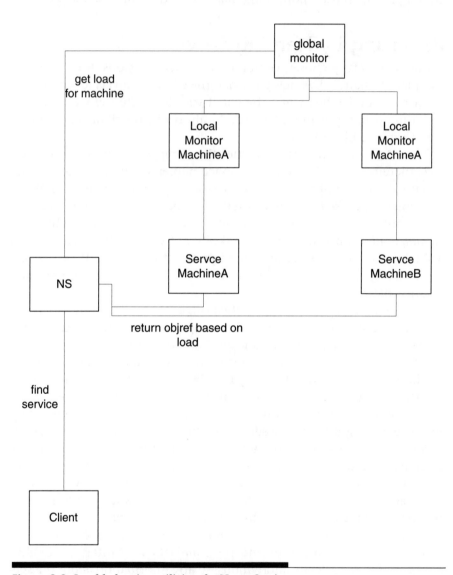

Figure 9-2. *Load balancing utilizing the Name Service*

used. If a system provides a service for persistent user preferences, a simple learning algorithm (using average statistics from previous sessions) can be used to learn the usage pattern for a user, and a client can send this to the Naming Service. A client that is aware of this extended functionality can find the context and narrow it to the extended interface, and then send the extra information with the request to resolve an object reference. This will not prevent other clients from using the *NamingContext* in the standard form; the service will just not be quite as optimized. An extended context interface could also allow access to the list of service instances, a possibility that we will discuss below.

Balancing by OAD

The Naming Service approach requires multiple service instances running and bound into the *NamingContext* before a request comes in. This works, but if the services are not used, then the idle processes take up resources and degrade the performance of other services; thus, an optimal solution is for the processes to start up when needed.

The function of the OAD is to map services to processes, and to manage the processes. It is responsible for starting up new processes or copies of services for incoming client requests. Standard activation policy possibilities include starting processes for each client connection or each client request. Also common is having a maximum number of processes and either reusing them or simply refusing more connections. Another common extension is process per user, even if a user can indirectly request connections from different client processes through other services.

Since most OADs work on a single machine, using them alone to balance load does not really add value unless the critical resources are file descriptors or threads. If an OAD that is RPC- or SNMP-aware can be found, it might solve the problem; otherwise, the solution is a federation of local OADs. One approach to this is to define a clique of OADs on various machines, the members of which always coordinate with the others when a request to start a process occurs. The other approach is to devise a consolidation service that will coordinate the OADs on various machines to provide automatic creation of processes. In either case the federation needs to know which machines a service can be started on, and on which machines there is an already-running process; for example, if the activation policy is per user, if a request comes to one OAD, it first needs to see if any other OAD has a process for the specified user.

Using the Naming Service as the balancing coordinator along with an OAD-based mechanism makes for good synergy. Many current vendor OADs allow for automatic service creation from an IOR. The IOR will actually point to the ORB's OAD and will cause a forwarding response from the OAD on first connection to the right process according to the activation policies. If a given OAD supports this, then storing these IORs in the Naming Service provides a decent and moderately dynamic solution.

If a still more dynamic solution is desired, the Naming Service can be responsible for growing the list of service instances. When the load on the currently running instances passes a threshold value, the Naming Service can contact the federated OAD and request a new process. The OAD federation would find a new machine that can run the service and does not already have one. If the OAD can start a new useful process, the Naming Service can add it to the list. When setting up such a system, it is important to provide a mechanism for service instances to be removed from the naming service list so that processes can be released.

Naming Service/OAD summary

Solutions involving Naming Services, traders, and OADs work well for addressing basic to medium-complex balancing needs. They also have the great advantage that they are nonintrusive to the services themselves, and completely transparent to the client. The only possible intrusion is the metrics collection, when you're opting for more precision. But often the same metrics needed for balancing will be important for monitoring the runtime system (especially if your system is complex enough to require sophisticated balancing) and this will collected anyway. This means that the load-balancing system can ride on top of the monitoring system.

Balancing by work

In some cases balancing among user connections is completely inappropriate due to the resource-intensive nature of the work done. As a systemwide technique the above works well, but on a service-by-service evaluation of balancing needs, it may well miss the mark. For example, if there are a few critically resource-intensive methods, to the extent that the rest of the request generates relatively little load, it is more important to balance the load among these expensive methods on a request-by-request basis rather than on a user basis. As this is very fine-grained, the reason to use it is to be very precise in allocating the work, and so a very accurate view of the load is needed. This does not have to use complex metrics. The rules can be as simple as not using a machine that is already processing a request. The metric, however, does need to be current and correct.

This kind of balancing involves sending each request to a different service instance. Therefore it is highly desirable that the service handling these requests be as stateless as possible. This avoids the need to replicate session state across machines. All the techniques we'll discuss benefit from being stateless, but some are more resilient than others.

Simplifying the service

The first option is to define a completely stateless service that handles only one type of request. Every time a client wants to make that kind of request, it obtains a new reference from a load-balancing Naming Service, makes the request, and forgets about the object reference. If the client needs to make the request again, it obtains a new reference from the Naming Service.

One of the drawbacks to this method that it depends on the client to use the mechanism responsibly. A larger possible drawback is a very unnatural breaking up of service interfaces. Since one of the most important goals of distributed object-oriented systems is proper modularization and encapsulation, this is a severe downside that may in turn revert a system to old RPC-style programming. On the upside, this technique can reuse the given load balancing mechanisms of a system.

Client responsible

Another option is to very deliberately leave it to the client to decide what kind of performance is needed throughout the client's life. This can be done with or without user intervention, although it can be very useful for the client application to ask the user for performance and priority requirements.

The client switches service instances when it can improve performance and when it is able to do so. If the service is stateful, but the client reaches a point where it can stand to lose the current session state, then the client application can drop the session and go back to the Naming Service. This lets the system shuffle its balance whenever it can, but also lets the client securely keep its session information. Another option is having the client ask the user for a performance minimum and then monitor the performance of requests. If the performance is dropping, the user can be given the option to abort current jobs and reissue them to another service instance.

The implementation of this technique often involves the client obtaining a list of service instances (perhaps from an extended version of a *NamingContext*) and checking the loads directly. This again allows the client to define its priority and performance criteria and choose appropriately.

Often this whole mechanism is hidden within an intelligent service proxy object (Figure 9-3). Many ORB vendors provide such an API hook, with which an object reference is automatically narrowed to a user-defined object type rather than the default generated proxy. All requests by necessity go through the proxy, so the proxy can make a decision for each method call as to which service instance the call will be made to. If the service is stateful, the proxy can decide to maintain a main session, but delegate those calls that do not require the state. Or it may maintain multiple sessions, duplicating only those calls (hopefully very few) that change the session state so it will be free to distribute all other calls. Another option is for the client proxy to cache the state locally, replicating it to services it wants to talk to.

The biggest drawback to this is having to maintain the client code. In addition, given that there are often many more clients then there are services, if all the clients are making multiple requests for metrics from the monitoring service, this will create a lot more traffic than a load-balancing Naming Service sitting on the same machine as the monitoring service. It is also a very narrow solution that may interfere with maintainability and change management of the services. This may also buck the growing trend towards thin clients.

The benefits include a possibly interesting and useful interaction with users, keeping coherent interfaces to services, and not impacting the services, especially in terms of state replication. Giving the client proxy the power to switch service instances and replicate state also couples a powerful fail-over mechanism to the load-balancing.

Façade

An in-between route is to façade the service (Figure 9-4). This method uses a version of the service that maintains a list of other service instances. Clients get a reference to this service and the implementation of this service delegates to the other service instances, which do the actual work. All the code that could be put in a smart proxy, except for code supporting user intervention, can be put in the façade, which can even include state replication. The façade thus functions as a remote proxy to the service, rather than a local proxy.

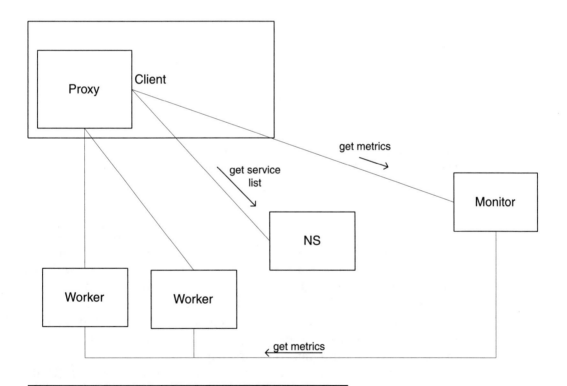

Figure 9-3. *Client responsible for balancing with smart proxies*

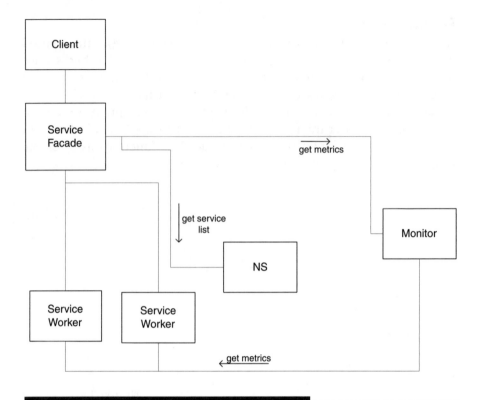

Figure 9-4. *Service façade, transparently balancing work*

Workers

Distilling the façade strategy leads to the idea of a main service with a number of worker slaves (Figure 9-5). The main service maintains the state, and any request that needs to be balanced is repackaged with the relevant session state and sent to one of the workers. In this case the interface for the workers does not need to be the same as the main service, so the main service can be stateful while the workers receive all the information they need for each request. All the client sees is the main service; the worker interface is completely hidden.

If a repackaging of the request can be placed into one object (all CORBA objects are represented in a Request object) then it can be useful to reverse

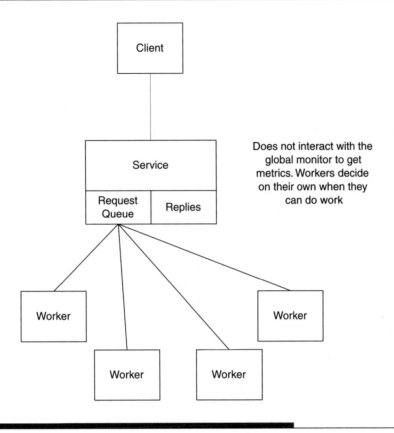

Figure 9-5. *Service with individual workers and request queue*

the balancing intelligence. If the main service needs to decide which worker can next handle a request, it needs to be able to compare machines and loads. Instead of doing this, the service could place the requests in a queue. Each worker, when it decides it can handle another request, grabs one from the queue and processes the request. Obviously this technique requires an asynchronous mechanism to get the results from the worker and pass them back to the client. This requires a tag on each job so that it can be traced back to the specific client request. Even though the worker-service interface must be asynchronous, the client-service interface can remain synchronous. The thread processing the client request can simply be suspended, blocking the client, until the reply is received from the worker.

Summary

The fail-over and load balancing strategies to be used for a particular architecture really depend on the nature of the architecture and its deployment environment. When designing systems, it is valuable to go over the characteristics enumerated at the beginning of the chapter and map them to the needs of the system. At the very least, most distributed systems benefit from a good logging system and require some basic activation management and consistent persistence mechanism. More complex systems will need fuller tracking and load balancing in order to guarantee robustness. The architect must always pick the best design elements for the job at hand.

Although system management has been a weak area in CORBA products, vendors have started to produce more sophisticated solutions. As this technology matures and becomes both more standard and more standardized, designing an architecture for deployment should become less of a do-it-yourself endeavor. Until then, the issues and strategies outlined in this chapter should serve as guide for evaluating requirements and designs for robust deployment.

Appendix

COM/CORBA Integration

In 1995, the OMG published a COM/CORBA Interworking Request for Propsals (RFP). The RFP was composed of two parts. Part A dealt with interworking between CORBA and the commercially available implementation of COM. Part B dealt with interworking between CORBA and DCOM, which was still in development at that time. The OMG ratified Part A of the COM/CORBA Interworking Specification in 1996 and Part B in 1998. There are currently commercial implementations of Part A.

Our goal in this appendix is take a look at the concepts and considerations put forth in the specification. To begin, we will consider motivations for COM/CORBA integration. Then, we will give a very brief overview of COM. Moving into the meat of our topic, we will discuss a conceptual model for bridging, examine features common to COM and CORBA, and investigate mapping issues. We will look at locating and managing distributed objects from the perspectives of both COM and CORBA. We will conclude by examining COM/CORBA distribution issues.

From Whence We COM

COM evolved from OLE, Object Linking and Embedding, a technology which was developed for the single-user, single-machine environment of Windows 3.1. OLE enabled users to create and manage compound documents, thereby maximizing code reuse within and across applications on the Windows platform. OLE2 was designed to extend the paradigm to the component level. OLE2 interfaces and protocols mediate dynamic component interaction on a desk top. COM, the Component Object Model, emerged as the standard that supports OLE2.

Motivation

Why create a bidirectional bridge for communication between COM and CORBA? What does their integration buy us? One answer to that question is that integrating the two would enable us to benefit from the inherent strengths of both standards. We could create and extend distributed systems using existing applications and components. From the CORBA perspective, we gain access to the mature GUIs found in COM-based applications like Excel and IDEs like Visual Basic. From the COM perspective, we achieve robust, platform-independent distribution based on an open architecture.

What's more, standardizing the integration process affords us an efficient, component-based approach. In addition to the best of what both models offer, we get well-defined integration interfaces and interoperable implementations.

In Terms of COM

Let's quickly define some COM terms:

- **OLE:** Object Linking and Embedding is an infrastructure that allows dynamic interaction between documents and between applications. Using OLE, we can embed a document created in one Windows application into a document created by another. OLE essentially allows for code to be reused at the application level.

- **OLE2:** OLE2 was an extension to OLE and improved the Component Object Model. It laid the groundwork for DCOM and ActiveX by providing support for automation.

- **COM:** The Component Object Model is a specification that defines component integration at the binary level and serves as the basis of OLE, Microsoft Transactional Service (MTS), and other Microsoft components. According to the COM specification, interfaces are implemented as C++ virtual function tables. Interaction with the vtable is provided by the *IUnknown* interface, from which all COM classes inherit. Accessing a COM interface requires static, compile-time knowledge of the interface's definition. In code, COM interfaces are declared as *interface* types that inherit from the *IUnknown* interface. An example of a simple COM interface is as follows:

```
//DocManager.idl
[object, uuid(...)]
interface IDocManager:IUnknown {
    HRESULT GetDocument([in] long docNum);
}
```

- **DCOM:** COM with its functionality extended to the network level.

- **Automation:** Automation makes the dynamic, runtime invocation of COM objects possible; it is conceptually equivalent to DII. The functionality is presented through the *IDispatch* interface; operations are located with a textual representation of an interface signature. *IDispatch* inherits from *IUnknown*, but does not allow direct access to *IUnknown* methods. Therefore, Automation interfaces cannot be invoked statically. In code, Automation interfaces are declared as *dispinterface* types that inherit from the *IDispatch* interface. Automation allows an application to expose functionality that can be utilized within another application or tool. An example is the Automation Interface to Microsoft Word which can be invoked from Excel's macro language (Visual BASIC for Applications, VBA).

- **Dual interfaces:** Dual interfaces are COM interfaces that inherit from the *IDispatch* interface. Functionally, they can be accessed both statically and dynamically. In code, Dual interfaces are declared as *interface* types that inherit from the *IDispatch* interface.

Bridging the Gap

A bridge is an implementation of the Interworking architecture. The Interworking architecture specifies how CORBA and COM can work together. Bridges perform the mapping between the COM and CORBA object models. Bridges use special proxy objects, referred to as views, to make an object from a foreign system appear to be native. Bridges provide CORBA views of COM objects and vice versa (Figures A-1 and A-2).

Metamodel

To begin our discussion about the issues involved in specifying a bridge between COM and CORBA, we will consider what their object models have in common. We will use these common concepts and features to develop a conceptual model that accurately represents the object models of both system. This metamodel, referred to in the specification as the Interworking model (see Figure 3), will serve as the starting point for creating a bidirectional mapping between the two.

The Interworking model describes an object as a discrete unit of functionality that is accessed through a published interface. This object has a life cycle: it is created and destroyed at discrete points in time. While the object is in existence, it can be identified by its reference. The

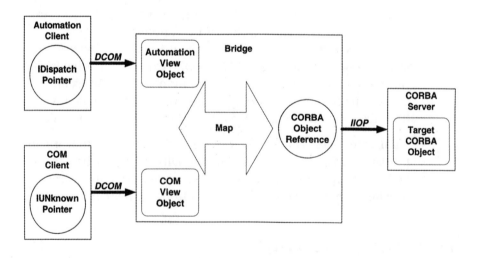

Figure A-1. *COM view of a CORBA object*

published interface is defined in terms of a set of fully described interface semantics, and this interface can also be assigned an identity. The interface can be composed of other interfaces according to a well-defined set of rules. Requests can target a specific object instance using a reference to that object. An object instance will service the request by invoking the desired operation in its implementation of the behavior. Parameters to requests are either object references or basic data types.

Object life cycle and identity

CORBA and COM have very different concepts of the life cycle of an object. CORBA objects are often long-lived; activation and passivation are done in a transparent fashion. Over the course of a CORBA object's lifetime, it may be activated (loaded into memory on the server) and passivated (stored in some persistent way) many times. The notion of an object in the CORBA world is decoupled from its instantiation state. Throughout its lifetime, activated and passivated states included, a CORBA object can be identified using the same object reference. Also,

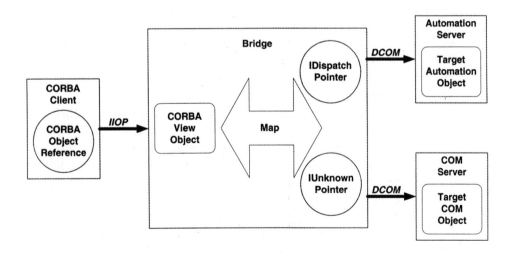

Figure A-2. *CORBA view of a COM object*

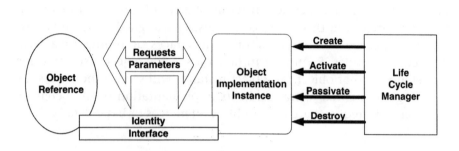

Figure A-3. *Interworking model*

the initial creation and ultimate destruction of a CORBA object are explicit events determined within the design of the application.

In contrast, the concept of a COM or Automation object is tightly coupled to its instantiated state. COM and Automation object references, implemented as in-memory pointers, don't exist for inactive objects and are not valid across instantiations. In addition, both COM and Automation objects are instantiated by a standard factory and with constructors that do not take parameters. Since reference counting is used to determine the fate of their existence, they are implicitly destroyed.

Mapping between COM and CORBA object models merits more discussion than we will give it in this appendix. That said, here are two possible scenarios.

If the interface in question is implemented by a CORBA object, the problem from the COM perspective is retaining a copy of the object's immutable, life-long CORBA object reference. This can be done by retrieving and "stringifying" the CORBA object reference (an IOR) and then storing it in a file. A subtle point to consider is that the object reference storage is not encapsulated by the CORBA object reference. If there are multiple references to the object within the COM component of the system, the CORBA object reference will be retained only by the reference holders who implement their own storage functionality.

If the interface is implemented on the COM side, the problem is correlating CORBA's "long-lived object" expectations with COM's transient nature. In COM, an object is identified by where it exists in memory. If its state needs to be retained, it is identified in some other way, such as a file. Since COM constructors don't take parameters, the COM objects have to have their state loaded into them after they are instantiated. The challenge is associating a newly born COM object with the state desired by a given CORBA client. One solution would be to implement COM target objects that provide factory functionality. The factory could be created without state, instantiate the object that is actually desired with the expected state, and return its reference to the CORBA client. The COM API function *CoGetInstanceFromFile* will load objects from files.

Interfaces and interface identity

CORBA interfaces are described in terms of OMG IDL. They are identified at runtime by a CORBA Interface Repository ID key, which is, by default, the fully scoped name of the interface. Alternately, you can use a Globally Unique Identifier (GUID), a 128-bit binary string, for the repository ID key by placing the *#pragma ID <interface_name> = <GUID>* preprocessor directive in the IDL file.

Both COM and Automation interfaces are described in term of MIDL. They are identified at runtime by Interface Identifiers (IIDs)—GUIDs. As we mentioned before, COM interfaces are statically typed. Automation interfaces are stored in type libraries for dynamic retrieval.

We need to map OMG IDL to MIDL and CORBA Interface Repository IDs to COM IIDs. Mapping OMG IDL to MIDL is accomplished with a naming convention. We will explain it with an example. The OMG IDL interface

```
module ContentManagement{
    module DocumentManagement{
        interface Text{
            ...
        }
    }
}
```

maps to the COM interface *IContentManagement_DocumentManagement_Text*, the Automation interface *DContentManagement_DocumentManagement_Text*, and the Dual interface *DIContentManagement_DocumentManagement_Text*.

COM IIDs can be generated by an algorithm that takes CORBA Interface Repository IDs and outputs GUIDs.

Interface composition

CORBA interfaces are defined in terms of existing interfaces according to the rules of C++ style inheritance. Both single and multiple inheritance are supported.

COM supports single inheritance. Multiple inheritance is accommodated by aggregating a set of interfaces and using the *QueryInterface(...)* method on the *IUnknown* interface to traverse them.

Newer Automation controllers, like Visual Basic, support aggregation and, for them, inheritance is built on top of and very similar to COM inheritance. For older versions, inheritance is implemented by lumping all of the derived methods into one interface. Keep in mind that both Automation and COM interfaces are expressed in terms of MIDL.

CORBA is flexible enough to replicate COM and Automation interfaces in the way that they are implemented in their native environments, so CORBA can implement a disjoint collection of interfaces to mimic COM aggregation or one all-inclusive interface for the older Automation controllers. The implementation is left up to vendors.

COM and Automation representations of CORBA inheritance are difficult to produce. A major consideration is that COM-based interfaces are sensitive to how their methods are ordered. If you took a single COM interface, ordered its methods from A to Z, and compiled it, and then took the same COM interface and ordered its methods from Z to A and compiled it again, they would be considered separate and unrelated in the COM world—remember, it's a binary standard. Automation differentiates between operations and attributes; *get* and *set* methods are attributes and all other methods are operations. Within Automation interfaces, attributes are listed before operations, *gets* are listed before *sets*, and everything is in A<Z<a<z order. Interfaces in inheritance relationships are grouped by inheritance level and then sorted according to the same rule.

In the mapping from CORBA to COM, there are three simple rules:

1. A CORBA interface without parents maps to a COM interface that inherits from *IUnknown*.

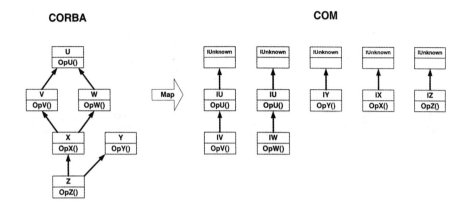

Figure A-4. *CORBA to COM inheritance mapping*

2. A CORBA interface with a single parent maps to a COM interface that inherits from the parent.

3. A CORBA interface with multiple parents maps to a COM interface that inherits from *IUnknown.*

The interfaces retain their identities across the mapping. Figure 4 is a diagram of the mapping. Notice that the interface names are mapped according the naming convention put forth in the *Interfaces* and *Interface Identity* section.

The CORBA to Automation mapping has to strike the delicate balance of being compatible with all Automation controllers while still maintaining the identity of all interfaces—or, enough identity so that the functionality of each interface is available. Here are the rules illustrated in Figure 5:

1. A CORBA interface without parents maps to an Automation interface that inherits from *IDispatch.*

2. A CORBA interface with a single parent maps to an Automation interface that inherits from the parent.

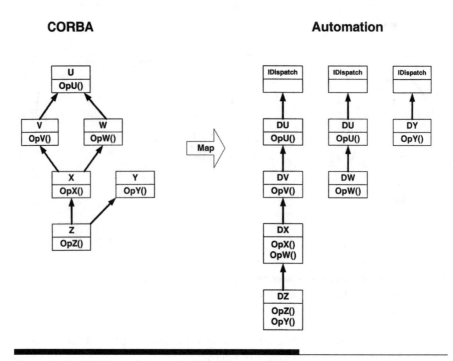

Figure A-5. *CORBA to Automation inheritance mapping*

3. A CORBA interface with multiple parents maps to an Automation interface that inherits from the left-most parent—after sorting rules are applied. The methods of all other parents are included in the interface's definition in their sorted order. In order to preserve the identity of the non left-most parents, their interfaces are defined again.

Requests

CORBA requests are bidirectional interactions in the form of method invocations. The actual request includes a reference to the target object, the name of the operation, and parameters. The reply includes return parameters and, in case of failure, exceptions. When a request is of the *oneway* type, there is no reply component.

COM and Automation requests are expressed essentially the same way as CORBA requests. The major difference is that COM requests don't return exceptions. Instead, they return a status parameter called *HRESULT*.

For the most part, the mapping between COM and CORBA for requests is straight forward and one-to-one. CORBA oneway requests are mapped to COM requests without return parameters. Also, because COM does not support dynamic invocation, CORBA DII/DSI-related interfaces are not mapped. Exceptions require special treatment and will be discussed in a section of their own below.

Parameters

CORBA interfaces have three types of parameters that must be explicitly declared: *in* parameters are passed to the target object, *out* parameters are passed from the target object, and *inout* parameters are passed both ways.

Similarly, COM and Automation interfaces support *[in]*, *[out]*, and *[inout]* parameters. *HRESULT* is an implicitly declared return parameter.

The parameter lists are maintained across the mapping. There are some exceptions, however. In order to accommodate the fact that the return value of all COM MIDL method invocations is *HRESULT*, explicit OMG IDL return values are mapped to *[retval,out]*, which is placed in the parameter list after all declared parameters. If the OMG IDL interface has a *raises* clause, a parameter that maps to a mechanism to retrieve the exception information is added onto the end of the COM operation's list of return exceptions. The exception retrieval functionality is explained more fully in the section on exceptions below.

Type Mapping

The mapping for basic types is almost one-to-one between CORBA and COM and between CORBA and Automation. COM and CORBA are able to exchange user defined types, enums, structs, and classes, in a straight forward manner. Automation represents types that can't be stored in its *VARIANT* type as native interfaces; so the mapping between CORBA and Automation is more involved. The simplest and most efficient way to communicate this information is in a table format. We will do that in the sections that follow. Special considerations will follow the tables.

Basic types

There are three special mappings to be considered in the basic type mapping.

- **Automation long to CORBA unsigned long** should return the *HRESULT DISP_E_OVERFLOW* when the Automation long parameter is a negative number.

- **CORBA unsigned long to Automation long** should return the *HRESULT DISP_E_OVERFLOW* when the CORBA unsigned long parameter is greater than the maximum value of an Automation long.

- **Automation long to CORBA unsigned short** should return the *HRESULT DISP_E_OVERFLOW* when the Automation long parameter is negative or is greater than the maximum value of a CORBA unsigned short.

Complex types

In order to provide a well-known interface for the mapping between CORBA non-object data types, like unions, and their Automation interface counterparts, the interworking specification supplies the interface *DICORBAComplexType*. Take special notice of the fact that a CORBA non-object data type is represented as an Automation interface which will be implemented as an Automation object. Automation objects are passed by reference while CORBA non-objects are passed by value. So, if we declare a CORBA *struct*, *myStruct*, it will always be passed by value in the CORBA world. However, if *myStruct* is passed into the Automation world for further distribution, there will be one copy of it being referenced by all interested clients. A change to *myStruct* by one client will be seen by all of them.

Exceptions

Exception types provide error reporting. Typically, there are two kinds of exceptions: system and user-defined. The mapping of exceptions is not straightforward.

Table A-1. *Basic types*

CORBA Type	COM Type	Automation Type
short	short 16-bit signed integer	short 16-bit unsigned integer
long	long 32-bit signed integer	long 32-bit signed integer
unsigned short	unsigned short 16-bit unsigned integer	long 32-bit signed integer
unsigned long	unsigned long 32-bit unsigned integer	long 32-bit signed integer
float	 32-bit IEEE floating point number	float 32-bit IEEE floating point number
double	double 64-bit IEEE floating point number number	double 64-bit IEEE floating point number
char	char 8-bit quantity limited to ISO Latin-1 character set	short 16-bit unsigned integer
char		unsigned char* 8-bit unsigned integer
octet	byte 8-bit opaque data type	short 16-bit unsigned integer
octet		unsigned char* 8-bit unsigned integer
boolean	bool 8-bit quantity limited to 0 and 1	VARIANT_BOOL True = -1, False = 0
string	LPSTR Null terminated 8-bit character string [string,unique] char*	BSTR Length-prefixed string. Prefix is an integer
bounded string	13B-2-4 13B-42	BSTR Length-prefixed string. Prefix is an integer
wstring	LPWSTR Null terminated Unicode string [string,unique] wchar_t*	BSTR Length-prefixed string. Prefix is an integer

Table A-2. *Complex types*

CORBA Type	COM Type	Automation Type
typedef	typedef	alias An alias with the scoped name
const	const 32-bit signed integer	alias An alias with the scoped name
enum	enum 8-bit opaque data type	enum 16-bit unsigned integer
struct	struct	DICORBAStruct An interface with property accessors for each structure member
sequence	struct A struct with a member to declare, a member to declare upward bound, and a pointer to an array	SAFEARRAY An array with lower and upper bounds
array	array 32-bit IEEE floating point number	SAFEARRAY An array with lower and upper bounds
union	union 64-bit IEEE floating point number	DICORBAUnion An interface with property accessors for the union discriminator and members
any	ICORBAAny An interface defined by the Interworking Architecture	DICORBAAny An interface defined by the Interworking Architecture
object	IUnknown An interface to the Automation view	IDispatch An interface to the Automation view

System

CORBA system exceptions have a well-defined structure. They contain three pieces of data: a completion status, a major code, and a minor code. The completion status is an *enum* with three possible values: *YES,*

NO, and *MAYBE*. The major code, a 32-bit unsigned integer, is specified by the CORBA specification and is intended to report general error information. The minor code, also a 32-bit unsigned integer, is defined by vendors and is intended to report more specific error information.

All COM operations return *HRESULT*. *HRESULT* is a 32-bit value the conveys success or failure in the first bit, the error source in the next 15 bits, and information about the error itself in the last 16 bits.

All Automation operations also return *HRESULT*. In newer automation controllers, like Visual Basic, the first bit of *HRESULT* can be used to trigger built-in error handling routines. In an effort to improve on COM's error handling abilities, Automation supplies an *EXCEPINFO struct* as the return value of the *IDispatch::Invoke()* method. The *EXCEPINFO struct* contains a string describing the source of the error, a string describing the error itself, the ID of the related help file, and a help file topic. The *struct* is intended to be used by humans and it cannot be extended. An *EXCEPINFO struct* can be accessed by assigning a pointer to the optional last parameter in the *IDispatch::Invoke()* parameter list. Non-null pointers denote that the client would like to access the *EXCEPINFO* object.

The Interworking Architecture defines a CORBA System exception major code to COM *HRESULT* mapping. The standard COM interface, *ISupportErrorInfo*, can used to convey a CORBA system exception's minor code and repository ID. Whether or not it is used is left up to vendors.

Automation system exceptions are mapped to *DICORBASystemException*. In order to make use of this interface, include an optional parameter at the end of the operation's parameter list. The implementation of the *DICORBASystemException* interface will function much the same way as the native Automation error handling system. The difference is that the built in Automation error-handling routines will not be triggered because the *HRESULT* bit will not be set to failure status. You could simply use Automation's native routines; however, the native routines do not give access to the data actually contained in the exception.

User-defined

CORBA user exception declaration and implementation is left to the developer. User-defined exceptions must be explicitly declared in the *raises* clause of an OMG IDL operation.

The specified mapping between CORBA/COM user exceptions is cumbersome. Similar to the Automation mechanism mentioned earlier, an optional pointer parameter is added onto the end of a COM mapping for a CORBA operation with a *raises* clause. The pointer references a COM *struct* that is a union of all exceptions declared in the raises clause. The COM *struct* provides a standard mechanism for gaining access to an undetermined number of secondary structures. These secondary structures actually represent the user-defined exceptions. Information contained in the COM *struct* can be retrieved by passing a pointer to the optional pointer parameter.

The exception-handling capabilities described for Automation system exceptions also apply for Automation user-defined exceptions. For a little extra work, COM implementations can make use of Automation exception-handling capabilities by way of the native COM interface *ISupportErrorInfo* and global functions *SetErrorInfo* and *GetErrorInfo*. The COM implementation could set error information with *SetErrorInfo*. A client could confirm that the implementation supports the exception handling mechanism with *ISupportErrorInfo* and retrieve it with *GetErrorInfo*.

Automation user exceptions are mapped to DICORIBASystemException. The functionality described above applies here as well.

Integration

In the context of the CORBA Interworking Architectures, integration boils down to being able to reference and invoke methods on COM objects from CORBA and vice versa. In this section, we will look at options for obtaining views from both perspectives.

COM and Automation objects from CORBA clients

The specification does not provide a standard way for a CORBA client to get an initial view of a COM or Automation object. A few options are possible. The simplest is to initiate creation of the target object in COM and then pass the reference into CORBA as is typical for callback architectures. Another approach would be to expose COM class factories to

CORBA clients with the *SimpleFactory* interface, one of the CORBA Life Cycle interfaces. *SimpleFactory* mimics the behavior of COM and Automation class factories by instantiating objects with no initialization parameters. Along the same lines, you could expose the native COM *IClassFactory* and Automation *DIClassFactory* interfaces to CORBA as well. The CORBA Naming Service is also an avenue for retrieving initial views.

As mentioned earlier, COM and Automation objects are inherently transient and special care must be taken to give them a persistent feel. Each time a reference is needed for an object that is not currently in memory, the object must be created and explicitly related to a desired state. The persistence will be transparent to the client if the vendor implements views that bind monikers.

Finally, when working with CORBA views of COM objects, it is important to remember that COM and Automation manage the life cycles of their objects by reference counting. The *Life CycleObject::remove()* method is supported by all CORBA views. It should always be called when the reference is no longer needed in order to prevent dangling views. View implementations that bind monikers can also release references to views in a fashion that is transparent to the client.

CORBA objects from COM and Automation clients

COM clients can obtain initial views of CORBA objects in much the same way that the CORBA views were obtained. The COM API presents a *CreateObject()* method that can be used to create views of CORBA objects. In addition, an initial view can be obtained by invoking the *CreateObject()* method of the *DICORBAFactory* interface, which is supplied by the Interworking Architecture. Using the Naming Service is a possibility as well.

These mechanisms, the native COM API, the *DICORBAFactory* interface and the Naming Service, also provide ways of retrieving views of existing objects. Resolving an IOR or a moniker are other options. Because CORBA object references are decoupled from the life cycle state of their corresponding objects, COM clients don't have to worry about explicitly releasing references to CORBA servers.

Distribution

Deployment models

Basically, a bridge can be deployed according to two models: it can reside on all client machines or it can reside on a single machine. Placing a bridge on each client machine can improve runtime performance in some cases and enables IIOP to be used for commucation throughout the system. It also takes advantage of CORBA's open, platform-independent and mature distributed architecture. You could also choose to deploy the bridge on a single machine and use DCOM for some or all distribution. Which solution is preferable? Where should your bridge reside? The only real answer, of course, is that it depends. Let us take a look at some general considerations.

How is your system currently architected?

If your system is completely Windows-centric, perhaps you should use DCOM for distribution. However, if your system has multiple platforms or will have multiple platforms, CORBA would provide the platform independence and portability you need.

What are your requirements for robustness and extensibility?

COM+ is promising improvements in security, better distributed life cycle management, and extended threading models. Even though Microsoft has expanded its product suite to include services like the Transaction Server, DCOM as a distributed architecture is not mature and its reliability and extensibility is an unknown. CORBA, on the other hand, has already survived many development cycles. Its open, standards-driven architecture allows for an application-driven response to object life cycle and threading issues.

What is the skill set of your staff?

An important consideration is the skill set of your staff. If your programmers are fluent with the languages and paradigms of object-oriented development, then CORBA could be a natural fit. However, if your developers are most familiar with a Visual Basic and the COM environment, then DCOM would be more desirable.

When you have considered all of these questions, you will have a preference for deploying your bridge. We would like to close this appendix by saying that we think is best to structure a system to take full advantage of the strengths of each of its components. Given a choice, we would build a CORBA-centric system that can also support COM clients. We would reap the benefits of CORBA's distribution capabilities and of COM's presentation capabilities. This is a fitting conclusion for a book about CORBA architectures.

References

Box, Don. *Essential COM*. Reading, Massachussetts: Addison Wesley Longman, Inc., 1998.

Brockschmidt, Kraig. *Inside OLE2*. Redmond, Washington: Microsoft Press, 1994.

Chung, P. Emerald. Huang, Yennun. Yajnik, Shalini. Liang, Deron. Shih, Joanne C. Wang, Chung-Yih. Frankel, David S., and Guttman, Michael K. *Resolving Differences in the Life Cycle of COMvs. CORBA*. Genesis Development Corporation 1996, 97. http://www.gendev.com/pubs/whitepapers.htm.

Genesis Development Corporation, *Objects*. http://www.gendev.com/pubs/whitepapers.htm, 1996,97.

Geraghty, Ronan. Joyce, Sean. Moriaty, Tom, and Noone, Gary. *COM_CORBA Interoperability*. Upper Saddle River, NJ: Prentice-Hall, Inc., 1999.

IONA Technologies PLC. *OrbixCOMet Desktop Programmer's Guide and Reference*. Dublin, Ireland, 1998.

Object Management Group, Inc. *Comparing ActiveX and CORBA/IIOP*, Framingham, Massachusetts, 1997, 1998, http://www.omg.org/library/activex.html, Object Management Group, Inc. *CORBA 2.3 -*

chapter 17 - Interworking Architecture. Framingham, Massachusetts, 1997. ftp.omg.org/pub/docs/formal/99-07-21.pdf.

Ouoin, Inc., *COM versus CORBA: A decision Framework, Version 1.3,* Cambridge, Massachusetts, June 1998.

Rosen, Michael, and Curtis, David. *Integrating CORBA and COM Applications.* New York, NY: John Wiley & Sons, Inc., 1998.

Wang, Yi-Min. *DCOM and CORBA Side by Side, Step by Step, and Layer by Layer,* Bell Laboratoies, Murray Hill New Jersey, 1997, http://www.bell-labs.com/~emerald/dcom_corba/Paper.html.

Index